The Australian Victories in France in 1918

Lieut.-General Sir John Monash, G.C.M.G., K.C.B., V.D., D.C.L., LL.D.

The Australian Victories in France in 1918

The Battles of the Australian Army on the Western Front During the Final Year of the First World War

ILLUSTRATED

Sir John Monash

The Australian Victories in France in 1918
The Battles of the Australian Army on the Western Front During the Final Year of the First World War
by Sir John Monash

ILLUSTRATED

First published under the title
The Australian Victories in France in 1918

Leonaur is an imprint of Oakpast Ltd
Copyright in this form © 2021 Oakpast Ltd

ISBN: 978-1-78282-960-7 (hardcover)
ISBN: 978-1-78282-961-4 (softcover)

http://www.leonaur.com

Publisher's Notes

The views expressed in this book are not necessarily those of the publisher.

Contents

Preface	9
Introduction	10
Back to the Somme	26
The Defence of Amiens	41
Hamel	56
Turning the Tide	72
The Battle Plan	81
The Battle Plan (Continued)	95
The Chase Begins	111
Exploitation	127
Chuignes	139
Pursuit	154
Mont St. Quentin and Péronne	170
A Lull	185
Hargicourt	199
America Joins In	218
Bellicourt and Bony	234
Montbrehain and After	248
Results	261

Appendix A	275
Appendix B	276
Appendix C	297

DEDICATED
TO THE
AUSTRALIAN SOLDIER
WHO BY HIS MILITARY VIRTUES, AND BY HIS DEEDS
IN BATTLE, HAS EARNED FOR HIMSELF A
PLACE IN HISTORY WHICH NONE
CAN CHALLENGE

Preface

The following pages, of which I began the compilation when still engaged in the arduous work of repatriation of the Australian troops in all theatres of war, were intended to be something in the nature of a consecutive and comprehensive story of the Australian Imperial Force in France during the closing phases of the Great War. I soon found that the time at my disposal was far too limited to allow me to make full use of the very voluminous documentary material which I had collected during the campaign. The realisation of such a project must await a time of greater leisure. So much as I have had the opportunity of setting down has, therefore, inevitably taken the form rather of an individual memoir of this stirring period.

While I feel obliged to ask the indulgence of the reader for the personal character of the present narrative, this may not be altogether a disadvantage. Having regard to the responsibilities which it fell to my lot to bear, it may, indeed, be desirable that I should in all candour set down what was passing in my mind, and should attempt to describe the ever-changing external circumstances which operated to guide and form the judgments and decisions which it became my duty to make from day to day. It may be that hereafter my exercise of command in the field and the manner in which I made use of the opportunities which presented themselves will be the subject of criticism. I welcome this, provided that the facts and the events of the time are known to and duly weighed by the critic.

My purpose has been to describe in broad outline the part played by the Australian Army Corps in the closing months of the war, and I have based upon that record somewhat large claims on behalf of the Corps. It would have overloaded the story to include in it any larger number of extracts from original documents than has been done. I may, however, assert with confidence that the statements, statistics and deductions made can be verified by reference to authoritative sources.

The photographs have been selected from a very large number taken, during the fighting and often under fire, by Captain G.H.

Wilkins, M.C. The maps have been prepared under my personal supervision, and are compiled from the official battle maps in actual use by me during the operations.

John Monash.

Introduction

THE AUSTRALIAN ARMY CORPS

The renown of the Australians as individual fighters, in all theatres of the Great War, has loomed large in the minds and imagination of the people of the Empire.

Many stories of the work they did have been published in the daily Press and in book form. But it is seldom that any appreciation can be discovered of the fact that the Australians in France gradually became, as the war progressed, moulded into a single, complete and fully organised army corps.

Seldom has any stress been laid upon the fact that because it thus became a formation fixed and stable in composition, fighting under a single command, and provided with all accessory arms and services, the corps was able successfully to undertake fighting operations on the grandest scale.

There can be little question, however, that it was this development which constituted the paramount and precedent condition for the brilliant successes achieved by these splendid troops during the summer and autumn of 1918—successes which far overshadowed those of any earlier period of the war.

For a complete understanding of all the factors which contributed to those successes, and for an intelligent grasp of the course of events following so dramatically upon the outbreak of the great German offensive of March 21st of that year, I propose to trace, very briefly, the genesis and ultimate development of the corps, as it became constituted when, on August 8th, it was launched upon its great enterprise of opening, in close collaboration with the army corps of its sister Dominion of Canada, that remarkable counter-offensive, which it maintained, without pause, without check, and without reverse, for sixty consecutive days—a period full of glorious achievement— which contributed, as I shall show in these pages, in the most direct and decisive manner, to the final collapse and surrender of the enemy.

In the days before the war, there was in the British Service no recognised or authorised organisation known as an army corps. When the Expeditionary Force was launched into the conflict in 1914, the army corps organisation was hastily improvised, and consisted at first merely of an army corps staff, with a small allotment of special corps troops and services, and of a fluctuating number of divisions. It was the *division* and not the *corps*, which was then the strategical unit of the army. Even when the necessity for the formation of army corps was recognised, it was still a fundamental conception that it was the division, and not the army corps, which constituted the fighting unit.

★★★★★★

A *division* consists of three infantry brigades, divisional artillery, three field companies of engineers, three field ambulances, a pioneer battalion, a machine-gun battalion, together with supply, sanitary and veterinary services. Its nominal strength is 20,000.

An *infantry brigade* consists of four infantry battalions, each of 1,000 men, and a light trench mortar battery.

Divisional artillery comprises two brigades each of four batteries, each of six guns or howitzers, also one heavy and three medium trench mortar batteries, and the divisional ammunition column.

This composition of a division was modified in detail during the course of the war.

★★★★★★

To each army corps were allotted at first only two, but later as many as four divisions, according to the needs and circumstances of the moment. But the component divisions never, for long, remained the same. The actual composition of every army corps was subject to constant changes and interchanges, and it was rare for any given division to remain for more than a few weeks in any one army corps.

The disadvantages of such an arrangement are sufficiently obvious to require no great elaboration; at the same time, it has to be recognised that, during the first three years of the war, at any rate, the army was undergoing a process of rapid expansion, and that, on grounds of expediency, it was neither possible nor desirable to adopt a policy of a fixed and immutable composition for so large a formation as an army corps.

Moreover, the special conditions of trench warfare made it imperative to create, under the respective armies, and in the respective zones of those armies, a subordinate administrative and tactical authority with a more or less fixed geographical jurisdiction. Thus, the frontage held by each of the five British Armies became subdivided into a series of corps frontages, and each corps commander had allotted to him a definite frontage, a definite depth and a definite area, for his administrative and executive direction.

It was within this corps area that he exercised entire control of all functions of a purely local and geographical character: such as the maintenance of all roads, railways, canals, telegraphs and telephones; the control of all traffic; the apportionment of all billeting and quartering facilities; the allocation and employment of all means of transport; the collection and distribution of all supplies, comprising food, forage, munitions and engineering materials; the conservation and distribution of all water supply; the sanitation of the area; the whole medical administration within, and the evacuation of sick and wounded from the area; the establishment and working of shops of all descriptions, both for general engineering and for Ordnance purposes; also of laundries, bathing establishments and rest camps; the creation of facilities for the entertainment and recreation of resting troops, and of schools for their military training and for the education of their leaders.

The corps commander was, in addition, directly responsible to the army commander for the tactical defence of his whole area, for the creation and maintenance of the entire system of field defences covering his frontage, comprising trench systems in numerous successive zones and field fortifications of all descriptions; for preparations for the demolition of railways and bridges to meet the eventuality of an enforced withdrawal; and for detailed plans for an advance into the enemy's territory whenever the opportune moment should arrive.

The extensive responsibilities thus imposed upon the corps commander, and upon the whole of his staff, obviously demanded an intimate study and knowledge of the whole of the corps area, such as could be acquired only by continuous occupation of one and the same area for a period extending over many months. It would therefore have been in the highest degree inconvenient to move such a complex organisation as an army corps staff from one area to another at short intervals of time.

On the other hand, the several divisions allotted to any given corps for the actual occupation and maintenance of the defences could not be called upon to carry out without relief or rest, trench duty for continuous periods longer than a few weeks at a time. During the first three years the number of divisions at the disposal of the British High Command was never adequate to provide each army corps in the front line with sufficient divisions to permit of a regular alternation out of its own resources of periods of trench duty and periods of rest. For a corps holding a two-division frontage, for example, it would have been necessary to provide a permanent strength of at least four divisions in order to permit of such a rotation.

The expedient generally adopted, therefore, was to withdraw altogether from the army corps, each division in turn, as it became due for a rest behind the line or was required for duty elsewhere, and to substitute some other available division from G.H.Q. or Army Reserve. The broad result was that such an deal as that of a fixed composition for an army corps proved quite unattainable, and there was a constant interchange of nearly the whole of the divisions of the army, who served in succession, for short periods, in many different corps, and under many different commanders.

To this general rule there was, from the outset of its formation, one striking exception, in the case of the Canadian Army Corps, consisting of the four Canadian divisions, which, with rare exceptions, and these only for short periods and for quite special purposes, invariably fought as a complete corps of fixed constitution.

It is impossible to overvalue the advantages which accrued to the Canadian troops from this close and constant association of all the four divisions with each other, with the corps commander and his staff, and with all the accessory corps services. It meant mutual knowledge of each other among all commanders, all staffs, all arms and services, and the mutual trust and confidence born of that knowledge. It was the prime factor in achieving the brilliant conquest of the Vimy Ridge by that corps in the early spring of 1917.

The consummation, so long and so ardently hoped for, of a similar welding together of all Australian units in the field in France into a single corps was not achieved in its entirety until a full year later, and it will be interesting to trace briefly the steps by which such a result, strongly pressed as it was by the Australian Government, was finally brought about.

Australia put into the field and maintained until the end, altogether five divisions of infantry, complete with all requisite artillery, engineers, pioneers and all supply, medical and veterinary services, in full conformity with the Imperial War Establishments laid down for such divisions. But the method and time of their formation and organisation, the manner and circumstances of their war preparation, and their employment as part of a corps varied considerably.

The First Australian Division, together with the Fourth Infantry Brigade, which was then under my command and subsequently became the nucleus of the Fourth Australian Division, were raised in Australia in 1914, immediately after the outbreak of war, were transported to Egypt, where they underwent their war training in the winter of 1915, and ultimately formed, with the New Zealand Contingent, the body known as the "Anzac" Corps, which carried out, on April 25th, the memorable landing on the Gallipoli Peninsula.

The Second Australian Division speedily followed, being raised in Australia during 1915, and the greater part of this Second Contingent joined the Anzac Corps in the later stages of the Dardanelles Expedition. Another independent Brigade (the Eighth) was also sent to Egypt in that year.

The raising of the Third Australian Division, early in 1916, was the magnificent answer which Australia made when public men and the Press declared that the Australian people would resent the Evacuation from Gallipoli, and the seemingly fruitless sacrifices which it entailed. This Division was shipped direct to England, and assembled on Salisbury Plain during the summer of 1916, where I assumed the command of it. There it underwent its war training under conditions far more advantageous than those which confronted the First and Second Divisions in the Egyptian desert. The Third Division entered the theatre of war in France in November, 1916.

In the meantime, the Evacuation of the Peninsula, in December, 1915, led to the assembly in Egypt of the First and Second Australian Divisions, the Fourth and Eighth independent infantry brigades and some thirty thousand reinforcements and convalescents.

Out of this supply of fighting material it was then decided to constitute two additional complete divisions, the Fourth Brigade forming the nucleus of the Fourth Australian division, while the 8th Brigade formed that of the Fifth Australian Division; the remaining brigades and the divisional troops were drawn from reinforcements, stiffened by a considerable contribution of veterans taken from the four infantry brigades who had carried out the landing on Gallipoli.

The Fourth and Fifth Divisions were thus formed in Egypt in February and March, 1916, and the conditions of their war training were even less satisfactory than those which had confronted the earlier divisions. The hot season speedily arrived; equipment, munitions and animals materialised slowly; training equipment and suitable training grounds were of the most meagre character; and upon all these difficulties supervened the urgent obligation to undertake the strenuous toil of organising and executing, on the Sinai desert, the field fortifications required for the defence of the Suez Canal zone.

The method in which the divisions then available in Egypt were to be grouped for the purposes of corps command was ripe for decision. It was then that the determination was reached to constitute two separate army corps, to be called respectively "First Anzac" and "Second Anzac". The former embodied the First, Second and Fifth Australian Divisions, under General Sir William Birdwood; the latter comprised the Fourth Australian and the New Zealand Divisions under Lieut.-General Sir Alexander Godley.

This was the organisation of the Australian troops when the time arrived, in May, 1916, for their transfer by sea from Egypt to the scene of the titanic conflict which had been for nearly two years raging on the soil of France and Belgium.

This grouping did not, however, persist for more than a few weeks. The opening of the great Somme offensive in July 1916 found the First, Second and Fourth Divisions operating under First Anzac in the valley of the Somme, while the Fifth Australian and the New Zealand Division constituted the Second Anzac Corps in the Armentières-Fleurbaix sector. There followed other interchanges as the campaign developed, and by November of 1916, the grouping stood with First Anzac employing the First, Second, Fourth and Fifth Divisions, while Second Anzac comprised the Third Australian, the New Zealand and the Thirty-Fourth British Divisions.

The series of offensive operations opening with the great and successful Battle of Messines on June 7th, 1917, found the Fourth Australian Division once again under the command of General Godley, only to be again withdrawn before the concluding phases of the Third Battle of Ypres, in September and October, 1917. The autumn offensive of 1917, aiming at the capture of the Passchendaele Ridge, was the first occasion on which the whole of the five divisions were simultaneously engaged in the same locality in a common enterprise; but even on that occasion they still remained distributed under two different corps commands, and had not yet achieved the long-desired unity of command and of policy.

This constant interchange of these divisions, unavoidable as it probably was, undoubtedly militated against the attainment of the highest standard of efficiency. Uniform in scope and purpose as military administration and tactical policy aims to be when considered on broad lines, yet in a thousand and one matters of detail, many of them of dominating importance, the personality and the individual idiosyncrasies of the corps commander and of his principal executive staff officers, are calculated to exercise a powerful influence upon the functioning of the whole corps.

Under each corps commander there grew up in course of time a particular code of rules, and policies, of technical methods and even of technical jargon—most of it in an unwritten form. This nevertheless tended towards efficiency so long as the whole of the component personnel of the corps remained stable, but imposed many difficulties upon divisions and other units which joined and remained under the corps for a short period only.

The result was that a divisional commander and his staff, accustomed to work in one environment, often found great difficulty, and occupied some appreciable period of time, in accommodating themselves to a new environment, in which doctrines of attack or defence, counter-attack or trench routine, supply or maintenance were, some or all of them, widely different from those to which they had formerly become accustomed. But, in the case of Dominion troops, there was a motive far overshadowing the desire for a removal of difficulties of merely a technical nature. It was one founded upon a sense of Nationhood, which prompted the wish, vaguely formed early in the war, and steadily crystallizing in the minds both of the Australian people and of the troops themselves, that all the Australian divisions should be brought together under a single leadership.

This ideal was associated with the hope that the commanders and staffs should to as large an extent as possible, consist solely of Australian officers, as soon as ever men sufficiently qualified became available. It is difficult to emphasise such a desire without appearing to display ingratitude to a number of brilliant general and other officers of the Imperial Regular Service. These men, at a time when Australia was still able to produce only few officers with the necessary training and experience to justify their appointment to the command of divisions and brigades, or to the senior administrative and general staffs, bore these burdens in a manner which reflected upon them the greatest credit, and earned for them the gratitude of the Australian people.

I refer, among many others, particularly to General Sir W. Birdwood, Major-Generals Sir H.B. Walker, Sir N.M. Smyth, V.C. and Sir H.V. Cox and Brigadier-Generals W.B. Lesslie and P.G.M. Skene. But as the war went on, this aspect of the national aspiration became steadily realised; one by one, the senior commands and staff appointments were taken over by Australian officers who had proved their aptitude and suitability for such responsibilities.

The other ideal of unity of command and close association with each other of all Australian units, proved slower of realisation. All concerned thought and hoped that it had been, at last, achieved in December, 1917, when it was decided to abolish the two "Anzac" Corps, and to constitute a single Australian Army Corps. This was effected by the transfer of the Third Australian Division from Second to First Anzac Corps, by altering the title of "Second Anzac" to "XXII. Corps", and by substituting for the name "First Anzac" the name "Australian Army Corps", which name it bore until the termination of the war.

The only regrettable feature of this development was the dissolution of the close comradeship which had existed between the troops from the sister Dominions of Australia and New Zealand.

Even then all hopes were doomed to disappointment. For the next four months the corps contained five divisions in name only. Almost at once, the Fourth Australian Division was withdrawn to serve under the VII. Corps in connection with the operations before Cambrai. Not many weeks later, when the German avalanche was loosed, the whole five divisions became widely scattered, and, for a time, the Third and Fourth Divisions served under the VII. British Corps, the Fifth Division under the III. Corps, and the First Division under the XV. Corps. It was not until April, 1918, that four out of the five divisions again came together under the control of the Australian Corps commander, at that time General Sir William Birdwood.

About the middle of May, 1918, this popular commander was appointed to the leadership of the Fifth British Army. In deference to his long association with the Australian Imperial Force, he was asked to retain his status as G.O.C., A.I.F. His responsibilities as the commander of an army, and its removal to quite a different area in the theatre of war, made it, however, impossible for him to take any active part in the direction of the further operations of the Australian Corps.

Owing to the vacancy thus created, the commander-in-chief, with the concurrence of the Commonwealth Government, did me the great honour to appoint me to the command of the Australian Army Corps, a command which I took over during the closing days of May and retained until after the armistice.

At that juncture the First Australian Division was still involved in heavy fighting, under the XV. Corps, in the Hazebrouck sector, and no amount of pressure which I could bring to bear succeeded in prevailing upon G.H.Q. to release this division. It was not until early in

August, 1918, on the very eve of the opening of the great offensive, that, at long last, all the five Australian divisions became united into one corps, never to be again separated. From that date onwards all five divisions embarked (for the first time in their history) upon a series of combined offensive operations, the story of which I have set myself the task of unfolding in these pages.

The Australian Army Corps had by that time evolved from a mere geographical organisation into one which, over and above its component infantry divisions, had acquired a large number of accessory arms and services, called corps troops, which formed no part of a division. It is desirable for the complete understanding of the battle plans of the offensive period, to consider the extent and nature of the whole of the fighting and maintenance resources of the corps.

These fell theoretically into two categories, comprising on the one hand those units properly designated as "Corps Troops", which possessed a fixed and unalterable constitution, and, on the other hand, those additional units, known as "Army Troops", whose number and character fluctuated in accordance with the varying needs of the situation, and with the requirements of the various operations.

These army troops, whenever detailed to act under the orders of the corps commander, became an integral part of the corps, and were to all intents and purposes corps troops, until such time as they had completed the tasks allotted to them. The corps troops were multifarious in character, and amounted in the aggregate to large numbers, occasionally exceeding 50,000, a number as great as that of three additional divisions, whose normal strength in the closing phases of the war never exceeded 17,000.

The headquarters of the army corps comprised upwards of 300 staff and assistant staff officers, clerks, orderlies, draughtsmen, motor drivers, grooms, batmen, cooks and general helpers. The corps cavalry consisted, in the case of the Australian Army Corps, of the 13th Regiment of Australian Light Horse, and was employed, in conjunction with the Australian Cyclist Battalion, for reconnaissance, escort and dispatch rider duty.

The corps signal troops were an extensive organisation, and controlled the whole of the signal communications throughout the corps area (except within the divisions themselves), being responsible for the establishment, upkeep and working of every method of communication, whether by telegraph, telephone, wireless, pigeons, messenger dogs, aeroplane, or dispatch rider. Apart from telegraphists, mechanics and electrical experts in considerable numbers, adequate for the very heavy signal traffic during battle, and even during periods of comparative quiet, corps signals also operated two Motor Air Line and two Cable Sections, for the laying out and maintenance of wires. Those within the corps area, at any one place and time, amounted to several hundreds of miles.

The whole of the mechanical transport, consisting of hundreds of motor lorries, for the collection and distribution of ammunition, food, forage and ordnance stores of all descriptions, was also under the direct control of corps headquarters. So also, were some half-dozen mobile ordnance workshops, for the repair of weapons and vehicles of all kinds. All these were permanent corps troops, but represented only a fraction of those serving under the orders of the corps commander.

Among the Administrative Services there was a large contingent of the labour corps comprising some 20 companies, for the construction and maintenance of all roads, and water supply installations, and for the handling, daily, of a formidable bulk and weight of artillery ammunition; also two or more motor ambulance convoys, for the evacuation of the sick and wounded out of the corps area, and a number of army troops companies of engineers, as well as two companies of Australian tunnellers, who were usually employed upon the construction and maintenance of bridges, locks, water transport mechanism, deep dugouts and battle stations.

But the fighting units of the corps troops formed by far the largest proportion, and comprised artillery, heavy trench mortars, air squadrons and tanks. The artillery alone merits more detailed consideration. It comprised a vast array of many different classes of guns for many different purposes, and classified into various categories by reference either to their calibres, their mobility or their tactical purposes.

Grouped according to calibre, all guns and howitzers of 4½-inch bore or less were strictly considered as field artillery which, although administered by the divisions, was almost invariably fought under the direct orders of the corps commander. All guns and howitzers of greater bore, up to the giant 15-inch, were known as heavy and siege artillery.

Regarded from the point of view of mobility, all field guns and that wonderfully useful weapon, the 60-pounder, were horse-drawn, the larger ordnance were tractor-drawn, and the very largest were mounted on railway trains and hauled by steam locomotive.

Finally, as regards tactical utilisation, some natures of ordnance were invariably employed for barrage or harassing fire, others for

The Australian Corps Commander—with the Generals of his Staff.

bombardment, others for counter-battery fighting, and yet others for anti-aircraft purposes.

The total ordnance under the orders of the Australian Army Corps naturally fluctuated according to the daily battle requirements, but amounted at times, during the period of the war under consideration, to as many as 1,200 guns of all natures and calibres, grouped in brigades each of four to six batteries, each of four to six guns.

This very formidable artillery equipment far transcended in quantity and dynamic power anything that had been envisaged in the previous years of the war, or in any previous war, as possible of administrative or tactical control under a single commander. It undoubtedly became a paramount factor in the victories which the corps achieved. The artillery of the corps is entitled to the proud boast that it earned the confidence and gratitude of the infantry.

It must be left to the imagination to conceive the complexity of the task of keeping this enormous mass of artillery regularly supplied with its ammunition, of multifarious types and in adequate quantities of each, of allocating to each brigade and even to each battery its appropriate task in the general plan, and of advancing the whole organisation over half-ruined roads and broken bridges, in order to keep up with the infantry as the battle moved forward from day to day. It would defy a detailed description intelligible to any but gunnery experts.

The Air Force had, by the summer of 1918, also achieved a great development. The numerous air squadrons had embarked upon a policy of specialisation in tactical employment, in accordance with the build and capacities of the aeroplanes with which they were equipped. Thus, gradually the whole range of utilisation became covered, from the small fast single-seater fighting scout, intended to engage and drive off enemy 'planes, to the slower two-seater reconnaissance machines, employed chiefly for photography and for the direction of artillery fire, and the giant long-distance bombing machines.

The Australian Corps had at its exclusive disposal at all times the No. 3 Squadron of the Australian Flying Corps, and employed the machines for reconnaissance prior to and after battle, and for contact and counter-attack work and artillery observation during battle. But, whenever the scope of the operations rendered it necessary, the resources of the corps in aircraft were enormously increased, and as many as a dozen squadrons were on occasions employed, during battle, in low flying pursuit of enemy infantry and transport, in production of smoke screens, in bombing, in ammunition carrying, and

The Valley of the Somme—looking East towards Bray, which was then still in enemy hands.

in dispatch bearing—over and above usual reconnaissance work designed to keep corps and divisional headquarters rapidly and minutely informed, from moment to moment, of the situation of the infantry in actual contact with the enemy.

Another branch of the air force activities under the direct control of the corps was the captive balloon service. Some five large captive or kite balloons, carrying trained artillery observers, regularly ascended along the corps front whenever the weather and the conditions of visibility permitted, to a height of from 2,000 to 3,000 feet, and with the aid of powerful telescopes and of telephone wires woven into the anchoring cables, kept the artillery regularly notified of all visible enemy movement, and of the occurrence of all suitable targets of opportunity, such as the flashes from enemy guns in action.

During battle one such balloon was invariably sent up well forward to observe as closely as possible the progress of the fighting, but the results were almost uniformly disappointing, because the smoke and dust of the barrage and the general murk of battle usually proved impenetrable to the air observer, tied as he was to a fixed position. The reports of these observers were usually confined to the laconic observation: "Can't see much, but all apparently going well."

The last of the major fighting units of corps troops remaining to be mentioned are the tanks. These extraordinary products of the war underwent a remarkable evolution during the two years which followed their first introduction on the battlefield in the Somme campaign of 1916. The standard of efficiency which had been reached by the early summer of 1918, in the most developed types of these curious monsters, as far outclassed that of the earlier types in both mechanical and fighting properties as the modern service rifle compared with the old Brown Bess of the Peninsular War. The tank crews had improved in like proportion, both in skill, enterprise and adaptability.

Nothing can be more unstinted than the acknowledgment which the Australian Corps makes of its obligation to the Tank Corps for its powerful assistance throughout the whole of the great offensive. Commencing with the Battle of Hamel, a large contingent of tanks participated in every important "set-piece" engagement which the corps undertook. The tanks were organised into brigades, each of three battalions, each of three companies, each of twelve tanks. During the opening phases, early in August, the tank contingent comprised a whole brigade of Mark V. Tanks, a battalion of Mark V. (Star) Tanks, and a battalion of fast armoured cars; in the later phases, during the assault on the Hindenburg Line, a second brigade of Mark V. Tanks and a battalion of Whippets also co-operated.

Such was the formidable array of fighting resources under the direct orders of the Australian Corps commander, and, together with the five Australian divisions, formed a fighting organisation of great strength and solidarity. It became an instrument for offensive warfare, as has been said by a high authority, which for size and power excelled all corps organisations which either this or any previous war had produced. It was an instrument which it was a great responsibility, as also a great honour, to wield in the task of shattering the still formidable military power of the enemy. For in the early summer of 1918, that power appeared to be still unimpaired, and still capable of inflicting serious reverses upon the Allied cause.

Early in 1918, owing to the depletion of human material, the Imperial divisions were reconstituted by a reduction of their infantry brigades from a four-battalion to a three-battalion basis, thus reducing the available infantry by twenty-five *per cent*. But in this reduction, the Australian divisions during the fighting period shared only to a very small extent. In March the strength of the 15 brigades of Australian infantry in the field was still 60 battalions.

The heavy fighting of March and April compelled the extinction of 3 battalions, one each respectively in the 9th, 12th and 13th Infantry Brigades; but the remaining 57 battalions of infantry remained intact until after the close of the actual fighting operations early in October. The corps was therefore enabled to maintain an additional twelve battalions over and above the then prevailing corresponding Imperial organisation.

It was thus the largest of all army corps ever organised, in this or any other war, by any of the combatants—the largest both in point of numbers and of military resources of all descriptions, approaching, and in one case exceeding, a full army command.

But even these great resources and responsibilities were added to, during the course of the operations, by the allocation, at successive times, to the Australian Corps of the 17th Imperial Division, the 32nd Imperial Division and the 27th and 30th American Divisions. Thus, during the closing days of September, 1918, the corps numbered a total of nearly 200,000 men, exceeding more than fourfold the whole of the British troops under the command of the Duke of Wellington at the Battle of Waterloo.

Of this total about one-half comprised Australian troops, the heavy artillery and other army units attached to the corps consisting of Imperial troops. The commanders and staffs from June, 1918, until the end consisted almost entirely of Australian officers, among whom the following were the senior:

Corps Commander	Lieut.-General Sir J. Monash, G.C.M.G., K.C.B., V.D.
Corps Chief-of-Staff	Brigadier-General T. A. Blamey, C.M.G., D.S.O.
Corps Artillery Commander	Brigadier-General W. A. Coxen, C.B., C.M.G., D.S.O.
Chief Engineer	Brigadier-General C. H. Foott, C.B., C.M.G.
1st Div. Commander	Major-General Sir T. W. Glasgow, K.C.B., D.S.O.
General Staff Officer	Lieut.-Colonel A. M. Ross, C.M.G., D.S.O.
Chief Admin. Officer	Lieut.-Colonel H. G. Viney, C.M.G., D.S.O.
2nd Div. Commander	Major-General Sir C. Rosenthal, K.C.B., C.M.G., D.S.O.
General Staff Officer	Lieut.-Colonel C. G. N. Miles, C.M.G., D.S.O.
Chief Admin. Officer	Lieut.-Colonel J. M. A. Durrant C.M.G., D.S.O.
3rd Div. Commander	Major-General Sir J. Gellibrand, K.C.B., D.S.O.
General Staff Officer	Lieut.-Colonel C. H. Jess, C.M.G., D.S.O.
Chief Admin. Officer	Lieut.-Colonel R. E. Jackson, D.S.O.
4th Div. Commander	Major-General E. G. Sinclair-Maclagan, C.B., D.S.O.
General Staff Officer	Lieut.-Colonel J. D. Lavarack, C.M.G., D.S.O.
Chief Admin. Officer	Lieutenant-Colonel R. Dowse, D.S.O.

All the above were Australian officers, and most of them were of Australian birth. There were also two senior staff officers of the Regular Army, Brigadier-General R.A. Carruthers, C.B., C.M.G., who was chief of the Administrative Services, and Brigadier-General L.D. Fraser, C.B., C.M.G., who was in immediate command of the heavy artillery of the corps. (For grouping of Australian brigades into divisions, see Appendix "A".)

CHAPTER 1
Back to the Somme

The early days of the year 1918 found the Australian Corps consisting of the First, Second, Third and Fifth Australian Divisions, while the Fourth had been transferred far south to co-operate in the later developments of the Cambrai fighting. The corps was then holding, defensively, a sector of the line in Flanders, which had in the previous years of the war become, at various times, familiar to all our divisions, and which extended from the River Lys at Armentières, northwards, as far as to include the southern half of the Messines Ridge.

It was, indeed, that very stretch of country, which in June, 1917, had been captured by our Third Division, in co-operation with the New Zealanders. Opposite its centre lay the town of Warneton, still in the hands of the enemy. Excepting for a small area of undulating ground in the extreme north of the corps sector, the country was a forbidding expanse of devastation, flat and woebegone, with long stretches of the front line submerged waist deep after every freshet in the River Lys, and with the greater part of our trench system like nothing but a series of canals of liquid mud. This unsavoury region formed, however, the most obvious line of approach for an enemy who, debouching from the direction of Warneton, aimed at the high land between us and the Channel ports; so that, tactically useless as were these mud flats, it was imperative that they should be strongly defended, in order to protect from capture the important heights of Messines, Kemmel, Hill 63, Mont des Cats and Cassel.

During the fighting of the preceding summer and early autumn, which gave the Australian troops possession of this territory, the locality was dry, practicable for movement, and reasonably comfortable for the front line troops. Now it was water-logged, often ice-bound, bleak and inhospitable. The precious months of dry weather, between August and October, 1917, had been allowed to pass without any comprehensive attempt on the part of those divisions which had relieved the Second Anzac Corps after its capture of this ground to perfect the defences of the newly-conquered territory. At any rate, there was little to show for any work that may have been attempted.

Now, in the very depth of the worst season of the year, the demand came to prepare the region for defence and resistance to the last; for the threat of a great German offensive in the opening of the 1918 campaigning season was already beginning to take shape. It was the Australian Corps which was called upon to answer that demand. There followed week after week of heart-breaking labour, much of it necessarily by night, in draining the flat land, in erecting acre upon acre of wire entanglements, in constructing hundreds of strong points, and concrete machine-gun emplacements. Trenches had to be dug, although the sides collapsed unless immediately revetted with fascines or sheet iron; roads had to be repaired, and vain attempts were made to provide the trench garrisons with dry and bearable underground living quarters.

The monotony of all this labour, which long after—when the Australians had disappeared from the scene and were again fighting on the Somme—proved to have been undertaken all in vain, was relieved only by an occasional raid, undertaken by one or other of our front line divisions, for the purpose of molesting the enemy and gathering information. The corps front was held by two divisions in line, one in support, and one resting in a back area; the rotation of trench duty gave each division about six weeks in the line.

My own command at that juncture still comprised the Third Australian Division, which I had organised and trained in England, eighteen months before. Although this division had never been on the Somme, it had seen a great deal of fighting in Flanders during 1917. During this period, therefore, and until the outbreak of the storm in the last days of March, 1918, my interest centred chiefly in the doings of the Third Division, although for a very short period I had the honour of commanding the corps during the temporary absence of Sir William Birdwood.

The information at our disposal led to the inevitable conclusion that, during January and February, the enemy was busy in transferring a great mass of military resources from the Russian to the Western Front. No one capable of reading the signs entertained the smallest doubt that he contemplated taking the offensive, in the spring, on a large scale. The only questions were, at what point would he strike? and what tactics would he employ?

Every responsible Australian commander, accordingly, during those months, applied himself diligently to these problems, formulated his doctrines of obstinate defence, and of the defensive offensive; and saw to it that his troops received such precognition in these matters as was possible at such a time and in such an environment. The principles of defence in successive zones, of the rapid development of infantry and artillery fire power, of the correct distribution of machine-guns, of rear-guard tactics, and questions of the best equipment for long marches and rapid movement were debated and resolved upon, in both official and unofficial conferences of officers.

All this discussion bore good fruit. Among the possible roles which the Australian divisions might be called upon to fill, when the great issue was joined, were those which involved these very matters. And so, the event proved; and the Australians then approached their new and unfamiliar tasks, not wholly unprepared by training and study for the difficulties involved.

It was on March 8th that the Third Division bade a last but by no means a regretful farewell to the mud of Flanders and Belgium—regions which it had inhabited almost continuously for the preceding sixteen months. The division moved back for a well-earned rest, to a pleasant countryside at Nielles-lez-Blequin, not far from Boulogne. It was lying there, enjoying the first signs of dawning spring when, on March 21st, the curtain was rung up for a great drama, in which the Australian troops were destined to play no subordinate part.

There followed many weeks of crowded and strenuous days, and the story of this time must, of necessity, assume the form of a personal narrative. Events followed one upon the other so rapidly, and the centre of interest changed so quickly from place to place and from hour to hour, that no recital except that of the future historian writing with a wealth of collected material at his disposal, could take upon itself any other guise than that of a record of individual experience.

The Germans attacked the front of the Fifth British Army on March 21st. The information which was at the disposal of our high command was not of such a nature that the promulgation of it would have been calculated to elevate the spirits of the army; consequently divisions situated as we were, in reserve, and, for the time being, entirely out of the picture, had to depend for our news partly upon rumour, which was always unreliable, and partly upon severely censored *communiqués*, framed so as to allay public anxiety. Nothing definite emerged from such sources, except that things were going ill and that fighting was taking place on ground far behind what had been our front line near St. Quentin. This hint was enough to justify the expectation that my division would not be left for long unemployed; and on the same day, March 21st, instructions were issued for all units to prepare for a move, to dump unessential baggage, to fill up all mobile supplies, and to stand by in readiness to march at a few hours' notice.

Orders came to move on March 22nd. The division was to move

east, that is, back into Flanders, and not south to the Somme Valley, as all had hoped. The prescribed move duly started, but by March 24th had been arrested, for orders had come to cancel the move and await fresh orders. Advanced parties, for billeting duty, were to proceed next morning by motor lorry to Doullens, and there await orders. Later came detailed instructions that the division was to be transferred from the Australian Corps to the Tenth Corps, which latter was to be G.H.Q. Reserve, and that the whole division was to be moved the next night to the Doullens area, the dismounted troops by rail, and the artillery and other mounted units by route-march. (The majority of the place-names mentioned in the remainder of this chapter will be found on Maps A or J.)

It was evident that the plans of the high command were the subject of rapid changes, in sympathy, probably, with fluctuations in the situation, which were not ascertainable by me. There followed a night and day of strenuous activity, during which arrangements were completed to entrain the three infantry brigades and the pioneers at three different railway stations, to start off the whole of the mounted units on their long march by road, and to ensure that all fighting troops were properly equipped with munitions, food and water, all ready for immediate employment. It was well that my staff responded capably to the heavy demands made upon them, and that all this preparatory work was efficiently done.

The entrainments commenced at midnight on the 25th and continued all night. At break of day on the 26th, after assuring myself that everyone was correctly on the move, I proceeded south by motorcar, in the endeavour to find the Tenth Corps Headquarters, and to report to them for orders. My fruitless search of that forenoon revealed to me the first glimpse of the true reason for that far-reaching disorganisation and confusion which confronted me during the next twenty-four hours.

Over three years of trench warfare had accustomed the whole army to fixed locations for all headquarters, and to settled routes and lines of inter-communication. The powerful German onslaught and the recoil of a broad section of our fighting front had suddenly disturbed the whole of this complex organisation. The headquarters of brigades, divisions, and even corps, ceased to have fixed locations where they could be found, or assured lines of telegraph or telephone communications, by which they could be reached. Everything was in a state of flux, and the process of getting into personal contact with each other suddenly took responsible leaders hours where it had previously taken minutes.

In its broad result, this disorganisation affected most seriously the retiring troops, by depriving them of the advantages of rapidly disseminated orders for properly co-ordinated action by a large number of corps and divisions withdrawing side by side. The consequence was, I am convinced, that the recoil—which may have been inevitable at first by reason of the intensity of the German attack, and because the defensive organisation of the Fifth Army had been unduly attenuated—was allowed to extend over a much greater distance, and to continue for longer, in point of time, than ought to have been the case.

Between Albert and St. Quentin there were in existence several lines of defence, which by reason of their topographical features, or the existence of trenches and entanglements, were eminently suitable for making a stand. Yet no stand was made, at any rate on a broad front, because there was no co-ordination in the spasmodic attempts to do so. I subsequently learned of more than one instance where brigades of infantry or of artillery found themselves perfectly well able to hold on, but were compelled to a continued retirement by the melting away of the units on their flanks.

I sought the Tenth Corps at Hautcloque, where they were to be. They were not there. I proceeded to Frevent, where they were said to have been the night before. They had already left. In despair, I proceeded to Doullens, resolved at least to ensure the orderly detrainment of my division and their quartering for the following night, and there to await further orders. A despatch rider was sent off to G.H.Q. to report my whereabouts, and the fact that I was without orders.

Arriving at Doullens, I tumbled into a scene of indescribable confusion. The population were preparing to evacuate the town *en masse*, and an exhausted and hungry soldiery was pouring into the town from the east and south-east, with excited tales that the German cavalry was on their heels. Influenced by the persistency of these reports, I determined to make, immediately, dispositions to cover the detrainment of my troops, so that some show of resistance could be made.

In the midst of all this stress and anxiety, I was favoured by a run of good luck. Within half an hour of my reaching Doullens, the first of my railway trains arrived, bringing Brigadier-General Rosenthal and a battalion of the 9th Brigade, sufficient troops, at any rate, to furnish a strong outpost line for covering the eastern approaches of Doullens, while the remainder of the brigade should arrive. These arrangements made, I motored to Mondicourt, where almost immediately afterwards a train arrived, bringing Brigadier-General McNicoll and the first battalion of the 10th Brigade.

There also arrived, almost simultaneously, that rumour with the ridiculous *dénouement*, that German armoured motorcars were approaching along the road from Albert and were within three miles of that point. Those armoured cars proved ultimately to be a train of French agricultural implements which a wheezy and rumbling traction engine was doing its best to salve. McNicoll likewise received orders to put out a line of outposts to cover Mondicourt railway station.

At this point, too, endless streams of dust-begrimed soldiers were straggling westwards. McNicoll collected many hundreds of them, and did not omit, by very direct methods, to prevail upon all of them who had not yet lost their rifles and essential equipment, to call a halt and join his own troops in the defensive dispositions which he was making.

My next business was to select a suitable central point at which to establish my headquarters, preferably where I could find a still intact telephone service. Again, by good luck I found a most suitable location in a small *château* at Couturelle, whose owner hospitably provided a much needed meal. It was there, soon after my arrival, that I learned of the presence in the neighbourhood of Major-General Maclagan; this news, implying as it did the presence also of some at least of the Fourth Australian Division, was a gleam of sunshine in an otherwise gloomy prospect. Report said that he was at Basseux, and thither I proceeded, in order to arrange, by personal conference with him, some plan for co-ordinated action.

Basseux rests on the main road from Doullens to Arras, which lies roughly parallel to the line along which, as subsequently transpired, the vanguard of the enemy was endeavouring to advance at that part of the front. That main road I found packed, for the whole of the length which I had to traverse, with a steadily retreating collection of heterogeneous units, service vehicles and guns of all imaginable types and sizes, intermingled with hundreds of civilian refugees, and farm waggons, carts, trollies and barrows packed high with pathetic loads of household effects. The retrograde movement was orderly and methodical enough, and there was nothing in the nature of a rout, but it was nevertheless a determined movement to the rear which evidenced nothing but a desire to keep moving.

I found Maclagan at about four o'clock. His division had already been on the move, by bus and route march, for three days without rest. The position to the east and south-east of him was obscure, and he also had posted a line of outposts in the supposed direction of the enemy, and was arranging to despatch his 4th Brigade to Hebuterne (which the enemy was reported to have entered), with orders to recapture that town. That the enemy was not very far away became evident from the fact that the vicinity of the hut in which we were conferring presently came under desultory long-range shell-fire.

There was nothing to be done except to arrange jointly to keep up an effective and as far as possible continuous line of outposts towards the south-east, and to await developments. Having made these arrangements I returned along the same crowded road, which was now also being leisurely shelled by the enemy, to Couturelle. There I found that the principal officers of my staff had arrived.

Thereupon orders were issued for the concentration, after detrainment, of my three brigades in the following areas, each with due outpost precautions, *viz*.: 9th Brigade at Pas, 10th Brigade at Authie, and 11th Brigade at Couin. My artillery was still distant a full day's march by road.

About nine o'clock that evening I received, by telephone, my first order from the Tenth Corps. It ran as follows:

> A staff officer has left some time ago on his way to you, carrying instructions for you to report personally at once to Corbie for orders. We have since heard that you are to go to Montigny instead.

It was nearly an hour before the staff officer arrived, having been delayed on the road by congestion of traffic. The instructions he carried transferred my division from the Tenth to the Seventh Corps, to whom I was to report personally, without delay, at Corbie. It was evident from the later telephone message that the Seventh Corps had been compelled to withdraw from Corbie, and was proceeding to Montigny.

This was the second stroke of good luck that day; for if the telephone message above recited had not overtaken the staff officer, it is quite probable that I should have already started for a wrong destination, and have had to waste valuable time at a most critical juncture. Had I failed to find General Congreve, the Seventh corps commander, *that same night*, it is almost certain that my division would have arrived on the Somme too late to prevent the capture of Amiens.

Setting out from Couturelle shortly after ten o'clock that night, accompanied by four of my Staff and two despatch-riders, with two motorcars and two motorcycles, in black darkness, on unfamiliar roads congested with refugee traffic, I did not reach Montigny until after midnight. I found General Congreve in the corner of a bare *salon* of stately proportions, in a deserted *château* by the roadside, seated with his chief of staff at a small table, and examining a map by the flickering light of a candle. The rest of the *château* was in darkness, but heaps of hastily dumped staff baggage impeded all the corridors. General Congreve was brief and to the point. What he said amounted to this:

> At four o'clock today my corps was holding a line from Albert to Bray, when the line gave way. The enemy is now pushing westwards and if not stopped tomorrow will certainly secure all the heights overlooking Amiens. What you must try and do is to get your division deployed across his path. The valleys of the Ancre and the Somme offer good points for your flanks to rest upon. You must, of course, get as far east as you can, but I know of a good line of old trenches, which I believe are still in good condition, running from Méricourt-l'Abbé towards Sailly-le-Sec. Occupy them, if you can't get further east.

At that juncture General Maclagan arrived and received similar crisp orders to bring his division into a position of support on the high land in the bend of the Ancre to the west of Albert. I gleaned further that the Seventh Corps was now the south flank corps of the Third Army, and that as the Fifth Army, south of the Somme, had practically melted away, while the French were retiring south-westerly and leaving an hourly increasing gap between their north flank and the Somme, General Byng had resolved to make every effort not only to maintain the flank of his Third Army on the Somme, but also to prevent it being turned from the south, while the commander-in-chief was taking other measures to attempt next day to fill the gap above alluded to.

It was already 1 a.m. of March 27th, and I had left my division twenty miles away. Everything depended now on quick decision and faultless executive action. It was fortunate that a telephone line to G.H.Q. had been found in good working order, and that the services of three large motorbus convoys could be arranged for to proceed at once to the Doullens area, in order to transport my infantry during the night to the place appointed. I worked with my staff till nearly break of day, considering and settling all detailed arrangements, and we then separated in various directions to our appointed tasks.

I proceeded myself a little after dawn, with one staff officer, to

Franvillers, which had been decided upon as the point for leaving the buses. There was yet no sign of any Australian troops, and the village was being hastily evacuated by the terror-stricken inhabitants. But there were ample and visible signs, far away on the high plateau beyond the Ancre Valley, that the German line of skirmishers was already on the move, slowly driving back the few troops of British cavalry who were, most valiantly, trying to delay their advance.

The next hour was one of intense suspense and expectancy; but my anxiety was relieved when there rolled into the village from the north, a motorbus convoy of thirty vehicles, crowded with good staunch Australian infantry of the 11th Brigade, and bringing also Brigadier-General Cannan and some of his brigade staff. It was not the first time in the war that the London motorbus—after abandoning the population of the great metropolis to enforced pedestrianism—had helped to save a most critical situation.

Almost immediately after, there arrived McNicoll, with a battalion of his 10th Brigade. Hour after hour a steady stream of omnibus convoys came in. No time was lost in assembling the troops, and in directing the infantry—company after company—down the steep, winding road to the little village of Heilly, and thence across the Ancre, to deploy on the selected line of defence indicated in the orders above recited.

The spectacle of that infantry will be ever memorable to me, as one of the most inspiring sights of the whole war. Here was the Third Division—the "new chum" division, which, in spite of its great successes in Belgium and Flanders, had never been able to boast, like its sister divisions, that it had been "down on the Somme"—come into its own at last, and called upon to prove its mettle. And then there was the thought that they were going to measure themselves, man to man, against an enemy who, skulking behind his field works, had for so long pounded them to pieces in their trenches, poisoned them with gas, and bombed them as they slept in their billets.

That, at any rate, was the point of view of the private soldier, and no one who saw those battalions, in spite of the fatigue of two sleepless nights, marching on that crisp, clear spring morning, with head erect and the swing and precision of a royal review parade, could doubt that not a man of them would flinch from any assault that was likely to fall upon them. Nor was there a man who did not fully grasp that upon him and his comrades was about to fall the whole responsibility of frustrating the German attempt to capture Amiens and separate the Allied Armies.

By midday, the situation was already well in hand, and by four o'clock I was able to report to the Seventh Corps that no less than six battalions were already deployed, astride of the triangle formed by the Ancre and the Somme, on the line Méricourt-Sailly-le-Sec, distributed in a series of "localities" defended by rifles and Lewis guns. As yet no artillery was available.

The 11th Brigade occupied this line to the south of the main road from Corbie to Bray, the 10th Brigade continued it to the north of the road, while the 9th Brigade was leaving the buses and assembling in the neighbourhood of Heilly.

So far, the pressure of the enemy upon my front had not been serious. It was obvious that he had, as yet, very little artillery at his disposal. We had not, however, found our front totally devoid of defenders. During the forenoon, a few troops of our cavalry, and a force under Brigadier-General Cummings, comprising about 1,500 mixed infantry, the remnants of a large number of different units of the Third Army, were slowly withdrawing under pressure from the advancing German patrols. These valiant "die-hards", deserving of the greatest praise in comparison with the many thousands of their comrades who had withdrawn from any further attempt to stem the onflowing tide, were now ordered to retire through my outpost line, thus leaving the Australian infantry at last face to face with the enemy.

These dispositions were completed only in the nick of time. All that afternoon the enemy appeared over the sky-line in front of us, both in lines of skirmishers and in numerous small patrols, endeavouring to work forward in the folds of the ground, and to sneak towards us in the gullies. But all of them were received with well directed rifle fire and the enemy suffered many losses. Towards nightfall the attempts to continue his advance died away.

That was, literally, the end of the great German advance in this part of the field, and although, as will be told later, the enemy renewed the attempt on several subsequent occasions to reach Amiens, he gained not a single inch of ground, but, on the contrary, was compelled in front of us to undertake a slow but steady retrograde movement.

Our reconnoitring patrols discovered, however, that the enemy already had possession of the village of Sailly-Laurette, and of Marett and Treux Woods, but that he was not yet in great strength on the crest of the plateau. Orders were issued to perfect the organisation of our defensive line, put out wire entanglements, dig-in machine-guns, and rest the troops in relays during the coming night, but not to attempt any forward movement until the next night.

My artillery and other mounted units were still half a day's march away; but Brigadier-General Grimwade, their commander, had been instructed to push on in advance, with the whole of the commanders of his brigades and batteries. They arrived on the scene in sufficient time to enable the whole situation to be examined in the daylight, and for detailed action to be decided upon. The artillery kept coming in during the whole of the following night, and although men and horses were almost exhausted after two days of forced marching, their spirits were never higher. Next morning found the guns already in action, and engaging all bodies of the enemy who dared to expose themselves to view.

I must now turn to the Fourth Australian Division. They had been less fortunate in several respects. Maclagan was directed to leave behind his 4th Brigade, which had on the 26th speedily become committed to important operations under the 62nd Division in front of Hebuterne, from which village this brigade had driven the enemy. This left him with only two Brigades, the 12th and 13th. He was faced with the obligation of bringing his already over-tired infantry, by route march, down from the Basseux area, to the high ground west and south-west of Albert. That town had fallen and the situation there had, by the 26th, also become very critical.

This march was, however, accomplished in strict accordance with orders, and was a remarkable feat of endurance by the troops of the 12th and 13th Brigades. There can be no doubt, however, that the effort was more than justified, for the mere presence, in a position of readiness, of these two Australian brigades, did much to steady the situation opposite Albert, by heartening the line troops and stimulating their commanders to hang on for a little longer. It was this last effort which brought to a standstill the German advance north of the Ancre, as the entry of the Third Division had stopped that to the south of that river.

After his two brigades had had only four hours' rest, Maclagan took over, with them, the control of the fighting front, opposite Dernancourt and Albert, which the Seventh Corps had allotted to him. Thus, by the night of the 27th, as the result of the rapid movements which I have described and the ready response of the troops, there was already in position the nucleus of a stout defence by five Australian brigades, stretching almost continuously from Hebuterne to the Somme, while another Australian brigade, the 9th, remained still uncommitted.

But the situation south of the Somme gave cause for the gravest anxiety. The north flank of the French was hourly retiring in a south-westerly direction, and the ever widening gap was filled only by a scratch force of odd units supported and assisted by a few elements of the First Cavalry Division. The right flank of our Third Army, therefore, lay exposed to the danger of being turned, if the enemy should succeed in pressing his advantage as far west as Corbie, and in crossing the river at or west of that town.

It was for this reason that, after a conference with General Congreve, late in the day, I decided to deploy my 9th Brigade along the Somme from Sailly-le-Sec westward as far as Aubigny, (2 miles west of Corbie)—far too extended a front for one brigade, but at least an effort to dispute the passage by the enemy of the existing bridges and lock-gates over the Somme.

The two following days were full of toil and hard travelling in establishing touch with divisional headquarters to the north and south of me, in arranging for co-ordinated action with them, and in gleaning all possible information as to the situation, and as to the number and condition of other troops available in an emergency.

It was an especial pleasure for the Australian troops to find themselves fighting in these days in close association with famous British Cavalry Regiments, and that these feelings were reciprocated may be gathered from the following letter from Major-General Mullens, who commanded the First Cavalry Division, which was devoting its energies to covering the gap between the Somme and the French flank:

> My Dear Monash,
> I was hoping to have come to see you, when the battle allowed, to thank you, your artillery commander, and your brigadiers who were alongside of my division, for your most valuable and encouraging support and assistance, especially on the 30th March, when we had a hard fight to keep the Bosche out of our position. I was very much struck by the courtesy of yourself and your officers in coming to see me personally, and for your own and their keen desire to do everything in their power to help. As you know, we had a curious collection of units to deal with, and it was a very real relief to know that I had your stout-hearted fellows on my left flank and that all worry was therefore eliminated as to the safety of my flanks.
> Your order for the placing of your heavy guns and batteries so

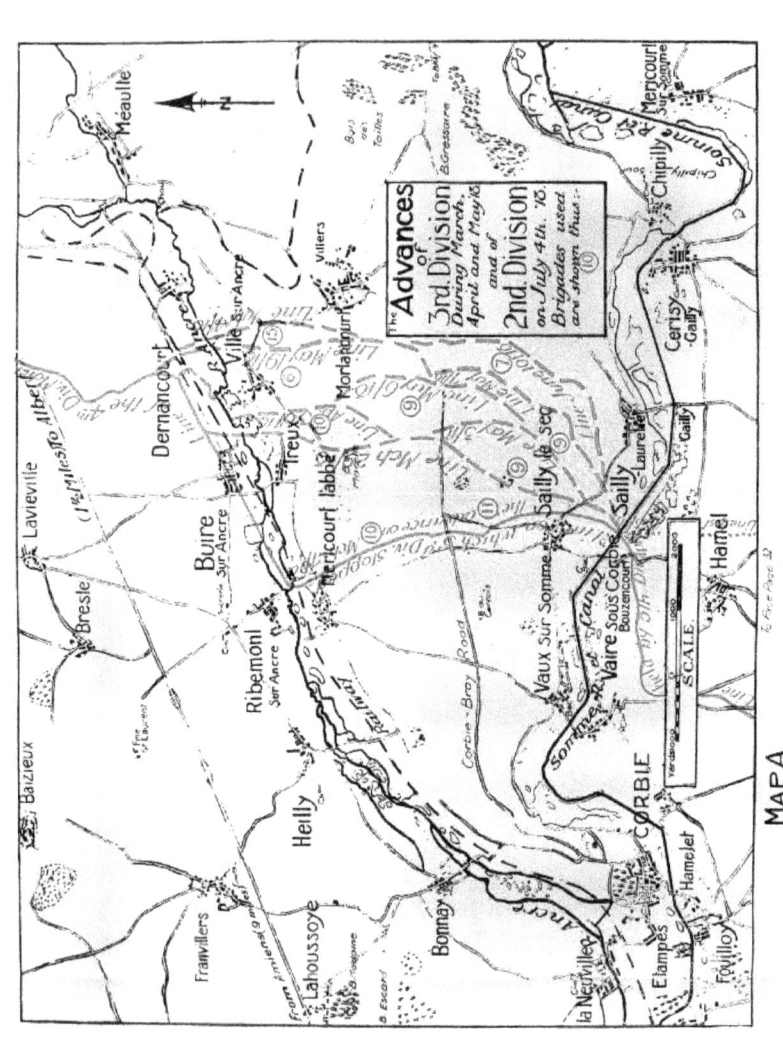

MAP A.

as to cover my front was of very real assistance, and incidentally they killed a lot of Huns, and what they did was much appreciated by us all. Will you convey to all concerned my own appreciation, and that of all ranks of the 1st Cavalry Division. It was a pleasure and an honour to be fighting alongside troops who displayed such magnificent *moral*. I only hope we may have the chance of co-operating with you again, and under more favourable circumstances.

      Yours sincerely,

          (Sgnd.)   R.L. Mullens.

On the night of March 29th, I advanced my line, pivoting on my right, until my left rested on the Ancre east of Buire, an extreme advance of over 2,000 yards, meeting some opposition and taking a few prisoners. This deprived the enemy of over a mile of valuable vantage ground on the crest of the plateau along which ran the main road from Corbie to Bray.

By that time, it was apparent that the enemy's artillery resources were hourly accumulating, and on the next afternoon he delivered a determined attack along my whole front, employing two divisions. The attack was completely repelled, with an estimated loss to the enemy of at least 3,000 killed. My artillery were firing over open sights and had never in their previous experience had such tempting targets.

On the previous day, however, the situation between the Somme and Villers-Bretonneux, and still further to the south, had become desperate; and much to my discomfiture I was ordered to hand over my 9th Brigade (Rosenthal) for duty with the 61st Division, in order to reinforce that dissolving sector. My importunity as to the necessity for maintaining the defence of my river flank, however, led the Seventh Corps commander to let me have, in exchange, the 15th Brigade (Elliott), which was the first brigade of the Fifth Australian Division to arrive from Flanders on the present scene of operations. This interchange of brigades was completed by the 30th.

That day was further marked by a concentrated bombardment of the village of Franvillers, in which I had established my headquarters. Although no serious loss was suffered, the responsible work of my staff was disturbed. On reporting the occurrence to General Congreve, he insisted upon my moving my headquarters back to St. Gratien, which move was completed the next day.

On April 4th the enemy attacked, in force, south of the Somme, and the village of Hamel was lost to us by the rout of the remnants of a very exhausted British division which had been sent in the night before to defend it. This success gave the enemy a footing upon a portion of Hill 104, and brought him to the eastern outskirts of Villers-Bretonneux. Three months later it cost the Australian Corps a concentrated effort to compel him to surrender these advantages.

One last and final attempt to break through the Australian phalanx north of the Somme was made by the enemy on April 5th. The full weight of this blow fell chiefly upon the gallant Fourth Australian Division. The Battle of Dernancourt will live long in the annals of military history as an example of dogged and successful defence. The whole day long the enemy expended division after division in the vain endeavour to compel two weak Australian brigades to loosen their hold on the important high ground lying west of Albert. He well knew that the capture by him of these heights involved the inevitable withdrawal of the Third Australian Division also, and that thereby the path to Amiens would again lie open.

The great German blow against the important railway centre of Amiens had been parried, and from this time onwards interest in this sphere of operations rapidly waned. It blazed up again for a few hours only when, three weeks later, the enemy made his final attempt to reach his goal, on this occasion by way of Villers-Bretonneux. North of the Somme, his activity quickly died down, and the attitude of both combatants gradually assumed the old familiar aspect of trench warfare, with its endless digging of trenches, line behind line, its weary trench routine, and its elaborate installation of permanent lines of communication and of administrative establishments of all descriptions.

South of the Somme, the Fifth Australian Division came into the line on April 5th, relieving a cavalry division on a frontage of about 5,000 yards, and thereby obviating any further necessity for the maintenance of my flank river defence. This duty had been performed for me in succession by the 15th Australian, the 104th Imperial and the 13th Australian Brigades (the latter then under Glasgow). My 9th Brigade still remained detached from me, operating under both the 18th and 61st British Divisions, and performed prodigies of valorous fighting in a series of desperate local attacks and counter-attacks, which took place between Villers-Bretonneux and Hangard, where the French northern flank then lay. In this service the 9th Brigade received gallant co-operation from the 5th Australian Brigade (of the 2nd Australian Division), which was now also arriving in this area, after having been relieved from trench garrison duty in the Messines-Warneton sector in Flanders.

The Fifth Division and these two detached brigades were, during this period, serving under the Third Corps (Butler), which had been reconstituted to fill the gap between the Somme and the flank of the French Army. The First Australian Division was already well on the way to follow the Second Division, when, on April 11th, it was hurriedly re-transferred to Flanders to assist in stemming the new German flood which was inundating the whole of that region, and which was not arrested until it had almost reached Hazebrouck. This task the First Australian Division performed most valiantly, thereby upholding the reputation already earned by its younger sister divisions for a capacity for rapid, ordered movement and decisive intervention at a critical juncture.

For some days there had been rumours that the Australian Corps Headquarters would shortly be transferred to the Amiens area, and would once again gather under its control the numerous elements of the four Australian divisions which were by now widely scattered, and had been fighting under the orders of three different Army Corps. There was the still more interesting and pregnant rumour that General Lord Rawlinson—relinquishing his post of British representative on the Supreme War Council at Versailles—was soon to arrive and to form and command a reconstituted Fourth British Army, which was to be composed of the Australian and the Third (British) Army Corps. (The Fourth Army had disappeared when, in 1917, General Rawlinson went to Versailles. The Fifth Army was not revived until June, 1918.)

Chapter 2
The Defence of Amiens

The Australian Corps Headquarters, under General Birdwood, commenced its activities at Villers-Bocage on April 7th, but soon after removed to the handsome seventeenth-century *château* at Bertangles, with its pleasant grounds and spacious parks. One by one the detached Australian brigades rejoined their divisions, and the divisions themselves came back under the orders of their own corps.

The comparative calm which had supervened upon all the excitement of the closing days of March and the first weeks of April was rudely broken when, before daybreak on April 24th, the enemy began a furious bombardment of the whole region extending from opposite Albert to a point as far south as Hangard. It was certain that this demonstration was the prelude of an infantry attack in force, but it was not until well after midday that the situation clarified, and it became known that the attack had been confined to the country south of the Somme, that it had struck the southern flank of the Fifth Australian Division, which had stood firm and had thereby saved the loss of the remainder of the tactically important Hill 104. But the town of Villers-Bretonneux, lying beyond the Australian sector, had fallen and the Germans were in possession of it.

It was imperative to retrieve this situation, or at least to make an attempt to do so. The nearest available reserve brigades of infantry were Australian, the 13th under Glasgow, and the 15th under Elliott. They were placed under the orders of the Third Corps, and by them directed to recapture the town.

Both brigades had to make long marches to reach the battleground. It was already dark before they had deployed on the appointed lines of departure. The details of this enthralling and wonderful night attack form too lengthy a story to find a place in this brief narrative; suffice it to say that when the sun rose on the third anniversary of Anzac Day, it looked down upon the Australians in full possession of the whole town, and standing upon our original lines of twenty-four hours before, with nearly 1,000 German prisoners to their credit. In this summary fashion, the last German attempt to split in two the Allied Armies failed ignominiously, and the attempt was never again renewed.

A comprehensive rearrangement of the whole Front in this much-contested region then took place. The appointment of Marshal Foch as Supreme Commander on the Western Front bore, as one of its first fruits, a clear decision as to the final point of junction between the French and the British Armies. This was fixed just south of Villers-Bretonneux, and not at the Somme Valley, as was thought desirable by some of the British commanders.

The new Fourth Army became the flank British Army in contact with the French. The Australian Corps became the south flank of that Army. Its sector extended, from the point named, northwards as far as the Ancre.

The Third Corps was transferred to the north of the Ancre, opposite Albert, and those two corps comprised, for some time to come, the whole of the Fourth Army resources.

The Australian Corps now organised its front with three divisions in line and one in reserve. My occupation, with the Third Australian Division, of the original sector between the Ancre and the Somme remained undisturbed, and my front line remained for a time stationary on the alignment gained on March 29th.

But the Third Division had had enough of stationary warfare, and the troops were athirst for adventure. They were tired of raids, which meant a mere incursion into enemy territory, and a subsequent withdrawal, after doing as much damage as possible.

Accordingly, I resolved to embark upon a series of minor battles, designed not merely to capture prisoners and machine-guns, but also to hold on to the ground gained. This would invite counter-attacks which I knew could only enhance the balance in our favour, and would seriously disorganise the enemy's whole defensive system, while wearing out his nerves and lowering the *morale* of his troops.

Four such miniature battles (see Map A), were fought in rapid succession, on April 30th and May 3rd, 6th and 7th, by the 9th and 10th Brigades, who were then in line. These yielded most satisfactory results. Not only did we capture several hundred prisoners and numerous machine-guns, but also advanced our whole line an average total distance of a mile. This deprived the enemy of valuable observation, and forced back his whole artillery organisation.

But these combats, and the numerous offensive patrol operations, which were also nightly undertaken along my whole front, did a great deal more. They yielded a constant stream of prisoners, who at this stage of the war had become sufficiently demoralised by their disappointments to talk freely, and impart a mass of valuable information as to movements and conditions behind the German lines.

The following list of 41 separate identifications, covering a total of over 300 prisoners, represents the fruits of these efforts during the period from March 27th to May 11th. From these it will be seen that during these six weeks I had been confronted by no less than six different German divisions:

No.	Date.	Identification.		
1	28.3.18	3 Gren. R.	1st	Div.
2	,,	13 I.R.	13	,,
3	,,	3 Gren. R.	1st	,,
4	,,	1 I.R.	1st	,,
	,,	13 I.R.	13	,,
5	,,	86 Fus. R.	18	,,
6	,,	1 I.R.	1st	,,
7	30.3.18	13 I.R.	13	,,
8	,,	31 I.R.	18	,,
9	31.3.18		18	,,
10	1.4.18	20 Foot Arty.		
11	2.4.18	3 ,, ,,		
12	2/3.4.18	1 R.R.Bav.Ft. Arty.		
13	,,	13 I.R.	13	Div.

14	4/5.4.18	1 M.W.Coy.	1st Div.	
15	6/7.4.18	3 Jäger Bn.		
16	9/10.4.18	31 I.R.	18	,,
17	11/12.4.18	31 I.R.	18	,,
18	13/14.4.18	86 Fus. R.	18	,,
19	,,	31 I.R.	18	,,
20	14/15.4.18	85 I.R.	18	,,
21	,,	31 I.R.	18	,,
22	17/18.4.18	229 R.I.R.	30	,,
23	18/19.4.18	231 R.I.R.	50	,,
24	,,	85 I.R.	18	,,
25	19/20.4.18	85 I.R.	18	,,
26	25/26.4.18	246 R.I.R.	54	Res. Div.
27	27/28.4.18	229 R.I.R.	50	,, ,,
28	28/29.4.18	247 R.I.R.	54	,, ,,
29	30/1.5.18	247 R.I.R.	54	,, ,,
30	3/4.5.18	357 I.R.	199	Div.
31	4/5.5.18	114 I.R.	199	,,
32	,,	31 I.R.	18	,,
33	5/6.5.18	237 R.I.R.	199	,,
34	,,	114 I.R.	199	,,
35	6/7.5.18	237 R.I.R.	199	,,
36	7/8.5.18	114 I.R.	199	,,
37	8/9.5.18	114 I.R.	199	,,
38	,,	237 R.I.R.	199	,,
39	,,	31 I.R.	18	,,
40	,,	357 I.R.	199	,,
41	,,	357 I.R.	199	,,

I.R.=Infantry Regiment ; R.I.R.=Reserve ditto.

While I was thus exerting a steady pressure on the enemy and gaining ground easterly, the Australian Corps line south of the Somme remained stationary, and each successive advance north of the river served only to accentuate the deep re-entrant which had been formed on the day when the loss of Hamel forced the British front line back along the Somme as far as Vaire-sous-Corbie.

While this was not very serious from the point of view of observation, because I was in possession of much the higher ground, and was able to look down, almost as upon a map, on to the enemy in the Hamel basin, yet I was beginning to feel very seriously the inconvenience of having, square on to my flank, such excellent concealed artillery positions as Vaire and Hamel Woods, which the enemy did not long delay in occupying.

Moreover, the whole of the slopes of the valley on my side of the river remained useless to me, because they were exposed to the full view of the enemy, so long as he was permitted to occupy the Hamel salient, which he had on April 5th driven into the very middle of what was now the corps front. I therefore made more than one attempt to persuade the then corps commander to undertake an operation for

German Prisoners taken by the Corps at Hamel, being marched to the rear.

the elimination in whole or in part of this inconvenient bend, but, for reasons doubtless satisfactory at that time, he declined to accept the suggestion. It fell to my lot myself to carry out this operation nearly two months later.

The Third Division was, however, relieved in the line by our Second Division on May 11th, and was withdrawn for a short but well-earned rest after six weeks of trench duty, following its first fateful rush into the thick of the battle.

It was on May 12th that I received the first intimation from General Sir William Birdwood that he was to be appointed to the command of a new Fifth Army, which the British War Council had decided to form, and that, upon his taking up these new duties, the task of leading the Australian Army Corps would devolve upon me.

In consequence of this and other changes, it was shortly afterwards decided, in consultation, that Glasgow should take over the command of the First Division, then still fighting at Hazebrouck, that Rosenthal should command the Second Division, and that Gellibrand should succeed me at the head of the Third Division.

Far, therefore, from being permitted a little respite from the strenuous labours of the preceding six weeks, I found myself confronted with responsibilities which, in point of numbers alone, exceeded six fold those which I had previously had to bear, but which, in point of difficulty, involved an even higher ratio.

There were numerous arms and services, under the corps, with whose detailed functions and methods of operation I had not been previously concerned. The other divisional commanders had hitherto been my colleagues, and I was now called upon to consider their personalities and temperaments as my subordinates. There was a vastly increased territory for whose administration and defence I would become responsible. I had to be prepared to enter an atmosphere of policy higher and larger than that which surrounded me as the commander of a division. And finally, there was the selection of my new staff.

My last executive work with the Third Division was the process of putting this Division back into the line, this time in the Villers-Bretonneux sector of our front. After handing over the division and all its outstanding current affairs to Major-General Gellibrand, I assumed command of the Australian Army Corps on May 30th, with Brigadier-General Blamey as my Chief-of-Staff.

★★★★★★

A farewell order to the Third Division was issued in the fol-

Visit of Monsieur Clemenceau group taken at Bussy on July 7th, 1918.

lowing terms:

As I am about to take up other duties the time has come when I must relinquish the command of the division. Closely associated with you as I have been, since the days of your first assembly and War Training in England, and, later, throughout all your magnificent work during the past nineteen months in the war zone, it is naturally a severe wrench for me to part from you.

I find it quite impossible to give adequate expression to my feelings of gratitude towards all ranks for the splendid and loyal support which you have, at all times, accorded to me. I am deeply indebted to my staff, to all commanders and to the officers and troops of all arms and services for a whole-hearted co-operation upon which, more than upon any other factor, the success of the division has depended.

It is my earnest hope, and also my sincere conviction, that the fine spirit and the high efficiency of the division will be maintained under the leadership of my successor, Brigadier-General Gellibrand; and if the men of the division feel, as I trust they do, an obligation to perpetuate for my sake the traditions built up by them during the period of my command, they can do so in no better way than by rendering to him a service as thorough and a support as loyal as I have been privileged to enjoy at their hands.

In formally wishing the division goodbye and good luck, I wish simply, but none the less sincerely, to thank each and all of you, for all that you have done.

    (Signed)   John Monash,
                                                              Major-General.

★★★★★★

I very soon became aware that, as corps commander, I was privileged to have access to a very large body of interesting secret information, which was methodically distributed daily by G.H.Q. Intelligence. This comprised detailed information of the true facts of all happenings on the fronts of all the Allies, the gist of the reports of our Secret Service, and very full particulars from which the nature and distribution of the enemy's military resources could be deduced with fair accuracy.

The numberings and locations of all his corps and divisions actually in the front line, on all the Allied fronts, was, of course, quite definitely known from day to day. The numberings of all formations lying in reserve were known with equal certainty, although their actual positions on any date were largely a matter of deduction by expert investigators. Of particular importance were the further deductions which could be drawn as to the condition of readiness or exhaustion of such reserve divisions, from known facts as to their successive appearance and experiences on any active battle front.

Our experts were thus able to classify the enemy divisions, and to determine from day to day the probable number, and even the probable numberings, of fit divisions actually available (after one, or after two, or after three days) to reinforce any portion of the front which was to be the object of an attack by us. They could also compute the number of fit divisions which the enemy had at his disposal at any time for launching an offensive against us.

All such data had a very direct bearing, not only on the probable course of the campaign in the immediate future, but also upon the responsibility which always weighed upon a corps commander of keeping his own sector in preparedness to meet an attack or to prevent such an attack from coming upon him as a surprise. He must therefore be alert to watch the signs and astute to read them aright.

One striking feature of the information at our disposal during the early part of June was the steady melting away of the enemy reserves as the consequence of his resultless, even if locally successful, assaults during the preceding two and a half months, against Amiens, in Flanders, and on the Chemin des Dames. But it was apparent that he still held formidable reserves of infantry, and a practically intact artillery, which he was bound to employ for at least one great and final effort to gain a decision.

The junction of the French and British Armies still offered a tempting point of weakness. As mine was now the flank British Corps, in immediate contact with General Toulorge's 31st French Corps, I could not afford to relax any of the precautions of vigilance or preparation which had been initiated by my predecessor for meeting such an attack. Consequently, during June, 1918, I ordered on the part of all my line divisions a maintenance of their energetic efforts to perfect the defensive organisations. I also undertook out of other corps labour resources the development of further substantial rear systems of defence, so that Amiens need not, in the event of a renewed attack, be abandoned to its fate without a prolonged struggle.

The First Australian Division was not yet a part of my new command, its continued presence in the Hazebrouck and Merris area, under the Fifteenth Corps, being still considered indispensable. My corps front now extended over a total length of ten miles, and I had but four divisions at my disposal to defend it. Three divisions held the line, one to the north and two to the south of the Somme. Only one division at a time could therefore be permitted a short rest, and this division formed my only tactical reserve.

All this added to the anxieties of the situation, and focussed the energies of the whole command on a constant scrutiny of all signs and symptoms that the enemy might be preparing to deliver his next blow against us. Active patrolling was maintained and continued to yield a steady stream of prisoners. A well conceived and planned minor enterprise by the Second Division, which was carried out on June 10th, and was Rosenthal's first divisional operation, gave us possession of a further slice of the important ridge between Sailly-Laurette and Morlancourt. It gained us 330 prisoners and 33 machine-guns. But no sign of any preparations on the part of the enemy for an attack upon us, in this zone, emerged from the careful investigations which followed this operation.

The days passed and evidences increased that the enemy was now beginning to devote his further attentions to the French front far to the south of us. At any rate, he continued to leave us unmolested, and the interrogations of our numerous prisoners all confirmed the absence of any preparations for an attack.

The defensive attitude which the situation thus forced upon us did not for long suit the present temper of the Australian troops, and I sought for a promising enterprise on which again to test their offensive power, on a scale larger than we had yet attempted in the year's campaign. There had been no Allied offensive, of any appreciable size, on any of our fronts, in any of the many theatres of war, since the close of the Passchendaele fighting in the autumn of 1917.

It was high time that the anxiety and nervousness of the public, at the sinister encroachments of the enemy upon regions which he had never previously trodden, should be allayed by a demonstration that there was still some kick left in the British Army. It was high time, too, that some commanders on our side of No Man's Land should begin to "think offensively", and cease to look over their shoulders in order to estimate how far it still was to the coast.

I was ambitious that any such kick should be administered, first, at any rate, by the Australians. A visit which I was privileged to pay to General Elles, commander of the Tank Corps, when he gave me a demonstration of the capacities of the newer types of tanks, only confirmed me in this ambition. Finally, the Hamel re-entrant had for two months been, as I have already explained, a source of annoyance and anxiety to me. It was for these reasons that I resolved to propose an operation for the recapture of Hamel, conditional upon being supplied with the assistance of tanks, a small increase of my artillery and an addition to my air resources.

I thereupon set about preparing a general plan for such a battle, which was to be my first corps operation. Having mentioned the matter first verbally to Lord Rawlinson, he requested me to submit a concrete proposal in writing. The communication is here reproduced, and will serve to convey an idea of the complexities involved in even so relatively small an undertaking:

Australian Corps.
21st June, 1918.

Fourth Army.

Hamel Offensive

1. With reference to my proposal for an offensive operation on the front of the "A" and "B" Divisions of this corps, with a view to the capture of Hamel Village and Vaire and Hamel Wood, etc., the accompanying map shows, in blue, the proposed ultimate objective line. This line has been chosen as representing the minimum operation that would appear to be worth undertaking, while offering a prospect of substantial advantages.

2. These advantages may be briefly summarised thus:

(*a*) Straightening of our line.

(*b*) Shortening of our line.

(*c*) Deepening our forward defensive zone, particularly east of Hill 104.

(*d*) Improvement of jumping-off position for future operations.

(*e*) Advancement of our artillery, south of the Somme.

(*f*) Denial to enemy of observation of ground near Vaux-sur-Somme, valuable for battery positions.

(*g*) Facilitating subsequent further minor advances north of the Somme.

(*h*) Disorganisation of enemy defences.

(*i*) Disorganisation of possible enemy offensive preparations.

(*j*) Inflicting losses on enemy personnel and material.

(*k*) Improvement of our observation.

(*l*) Maintenance of our initiative on this corps front.

3. The disadvantages are those arising from the necessity of bringing into rapid existence a new defensive system on a frontage of 7,000 yards and also the particular incidence, at the present juncture, of the inevitable losses, small or large, of such an operation in this corps.

4. In view of the unsatisfactory position of Australian reinforcements, any substantial losses would precipitate the time when the question of the reduction in the number of Australian divisions would have to be seriously considered.

It is for higher authority to decide whether a portion of the present resources in Australian manpower in this corps would be more profitably ventured upon such an operation as this, which is in itself a very attractive proposition, rather than to conserve such resources for employment elsewhere.

5. Detailed plans can only be prepared after I have had conferences with representatives of all Arms and Services involved, but the following proposals are submitted as the basis of further elaboration:

(*a*) The operation will be primarily a tank operation—at least one and preferably two battalions of tanks to be employed.

(*b*) The whole battle front will be placed temporarily under command of one divisional commander—by a temporary readjustment of inter-divisional boundaries.

(*c*) The infantry employed will comprise one division plus a brigade, *i.e.*, 4 infantry brigades, totalling, say, 7,500 bayonets; about one-half of this force to be employed in the advance and the other half to hold our present front defensively, taking over the captured territory within 48 hours after Zero. ("Zero" refers to the day and hour, not yet determined, on which the battle is to begin.)

(*d*) The action will be designed on lines to permit of the tanks effecting the capture of the ground; the roles of the infantry following the tanks will be:

(*i*) to assist in reducing strong points and localities.

(*ii*) to "mop up".

(*iii*) to consolidate the ground captured.

(*e*) Apart from neutralising all enemy artillery likely to engage our troops, our artillery will be employed to keep under fire enemy centres of resistance and selected targets—in front of the advance of the tanks. Artillery detailed for close targets will work on a prearranged and detailed time-table which will be adjusted to the time-table of the tank and infantry advance. Sufficient "silent" field artillery supplied before the battle should be emplaced in advanced positions, to ensure an effective protective barrage to cover consolidation on the blue line, and to engage all localities from which enemy counter-attacks can be launched. ("Blue Line", arbitrarily so called, because this line was drawn on the accompanying map in blue. It was to be the final objective for the day.) It is estimated that, in addition to the resources of the corps, four field artillery brigades will be required for, say, four days in all.

(*f*) Engineer stores in sufficient quantities to provide for the complete organisation of the new defences will require to be dumped beforehand as far forward as practicable.

(*g*) No additional machine-guns, outside of corps resources, will be required.

(*h*) Contact and counter-attack planes and low-flying bombing planes prior to and during advance must be arranged for.

(*i*) Artillery and mortar smoke to screen the operations from view of all ground north of the Somme in the Sailly-Laurette locality are required.

6. As to the date of the operations, the necessary preparations will occupy at least seven days after authority to proceed has been given. As an inter-divisional relief is planned to occur on June 28th-29th and 29th-30th, it would seem that this operation cannot take place earlier than the first week in July. The postponement of this relief would not be desirable for several reasons.

7. Valuable training in the joint action of tanks and infantry can be arranged, probably in the territory west of the Hallue Valley—provided that one or two tank companies can be detached for such a purpose. Thorough liaison prior to and during the operation between all tank and all infantry commanders would have to be a special feature. For this reason, only infantry units not in the line can be considered as available to undergo the necessary preparation.

(Sgd.)   John Monash,
                                                       Lieut.-General.
                                         Cmdg. Australian Corps.

Approval to these proposals was given without delay; the additional resources were promised, and preparations for the battle were immediately put in hand. As I hope, in a later context, to attempt to describe the evolution of a battle plan, and the comprehensive measures which are associated with such an enterprise, it will not be necessary to do so here.

It was the straightening of the corps front, as an essential preliminary to any offensive operations on a still larger scale, to be undertaken when the opportune moment should arrive, that made the Hamel proposal tactically attractive; it was the availability of an improved type of tank that gave it promise of success, without pledging important resources, or risking serious losses.

The new Mark V. Tank had not previously been employed in battle. It marked a great advance upon the earlier types. The epicyclic gearing with which it was now furnished, the greater power of its engines, the improved balance of its whole design gave it increased mobility, facility in turning and immunity from foundering in ground even of the most broken and uneven character. It could be driven and steered by one man, where it previously took four; and it rarely suffered suspended animation from engine trouble.

But, above all, the men of the Tank Corps had, by the training which they had undergone, and by the spirited leadership of Generals Elles, Courage, Hankey and other tank commanders, achieved a higher standard of skill, enterprise and *morale*; they were now, more than ever, on their mettle to uphold the prestige of the Tank Corps.

All the same, the tanks had become anathema to the Australian troops. For, at Bullecourt more than a year before, they had failed badly, and had "let down" the gallant infantry, who suffered heavily in consequence; a failure due partly to the mechanical defects of the tanks of those days, partly to the inexperience of the crews, and partly to indifferent staff arrangements, in the co-ordination of the combined action of the infantry and the tanks.

It was not an easy problem to restore to the Australian soldier his lost confidence, or to teach him the sympathetic dependence upon the due performance by the tanks of the roles to be allotted to them, which was essential to a complete utilisation of the possibilities which were now opening up. That the tanks, appropriately utilised, were destined to exert a paramount influence upon the course of the war, was apparent to those who could envisage the future.

This problem was intensified because the battalions of the Fourth Division who were to carry out the infantry tasks at Hamel were the very units who had undergone that unfortunate experience at Bullecourt. But, on the principle of restoring the nerves of the unseated rider by remounting him to continue the hunt, it was especially important to wean the Fourth Division from their prejudices.

Battalion after battalion of the 4th, 6th and 11th Brigades of infantry was brought by bus to Vaux, a little village tucked away in a quiet valley, north-west of Amiens, there to spend the day at play with the tanks. The tanks kept open house, and, in the intervals of more formal rehearsals of tactical schemes of attack, the infantry were taken over the field for "joy rides", were allowed to clamber all over the monsters, inside and out, and even to help to drive them and put them through their paces. Platoon and company leaders met dozens of tank officers face to face, and they argued each other to a standstill upon every aspect that arose.

Set-piece manoeuvre exercises on the scale of a battalion were designed and rehearsed over and over again; red flags marked enemy machine-gun posts; real wire entanglements were laid out to show how easily the tanks could mow them down; real trenches were dug for the tanks to leap and straddle and search with fire; real rifle grenades were fired by the infantry to indicate to the tanks the enemy strong points which were molesting and impeding their advance. The tanks would throw themselves upon these places, and, pirouetting round and round, would blot them out, much as a man's heel would crush a scorpion.

It was invaluable as mere training for battle, but the effect upon the spirits of the men was remarkable. The fame of the tanks, and all the wonderful things they could do, spread rapidly throughout the corps. The "digger" took the tank to his heart, and ever after, each tank was given a pet name by the company of infantry which it served in battle, a name which was kept chalked on its iron sides, together with a panegyric commentary upon its prowess.

There remained, however, much to be arranged, and many difficult questions to be settled, as regards the tactical employment of the tanks. I can never be sufficiently grateful to Brigadier-General Courage, of the 5th Tank Brigade, for his diligent assistance, and for his loyal acceptance of the onerous conditions which the tactical methods that I finally decided upon imposed upon the tanks.

These methods involved two entirely new principles. Firstly, each tank was, for tactical purposes, to be treated as an infantry weapon; from the moment that it entered the battle until the objective had been gained it was to be under the exclusive orders of the infantry commander to whom it had been assigned.

Secondly, the deployed line of tanks was to advance, *level with the infantry*, and pressing close up to the barrage. This, of course, subjected the tanks, which towered high above the heads of the neighbouring infantry, to the danger of being struck by any of our own shells which happened to fall a little short. Tank experts, consulted beforehand, considered therefore that it was not practicable for tanks to follow close behind an artillery barrage. The Battle of Hamel proved that it was.

Chapter 3
Hamel

The larger questions relating to the employment of the tanks at the Battle of Hamel having been disposed of, the remaining arrangements for the battle presented few novel aspects. Their manner of execution, however, brought into prominence some features which became fundamental doctrines in the Australian Corps then and thereafter.

Although complete written orders were invariably prepared and issued by a general staff whose skill and industry left nothing to be desired, very great importance was attached to the holding of conferences, at which were assembled every one of the senior commanders and heads of departments concerned in the impending operation. At these I personally explained every detail of the plan, and assured myself that all present applied an identical interpretation to all orders that had been issued.

Questions were invited; difficulties were cleared up; and the conflicting views of the different services on matters of technical detail were ventilated. The points brought to an issue were invariably decided on the spot. The battle plan having been thus crystallised, no subsequent alterations were permissible, under any circumstances, no matter how tempting. This fixity of plan engendered a confidence throughout the whole command which facilitated the work of every commander and staff officer. It obviated the vicious habit of postponing action until the last possible moment, lest counter orders should necessitate some alternative action. It was a powerful factor in the gaining of time, usually all too short for the extensive preparations necessary.

The final Corps Conference for the Battle of Hamel was held at Bertangles on June 30th, and the date of the battle itself was fixed for July 4th. This selection was prompted partly by the desire to allow ample time for the completion of all arrangements; but there were also sentimental grounds, because this was the anniversary of the American national holiday, and a considerable contingent of the United States Army was to co-operate in the fight.

For some weeks previously the 33rd American Division, under Major-General John Bell, had been training in the Fourth Army area, and its several regiments had been distributed, for training and trench experience, to the Australian and the III. Corps. I had applied to the Fourth Army and had received approval to employ in the battle a contingent equivalent in strength to two British battalions, or a total of about 2,000 men, organised in eight companies. The very proper condition was attached, however, that these Americans should not be split up and scattered individually among the Australians, but should fight at least as complete platoons, under their own platoon leaders.

All went well until three days before the appointed date, when General Rawlinson conveyed to me the instruction that, the matter having been reconsidered, only 1,000 Americans were to be used. Strongly averse, as I was, from embarrassing the infantry plans of General Maclagan, to whom I had entrusted the conduct of the actual assault, it was not then too late to rearrange the distribution.

The four companies of United States troops who, under this decision, had to be withdrawn were loud in their lamentations, but the remaining four companies were distributed by platoons among the troops of the three Australian brigades who were to carry out the attack—each American platoon being assigned a definite place in the line of battle. The dispositions of the main body of Australian infantry were based upon this arrangement.

In the meantime, somewhere in the upper realms of high control, a discussion must have been going on as to the propriety of after all allowing any American troops at all to participate in the forthcoming operations. Whether the objections were founded upon policy, or upon an under-estimate of the fitness of these troops for offensive fighting, I have never been able to ascertain; but, to my consternation, I received about four o'clock on the afternoon of July 3rd, a telephone message from Lord Rawlinson to the effect that it had now been decided that no American troops were to be used the next day.

I was, at the moment, while on my daily round of visits to divisions and brigades, at the headquarters of the Third Division, at Glisy, and far from my own station. I could only request that the army commander might be so good as to come at once to the forward area and meet me at Bussy-les-Daours, the headquarters of Maclagan—he being the commander immediately affected by this proposed change of plan. In due course we all met at five o'clock, Rawlinson being accompanied by Montgomery, his chief-of-staff.

It was a meeting full of tense situations—and of grave import. At that moment of time, the whole of the infantry destined for the assault at dawn next morning, including those very Americans, was already well on its way to its battle stations; the artillery was in the act of dissolving its defensive organisation with a view to moving forward into its battle emplacements as soon as dusk should fall; I well knew that even if orders could still with certainty reach the battalions concerned, the withdrawal of those Americans would result in untold confusion and in dangerous gaps in our line of battle.

Even had I been ready to risk the success of the battle by going ahead without them, I could not afford to take the further risk of the occurrence of something in the nature of an "international incident" between the troops concerned, whose respective points of view about the resulting situation could be readily surmised. So, I resolved to take a firm stand and press my views as strongly as I dared; for even a corps commander must use circumspection when presuming to argue with an army commander.

However, disguised in the best diplomatic language that I was able to command, my representations amounted to this: firstly, that it was already too late to carry out the order; secondly, that the battle would have to go on either with the Americans participating, or not at all; thirdly, that unless I were expressly ordered to abandon the battle, I intended to go on as originally planned; and lastly, that unless I received such a cancellation order before 6.30 p.m. it would in any case be too late to stop the battle, the preliminary phases of which were just on the point of beginning.

As always, Lord Rawlinson's charming and sympathetic personality made it easy to lay my whole case before him. He was good enough to say that while he entirely agreed with me, he felt himself bound by the terms of a clear order from the commander-in-chief. My last resource, then, was to urge the argument that I felt perfectly sure that the commander-in-chief when giving such an order could not have had present to his mind the probability that compliance with it meant the abandonment of the battle, and that, under the circumstances, it was competent for the senior commander on the spot to act in the light of the situation as known to him, even to the extent of disobeying an order.

Rawlinson agreed that this view was correct provided the commander-in-chief was not accessible for reference. Repeated attempts to raise General Headquarters from Bussy eventually elicited the information that the field marshal was then actually on his way from Versailles, and expected to arrive in half an hour. Thereupon Rawlinson promised a decision by 6.30, and we separated to rejoin our respective headquarters.

In due course, the army commander telephoned that he had succeeded in speaking to the field marshal, who explained that he had directed the withdrawal of the Americans in deference to the wish of General Pershing, but that, as matters stood, he now wished everything to go on as originally planned. And so—the crisis passed as suddenly as it had appeared. For, to me it had taken the form of a very serious crisis, feeling confident as I did of the success of the forthcoming battle, and of the far-reaching consequences which would be certain to follow. It appeared to me at the time that great issues had hung for an hour or so upon the chance of my being able to carry my point.

An interesting episode, intimately bound up with the story of this battle, was the visit to the corps area on July 2nd of the prime minister of the commonwealth, Mr. W.M. Hughes, and Sir Joseph Cook, the minister of the navy. They arrived all unconscious of the impending enterprise, but only by taking them fully into my confidence could I justify my evident pre-occupation with other business of first-class importance. Most readily, however, did they accommodate themselves to the exigencies of the situation.

Both ministers accompanied me that afternoon on a tour of inspection of the eight battalions who were then already parading in full battle array, and on the point of moving off to the assembly positions from which next day they would march into battle. The stirring addresses delivered to the men by both ministers did much to hearten and stimulate them. As they were on their way to an Inter-Allied War Council at Versailles, the personal contact of the ministers with the actual battle preparations had the subsequent result of focussing upon the outcome of the battle a good deal of interest on the part of the whole War Council.

The fixing of the exact moment for the opening of a battle has always been the subject of much controversy. As in many other matters, it becomes in the end the responsibility of one man to make the fatal decision. The Australians always favoured the break of day, as this gave them the protection of the hours of darkness for the assembly of the assaulting troops in battle order in our front trenches. But there must be at least sufficient light to see one's way for two hundred yards or so, otherwise direction is lost and confusion ensues.

The season of the year, the presence and altitude of the moon, the prospect of fog or ground mist, the state of the weather, and the nature and condition of the ground are all factors which affect the proper choice of the correct moment. To aid a decision, careful observations were usually made on three or four mornings preceding the chosen day. A new factor on this occasion was the strong appeal by the tanks for an extra five minutes of dawning light, to ensure a true line of approach upon the allotted objective, whether a ruined village, or a thicket, or a field work.

The decision actually given by me was that "Zero" would be ten minutes past three, and every watch had been carefully synchronized to the second, to ensure simultaneous action. A perfected modern battle plan is like nothing so much as a score for an orchestral composition, where the various arms and units are the instruments, and the tasks they perform are their respective musical phrases. Every individual unit must make its entry precisely at the proper moment, and play its phrase in the general harmony. The whole programme is controlled by an exact time-table, to which every infantryman, every heavy or light gun, every mortar and machine-gun, every tank and aeroplane must respond with punctuality; otherwise there will be discords which will impair the success of the operation, and increase the cost of it.

The morning of July 4th was ushered in with a heavy ground mist. This impeded observation and made guidance difficult, but it greatly enhanced the surprise. The unexpected occurrence of this fog lessened the importance of the elaborate care which had been taken to introduce into the artillery barrage a due percentage of smoke shell, and to form smoke screens by the use of mortars on the flanks of the attack. But the fog largely accounted for the cheap price at which the victory was bought.

No battle within my previous experience, not even Messines, passed off so smoothly, so exactly to time-table, or was so free from any kind of hitch. It was all over in ninety-three minutes. It was the perfection of team work. It attained all its objectives; and it yielded great results. The actual assault was delivered, from right to left, by two battalions of the 6th Brigade, three battalions of the 4th Brigade, and three battalions of the 11th Brigade. It was also part of the plan that advantage was taken by a battalion of the 15th Brigade to snatch from the enemy another slice of territory far away in the Ancre Valley, opposite Dernancourt, and so, by extending the battle front, further to distract him.

The attack was a complete surprise, and swept without check across the whole of the doomed territory. Vaire and Hamel Woods fell to the 4th Brigade, while the 11th Brigade, with its allotted tanks, speedily mastered Hamel Village itself. The selected objective line was reached in the times prescribed for its various parts, and was speedily consolidated. It gave us possession of the whole of the Hamel Valley, and landed us on the forward or eastern slope of the last ridge, from which the enemy had been able to overlook any of the country held by us.

Still more important results were that we gathered in no less than 1,500 prisoners, and killed and disabled at least as many more, besides taking a great deal of booty, including two field guns, 26 mortars and 171 machine-guns—at a cost to us of less than 800 casualties of all kinds, the great majority of whom were walking wounded. The tanks fulfilled every expectation, and the suitability of the tactics employed was fully demonstrated. Of the 60 tanks utilised, only 3 were disabled, and even these 3 were taken back to their rallying points under their own power the very next night. Their moral effect was also proved, and, with the exception of a few enemy machine-gun teams, who bravely stood their ground to the very last, most of the enemy encountered by the tanks readily surrendered.

Shortly after the battle, G.H.Q. paid the Australian Corps the compliment of publishing to the whole British Army a General Staff brochure, containing the complete text of the orders, and a full and detailed description of the whole of the battle plans and preparations, with an official commentary upon them. (Staff-Sheet No. 218: "Operations of the Australian Corps against Hamel, etc.," published July, 1918.)

The last paragraph of this document, which follows, expresses tersely the conclusions reached by our High Command:

> 81. The success of the attack was due:
> (*a*) To the care and skill as regards every detail with which the plan was drawn up by the Corps, Division, Brigade and Battalion Staffs.
> (*b*) The excellent co-operation between the infantry, machine-gunners, artillery, tanks and R.A.F.
> (*c*) The complete surprise of the enemy, resulting from the manner in which the operation had been kept secret up till zero hour.
> (*d*) The precautions which were taken and successfully carried out by which no warning was given to the enemy by any previous activity which was not normal.
> (*e*) The effective counter-battery work and accurate barrage.
> (*f*) The skill and dash with which the tanks were handled, and the care taken over details in bringing them up to the starting

line.

(*g*) Last, but most important of all, the skill, determination and fine fighting spirit of the infantry carrying out the attack.

Of the extent to which the tactical principles, and the methods of preparation which had been employed at Hamel, came to be utilised by other corps in the later fighting of 1918 no reliable record is yet available to me. But within the corps itself this comparatively small operation became the model for all enterprises of a similar character, which it afterwards fell to the lot of the corps to carry out.

The operation was a small one, however, only by contrast with the events which followed, although not in comparison with some of the major operations which had preceded it—by reference to the number of troops engaged, although not to the extent of territory or booty captured. Although only eight battalions (or the equivalent of less than one division) were committed in the actual assault, the territory recovered was more than four times that which was, in the pitched battles of 1917, customarily allotted as an objective to a single division. The number of prisoners in relation to our own casualties was also far higher than had been the experience of previous years. Both of these new standards which had thus been set up may be regarded as flowing directly from the employment of the tanks.

Among other aspects of this battle which are worthy of mention is the fact that it was the first occasion in the war that the American troops fought in an offensive battle. The contingent of them who joined us acquitted themselves most gallantly and were ever after received by the Australians as blood brothers—a fraternity which operated to great mutual advantage nearly three months later.

This was the first occasion, also, on which the experiment was made of using aeroplanes for the purpose of carrying and delivering small-arms ammunition. The "consolidation" of a newly-captured territory implies, in its broadest sense, its organisation for defence against recapture. For such a purpose the most rapidly realisable expedient had been found to be the placing of a predetermined number of machine-guns in previously chosen positions, arranged chequer-wise over the captured ground. According to such a plan, suitable localities were selected by an examination of the map and a specified number of Vickers machine-gun crews were specially told off for the duty of making, during the battle, by the most direct route, to the selected localities, there promptly digging in, and preparing to deal with any attempt on the part of the enemy to press a counter-attack.

The main difficulty affecting the use of machine-guns is the maintenance for them of a regular and adequate supply of ammunition. Heretofore this function had to be performed by infantry ammunition carrying parties. It required two men to carry one ammunition box, holding a thousand rounds, which a machine-gun in action could easily expend in less than five minutes. Those carrying parties had to travel probably not less than two to three miles in the double journey across the open, exposed both to view and fire. Casualties among ammunition carriers were always substantial.

It was therefore decided to attempt the distribution of this class of ammunition by aeroplane. Most of the machines of the corps squadron were fitted with bomb racks and releasing levers. It required no great ingenuity to adapt this gear for the carrying by each plane of two boxes of ammunition simultaneously, and to arrange for its release, by hand lever, at the appropriate time. It remained to determine, by experiment, the correct size and mode of attachment for a parachute for each box of ammunition, so that the box would descend from the air slowly, and reach the ground without severe impact.

It was Captain Wackett, of the Australian Flying Corps, who perfected these ideas, and who trained the pilots to put them into practice. Each machine-gun crew, upon reaching its appointed locality, spread upon the ground a large V-shaped canvas (V representing the word "Vickers") as an intimation to the air of their whereabouts, and that they needed ammunition. After a very little training, the air-pilots were able to drop this ammunition from a height of at least 1,000 feet to well within 100 yards of the appointed spot. In this way, at least 100,000 rounds of ammunition were successfully distributed during this battle, with obvious economy in lives and wounds. The method thus initiated became general during later months.

The corps also put into practice, on this occasion, a stratagem which had frequently on a smaller scale been employed in connection with trench raids. Our artillery was supplied with many different types of projectile, but among them were both gas shell and smoke shell. The latter were designed to create a very palpable smoke cloud, to be employed for the purpose of screening an assault, but were otherwise harmless. The former burst, on the other hand, with very little evolution of smoke, but with a pronounced and easily recognised smell, and their gas was very deadly.

My practice was, therefore, during the ordinary harassing fire in periods between offensive activities, always to fire both classes of shell *together*, so that the enemy became accustomed to the belief at the least that our smoke shells were invariably accompanied by gas shell, even if he did not believe that it was the smoke shell which alone gave out the warning smell. The effect upon him of either belief was, however, the same; for it compelled him in any case to put on his gas mask in order to protect himself from gas poisoning.

On the actual battle day, however, we fired smoke shell *only*, as we dared not vitiate the air through which our own men would shortly pass. But the enemy had no rapid means of becoming aware that we were firing only harmless smoke shell. He would, therefore, promptly don his gas mask, which would obscure his vision, hamper his freedom of action, and reduce his powers of resistance. On July 4th both the 4th and 11th Brigades accordingly took prisoner large numbers of men who were found actually wearing their gas masks. The stratagem had worked out exactly as planned.

The battle was over, and when the results were made known there followed the inevitable flow of congratulatory messages from superiors, and colleagues and friends, from all parts of the Front and from England. The following telegrams received from the Commonwealth Prime Minister were particularly gratifying:

> 1. On behalf of Prime Minister of Britain, and also of Prime Ministers of Canada, New Zealand and Newfoundland, attending Versailles Council, I am commissioned to offer you our warmest congratulations upon brilliant success of Australian Forces under your command, and to say that the victory achieved by your troops is worthy to rank with greatest achievements of Australian Armies.
>
> 2. My personal congratulations and those of the Government of Commonwealth on brilliant success of battle. Please convey to officers and men participating in attack warmest admiration of their valour and dash and manner in which they have maintained highest traditions of Australian Army. I am sure that achievement will have most considerable military and political effect upon Allies and neutrals, and will heighten morale of all Imperial Forces.
>
> 3. In company with Mr. Lloyd George and General Rawlinson today saw several hundred of prisoners taken by Australian Troops in battle before Hamel. Rawlinson expressed to me the

opinion that the operation was a brilliant piece of work. Please convey this to troops.

The following message transmitted to me by the commander of the Fourth Army was also received from the field marshal commanding-in-chief:

> Will you please convey to Lieutenant-General Sir John Monash and all ranks under his command, including the tanks and the detachment of 33rd American Division, my warm congratulations on the success which attended the operation carried out this morning, and on the skill and gallantry with which it was conducted. D. Haig.

A steady stream of visitors also set in, including numbers of general staff officers, who had been sent down from other corps and armies to gather information as to the methods employed. Everyone, of course, recognised that there was only one war, and that it was to the mutual benefit of all that all expedients calculated to accelerate the end of it should become the common property of all. My staff were accordingly kept busy for many days with maps and diagrams explaining the lines on which the enterprise had been carried out.

The most distinguished and most welcome of all our visitors, however, was Monsieur Clemenceau, the veteran statesman of France, who, in spite of the physical effort, immediately after the sitting of the Versailles War Council had closed, made haste to travel to the Amiens area, and to visit the corps for the special purpose of thanking the troops. He arrived on July 7th, and a large assemblage of Australian soldiers who had participated in the battle, and who were resting from their labours near General Maclagan's headquarters at Bussy, were privileged to hear him address them in English in the following terms:

> I am glad to be able to speak at least this small amount of English, because it enables me to tell you what all French people think of you. They expected a great deal of you, because they have heard what you have accomplished in the development of your own country. I should not like to say that they are surprised that you have fulfilled their expectations. By that high standard they judge you, and admire you that you have reached it. We have all been fighting the same battle of freedom in these old battlegrounds. You have all heard the names of them in history. But it is a great wonder, too, in history that you should be

here fighting on the old battlefields, which you never thought, perhaps, to see. The work of our fathers, which we wanted to hand down unharmed to our children, the Germans tried to take from us.

They tried to rob us of all that is dearest in modern human society. But men were the same in Australia, England, France, Italy, and all countries proud of being the home of free people. That is what made you come; that is what made us greet you when you came. We knew you would fight a real fight, but we did not know that from the very beginning you would astonish the whole Continent with your valour. I have come here for the simple purpose of seeing the Australians and telling them this. I shall go back tomorrow and say to my countrymen: 'I have seen the Australians; I have looked into their eyes. I know that they, men who have fought great battles in the cause of freedom, will fight on alongside us, till the freedom for which we are all fighting is guaranteed for us and our children.'

The French inhabitants of the Amiens district were also highly elated at the victory. The city itself had been, for some weeks, completely evacuated, by official order. Not only had it become the object of nightly visitations by flights of Gothas; but also, somewhere in the east and far beyond the reach of my longest range guns, the enemy had succeeded in emplacing a cannon of exceptionally large calibre, range and power, which took its daily toll of the buildings of this beautiful city.

The anniversary of the French national *fête* was approaching, and the prefect of the Department of the Somme, Monsieur Morain—appreciating the significance of the Hamel victory as a definite step towards the ultimate disengagement of the city from the German terror—determined to make the celebration of this *fête* not only a compliment to the Australian Corps, but also a proof of the unquenchable fortitude of the people of his department.

Accordingly, in the Hôtel de Ville, in the very heart of the deserted city, amidst the crumbling ruins of its upper stories, and of the devastation of the surrounding city blocks, he presided at a humble but memorable repast, which had been spread in an undamaged apartment, inviting to his board a bare twenty representatives of the French and British Armies, and of the city of Amiens. While we toasted the king and the republic, and voiced the firm resolve of both Allies to see the struggle through to the bitter end, the enemy shells were still

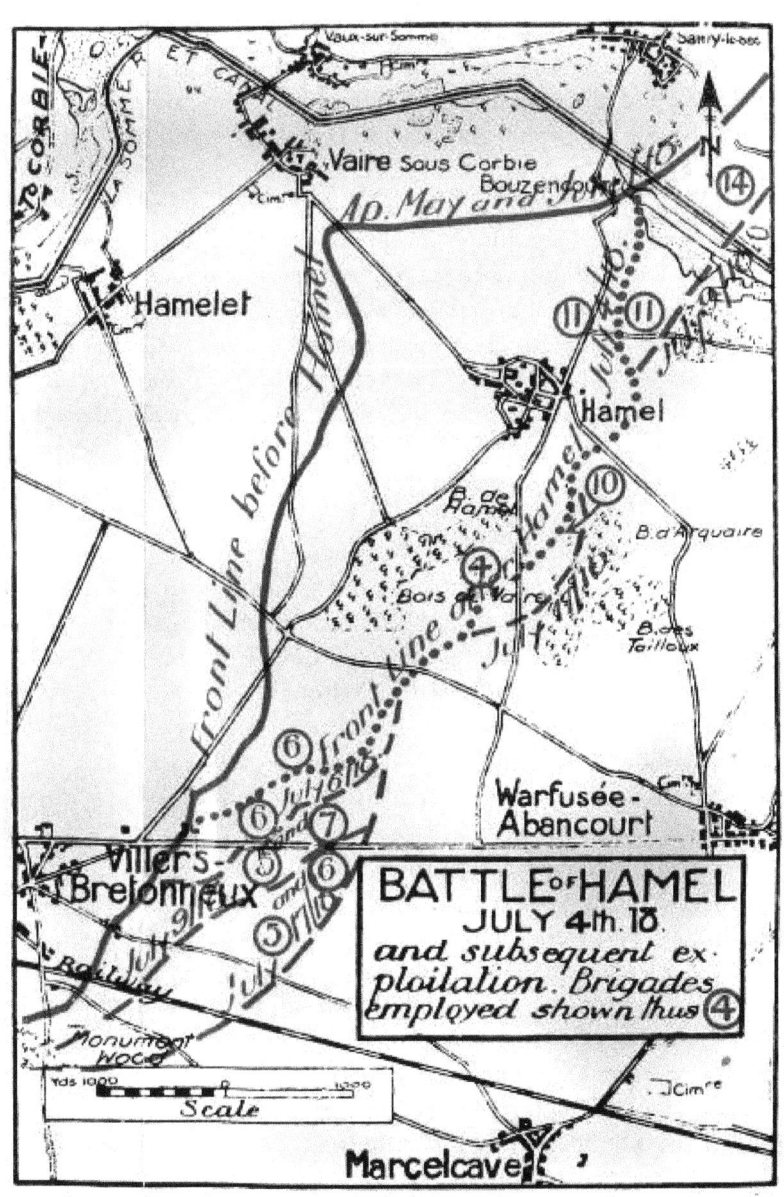

thundering overhead.

But other matters than rejoicings in a task thus happily accomplished compelled my chief attention during the remaining days of this July. I had to study and gauge accurately the tactical and strategical results of the victory of Hamel, and to lose no time in using the advantage gained. The moral results both on the enemy and on ourselves were far more important, and deserve far more emphasis than do the material gains.

It was, as I have said, the first offensive operation, on any substantial scale, that had been fought by any of the Allies since the previous autumn. Its effect was electric, and it stimulated many men to the realisation that the enemy was, after all, not invulnerable, in spite of the formidable increase in his resources which he had brought from Russia. It marked the termination, once and for all, of the purely defensive attitude of the British front. It incited in many quarters an examination of the possibilities of offensive action on similar lines by similar means—a changed attitude of mind, which bore a rich harvest only a very few weeks later.

But its effect on the enemy was even more startling. His whole front from the Ancre to Villers-Bretonneux had become unstable, and was reeling from the blow. It was only the consideration that I had still to defend a ten-mile front, and had still only one division in reserve in case of emergency, that deterred me from embarking at once upon another blow on an even larger scale. But I seized every occasion to importune the army commander either to narrow my front, or to let the First Division from Hazebrouck join my command, or both; but so far without result.

The only course that remained open to me was to initiate immediate measures for taking the fullest advantage of the enemy's demoralization by exploiting the success obtained to the utmost possible extent. No later than on the afternoon of the Battle of Hamel itself, orders were issued to all three line divisions to commence most vigorous offensive patrolling all along the corps front, with a view not merely to prevent the enemy from re-establishing an organised defensive system, but also ourselves to penetrate the enemy's ground by the establishment therein of isolated posts, as a nucleus for subsequent more effective occupation.

Enterprise of such a nature appeals strongly to the sporting instinct of the Australian soldier. Divisions, brigades and battalions vied with each other in predatory expeditions, even in broad daylight, into the enemy's ground, and a steady stream of prisoners and machine-guns flowed in. On the nights of July 5th and 6th, the Fifth Division, now in the sector between the Ancre and the Somme, possessed themselves with very little effort of a strip of some three hundred acres of hostile positions, bringing our front line so near to Morlancourt as to make that village no longer tenable by the enemy.

On the same nights, and again on July 8th and 9th, the Second and Fourth Divisions advanced their lines by an average of two hundred to three hundred yards along their respective fronts, and this advance was, in the case of the Second Division, particularly valuable in carrying our front line over the crest of the plateau of Hill 104, and giving us clear and unbroken observation far into the enemy's country, in the directions of Warfusee and Marcelcave.

It was a period replete with instances of individual enterprise and daring adventure. One incident, characteristic of the varied efforts of these days, was the capture, single-handed, and in broad daylight, by Corporal W. Brown, V.C., of the 20th Battalion, Second Division, of an officer and eleven men of the German Army, whom he stalked as they lay skulking in a trench dug-out not far from his observation post, and terrorised into submission by the threat of throwing a bomb at them.

But perhaps the best testimony of the successful activities of my troops during this period, and of the serious impression which they made upon the enemy, can be gathered by extracts from his own documents, a number of which were captured during this and subsequent fighting. Of these, the following, issued by the Second German Army Headquarters (Von der Marwitz), are among the more interesting:

> The enemy has in his minor enterprises again taken prisoner a complete front line battalion and part of a support battalion. The reason is our faulty leadership.
>
> The enemy penetrated the forward zone of the 108th Division by means of large patrols at midnight, on July 8th, 1918, without any artillery preparation, and again on the same night at 11 p.m., with artillery preparation, astride of the Marcelcave-Villers-Bretonneux railway. He occupied the trenches where our most advanced outposts lay, and took the occupants, comprising fifteen men, prisoner. The larger part of the forward zone has been lost.
>
> In the case of the present trench division, it has often happened that *complete* picquets have disappeared from the forward zone

Railway Gun, 11.2-inch Bore—captured near Rosières on August 8th, 1918.

German Depot of Stores—captured on August 8th, 1918.

without a trace.

All the above refers to the period between July 4th and 12th. We read again under date July 13th:

> During the last few days the Australians have succeeded in penetrating, or taking prisoner, single posts or picquets. They have gradually—sometimes even in daylight—succeeded in getting possession of the majority of the forward zone of a whole division.
>
> Troops must fight. They must not give way at every opportunity and seek to avoid fighting, otherwise they will get the feeling that the enemy are superior to them.

One last extract from these interesting papers:

> The best way to make the enemy more careful in his attempt to drive us bit by bit out of the outpost line and forward zone is to do active reconnaissance and carry out patrol encounters oneself. In this respect absolutely nothing seems to have been done. If the enemy can succeed in scoring a success without any special support by artillery or assistance from special troops, we must be in a position to do the same.

Our line in front of Villers-Bretonneux had for months run very close to the eastern outskirts of that town, a circumstance which cramped and embarrassed our defence of it. The enemy could peer into its streets and sweep them with machine-guns. He had held in strength a locality known as Monument Wood, the ruins of a once prosperous orchard, and his possession of it had been a source of annoyance both to us and to the French, for it lay just opposite the international boundary posts.

The time seemed opportune for a set-piece operation designed to advance our line opposite the town by 1,000 yards, on a broad front, to dislodge the enemy from Monument Wood, gain valuable elbow room, and obtain mastery of the remainder of the plateau on which the town was built. I had actually completed the draft of a plan for such an operation, and had held a preliminary conference with my staff to discuss it, when it became apparent that the nightly encroachments which the Second Division were effecting in this region would, in the course of a few days, achieve the capture of the whole of this territory without any special organised effort at all.

And so, it proved; for before the middle of July, Rosenthal had succeeded in possessing himself, by such a process of "peaceful penetration", of the whole of the coveted area. It was a further evidence of the serious demoralisation which our aggressive attitude of the preceding months had wrought among the German forces opposed to us.

The era of minor aggression by the Australian Corps was, however, about to draw to a close, and the situation was rapidly beginning to shape itself for greater events.

Chapter 4
Turning the Tide

The course of events during June and July pointed to the conclusions, firstly, that the enemy contemplated no further offensive operations in the Somme Valley, and, secondly, that the condition of the whole German Second Army, astride of the Somme, offered every temptation to us to seize the initiative against it.

So far as the Australian Corps was concerned, however, my total frontage, which had been increased (as the result of our exploitation) to over eleven miles, precluded the possibility, with only four divisions at my disposal, of maintaining, even if I could succeed in initiating, an ambitious offensive. The time was nevertheless ripe for action on a scale far more decisive than had become orthodox in the British Army in the past. Efforts on that method had been confined to a thrust, limited in point both of distance and of time, and followed by a period of inaction; they had often given the enemy ample leisure to recover, and to reorganise his order of battle.

To maintain an offensive, day after day, indefinitely, would require sufficient resources, particularly in infantry, to allow divisions to be used alternatingly. Only in such a way, by having rested divisions always available to alternate with tired divisions, could a continuous pressure be maintained.

I took every opportunity of pressing these views upon the army commander, and expressed the readiness of the Australian Corps to undertake and maintain a long sustained offensive, provided that arrangements could be made to shorten my frontage from a three to a two-division battle front, and to increase my resources, from the present four, to five or even six divisions. It was further essential that in any advances attempted by us, other corps must co-operate on both flanks.

It would be bad tactics to drive into the enemy's front a salient with a narrow base, for such a salient would make our situation worse instead of better, affording to the enemy the opportunity of artillery attack upon it from both its flanks as well as from its front. The salient must therefore be broad based in relation to its depth, and the base must ever widen as the head of the salient advances.

This principle implied that a large-scale operation of such a nature must be begun on a whole army front, and that, even at its inception, at least three corps must co-operate, to be aided by the entry of additional corps on the outer flanks as the central depth developed. In other words, it was a project implying a large commitment of resources, and the urgent question was whether the time was yet ripe for taking the risks involved.

The matter, however, now became a subject at least worthy of practical discussion, and, during the days which followed Hamel, the staffs of both the corps and army were kept busy with the investigation of data, maps, and information, while the availability of additional resources in guns, tanks and aeroplanes became the subject of anxious inquiry.

A circumstance which troubled me sorely was the fact that my corps stood on the flank of the British Army, and that the troops on my right belonged to the French Army. The relations between the Australian troops and the *tirailleurs* and *Zouaves* of the 31st French Corps (General Toulorge) had always been the very friendliest, and the joint "international" posts had been the scenes of hearty fraternization and of the evolution of a strange common vernacular.

This comradeship of *"poilu"* with "digger" did not, however, lessen the difficulties incidental to the joint conduct of a major operation of war by two corps of different nationalities, speaking different languages, with diverse tactical conceptions, and, above all, of substantially divergent temperaments. The French are irresistible in attack as they are dogged in defence, but whether they will attack or defend depends greatly on their temperament of the moment. In this they are totally unlike the British or Australian soldier who will at any time philosophically accept either role that may be prescribed for him.

In short, it was not possible to hope for an effective co-ordination of effort, controlled particularly by the minute observance of a timetable, on the part of the Australian and its adjacent French Corps, and I felt quite unprepared to count upon it. It was for this reason that I expressed to the army commander the hope that a British Corps might be obtainable to operate on my right flank in any undertaking that should be decided upon. Understanding that the greater part of the Canadian Corps was then unemployed, resting in a back area, I ventured to hope that this corps might be made available, in the event of a decision that the proposal should be proceeded with.

My hesitation to accept the French as colleagues in such a battle was based not altogether on theoretical or sentimental grounds. The steady progress in mopping up enemy territory to the east of Villers-Bretonneux, which had been made by my south flank division (the Second) as the aftermath of Hamel, soon produced a contortion of the Allied front line at this point which bade fair to prove just as troublesome to me as had been the great re-entrant opposite Hamel, which that battle had been specially undertaken to eliminate.

No persuasions on my part, or on that of my flank division, could induce the adjacent French division to extend any co-operation in these advances or to adopt any measures to flatten out the re-entrant which, growing deeper every day, threatened to expose my right flank. I am convinced that such hesitation was based upon no timidity, but was the result wholly of an entirely different outlook and policy from those which the Australian Corps was doing its best to interpret. But the experience of it made the prospect of punctual co-operation on their part in much more serious undertakings distinctly less encouraging.

The proposed offensive involved, therefore, far-reaching redispositions, comprising a substantial displacement southward of the inter-Allied boundary, a lengthening by several miles of the whole British Western front, and an entire rearrangement of the respective fronts of the Third and Fourth British Armies. It is not surprising that a decision was deferred, while the project was being critically investigated from every point of view.

Then, suddenly, a new situation arose. On July 15th, the enemy opened a fresh attack against the French in the south. The scale on which he undertook it immediately made it patent to all students of the situation that he was probably employing his whole remaining reserves of fit, rested divisions; that he meant this to be his decisive blow; and that whether he gained a decision or not, it would be his last effort on the grand scale.

It did not succeed; for just as he had once again reached the line of the Marne and had on July 17th achieved his "furthest south" at Château-Thierry, a beautifully timed counter-stroke by the French and Americans upon the western face of the salient, extending from Soissons to the Marne, resulted on July 18th in the capture by the Allies on that day alone, of 15,000 prisoners and 200 guns.

It was the end of German offensive in the war. Their mobile reserves were exhausted, and they were compelled slowly to recede from the Château-Thierry salient. The appropriate moment, for which Foch and Haig had doubtless been waiting for months, had at last arrived to begin an Allied counter offensive, and it was only a question of deciding at what point along the Franco-British front the effort should be made, and on what date it should open.

Doubtless influenced by the reasons already discussed, the choice fell upon that portion of the front of the Fourth Army which lay south of the Somme; in other words, upon the southern portion of the Australian Corps front. The date remained undecided, but the requisite redisposition of armies and corps was so extensive that no time was to be lost in making a beginning.

It was on July 21st that General Rawlinson first called together the corps commanders who were to be entrusted with this portentous task. The strictest secrecy was enjoined, and never was a secret better kept; with the exception of the field marshal and his army commanders, none outside of the Fourth Army had any inkling of what was afoot until the actual moment for action had arrived.

Yet an observant enemy agent, if any such there had been in the vicinity, might well have drawn a shrewd conclusion that some mischief was brewing, had he happened along the main street of the prettily-situated village of Flexicourt, on the Somme, on that bright summer afternoon, and had observed in front of a pretentious white mansion, over which floated the black and red flag of an army commander, a quite unusual procession of motorcars, ostentatiously flying the Canadian and Australian flags and the red-and-white pennants of two other corps commanders.

There were present at that conference, General Currie, the Canadian, General Butler, of the Third Corps, General Kavanagh, of the Cavalry Corps, and myself, while senior representatives of the Tanks and Air Force also attended. Rawlinson unfolded the outline of the whole army plan, and details were discussed at great length in the light of the views held by each corps commander as to the tasks which he was prepared to undertake with the resources in his hands or promised to him.

The conditions which I had sought in my previous negotiations with the army commander were, I found, conceded to me almost to the full extent. My battle front was to be reduced from eleven miles to a little over 7,000 yards. It would, in fact, extend from the Somme, as the northern, to the main Péronne railway, as the southern flank. And—what was equally important, and profoundly welcome—the First Australian Division was shortly to be relieved in Flanders, and would at last join my corps, thus for the first time in the war bringing all Australian field units in France under one command.

The Canadians were to operate on my right, and further south again the First French Army (Debenay) was to supply a corps to form a defensive flank for the Canadians. The Third British Corps was to carry out for me a similar function on my northern flank. Thus, four Corps in line were to operate, the two central Corps carrying out the main advance, while the two outer flank Corps would be employed further to broaden the base of the great salient which the operation would create.

The Cavalry Corps would appear in the battle area also, with all preparations made for a rapid exploitation of any success achieved. The utility of the cavalry in modern war, at any rate in a European theatre, has been the subject of endless controversy. It is one into which I do not propose to enter. There is no doubt that, given suitable ground and an absence of wire entanglements, cavalry can move rapidly, and undertake important turning or enveloping movements. Yet it has been argued that the rarity of such suitable conditions negatives any justification for superimposing so unwieldy a burden as a large body of cavalry—on the bare chance that it *might* be useful—upon already overpopulated areas, billets, watering places and roads.

I may, however, anticipate the event by saying that the First Cavalry Brigade was duly allotted to me, and did its best to prove its utility; but I am bound to say that the results achieved, in what proved to be very unsuitable country beyond the range of the infantry advance, did not justify the effort expended either by this gallant brigade or by the other arms and services upon whom the very presence of the cavalry proved an added burden.

For the full understanding of subsequent developments both during and after the battle it becomes of special importance to consider the proposed role of the Third Corps in relation to my left flank. It is to be remembered that the Fourth Army decided that the River Somme was to be the tactical boundary between the two northern corps. It was not competent for me to criticize this decision at the time, but I am free now to say that I believed such a boundary to have been unsuitable, and the event speedily proved that it was.

It is always, in my opinion, undesirable to select any bold natural or artificial feature—such as a river, ravine, ridge, road or railway—as a boundary. It creates, at once, a divided responsibility, and necessitates between two independent commanders, and at a critical point, a degree of effective co-operation which can rarely be hoped for. It is much better boldly to place a unit, however large or small, *astride* of such a feature, so that both sides of it may come under the control of one and the same commander.

This was especially the case in this part of the Somme Valley which is broad, and has an ill-defined central line, tortuous, and with the slopes on either side tactically interdependent; but most of all because, as I have already described, the high plateau on the north completely overlooks the relatively lower flats on the south of the river. The point I am trying to make should be borne in mind, for I believe it has been fully borne out by subsequent events.

The decision standing, however, as it did, it fell to the task of the Third Corps to make an assault (concurrently with that of the Australian Corps south of the river) for the capture of the whole of that reach of the river known as the Chipilly Bend, and of all the high ground on the spur which that bend enfolds. The object was to deprive the enemy of all ground from which he could look down upon my advancing left flank, or from which he could bring rifle or artillery fire to bear upon it.

The Third Corps was to operate on the front of one division, the 58th, which, pivoting its left upon the Corbie-Bray road, was to advance its right—in sympathy with the advance of the left of the Australian Corps—until it rested upon the river about one mile downstream from Etinehem. It was a movement the success of which was rendered promising by the nature of the ground and the disorganised condition of the enemy between the Ancre and the Somme.

As regards my right flank, this was to rest as stated upon the main railway. The Canadian Corps, of four divisions, would take over from the French a frontage of about 6,000 yards and deliver a thrust parallel to and south of the railway, in the direction of Caix and Beaucourt, and would aim at the seizure of the important Hill 102, immediately to the west of the latter locality. At no time did any question of the security of my right flank furnish me with any cause for anxiety; the prowess of the Canadian Corps was well known to all Australians, and I knew that, to use his own expressive vernacular, it was General Currie's invariable habit to "deliver the goods".

The comprehensive project thus outlined at the conference of July 21st involved, as a preliminary step, a far-reaching redisposition of very large bodies of troops over a very wide front. With the readjustment of the boundaries between the Third and Fourth British Armies we are not particularly concerned, because this affected a region, north of the Ancre, which lay well outside of the battle area. Nor did the internal readjustment of the northern part of the Fourth Army front present any difficulty, as it meant nothing more than a routine "relief" by the 58th Division of the Fifth Australian Division which was at this juncture holding that part of my corps sector which lay between the Somme and the Ancre.

But the southern half was a very different matter. The First French Army was to give up to the British a section of about four miles, extending from Villers-Bretonneux to Thennes. This was ultimately to be taken over by the Canadian Corps as a battle front, but that corps still had two of its divisions in the line in the neighbourhood of Arras.

Moreover, it was of the utmost importance to conceal from the enemy until the last possible moment any change in our dispositions. This meant concealing them from our own troops also, because the loss by us of a single talkative prisoner would have been sufficient to disclose to the enemy at least the suspicion, if not the certainty, that an attack was in preparation.

After examining the problem and discussing several alternative solutions, it was ultimately decided at this conference that, five or six days before the date fixed for the attack, the French would be relieved in this sector by a division, not of Canadians, but of Australians; that under cover of and behind this Australian division, the Canadian Corps would come in from the north, and would proceed to carry out its battle preparations; and finally that the actual appearance of Canadian troops in the front line would not ensue until three days before the battle.

During the preceding two days, the Australian troops would be gradually withdrawn from the sector, leaving only one Brigade in occupation of the line, to be backed up by the incoming Canadians in the unexpected contingency of an attack by the enemy. This last brigade would quietly melt away, leaving the Canadians in full possession of the field.

It was hoped that, during the days of the temporary Australian occupation of the sector, nothing would happen which might disclose to the enemy that the French had left it; and even if we were to have the misfortune to lose from this sector any Australian prisoners to the enemy, it was further hoped that, if kept in total ignorance of the inflow of Canadians, such prisoners would be unable to make any embarrassing disclosures. The *dénouement*, which will be told later, showed that this judgment of possibilities was a shrewd one, and that such precautions were not taken in vain.

At this period of the war, large numbers of Americans had already arrived in France, but only few of them were yet ready to take their places in the line of battle. The time had not yet arrived, therefore, when, by taking over large sections of the Western front they could help to shorten the French and British frontages. The British front was, therefore, still so extended that the mobile reserve divisions at the disposal of the field marshal were few.

This consideration made the contemplated reliefs and interchanges of corps and divisions, and their transference from one part of our front to another a matter of great complexity, and one which required time to execute. Each stage of the process was contingent upon the due completion of a previous stage. It is, moreover, a process which cannot be unduly hastened, without serious discomfort and fatigue to the troops and animals concerned.

Troops destined for battle must be kept in the highest physical condition. This means good feeding, comfortable housing, and adequate rest. A couple of weary days and sleepless nights spent in crowded railway trains, with cold food and little exercise, are sufficient to play havoc with the fighting trim of even a crack battalion. So, the daily stages of the journey must be short, and comfortable billets must be in readiness for each night's halt. The day's supplies must arrive punctually and at the right railhead, to ensure hot, well-cooked meals.

With the very limited number of serviceable railway lines which remained available behind the British front—and with the congestion of traffic resulting from the daily transportation of many thousands of tons of artillery ammunition and other war stores—it was not surprising that as the result of the deliberations of the conference it was resolved to advise the commander-in-chief that it would take not less than five days to rearrange our order of battle on the lines decided upon, and another five days, after corps and divisions had taken over their battle fronts, to enable them to complete their preparations.

Thus, the Fourth Army could be ready at ten days' notice, and the conference broke up, pledged to secrecy and complete inaction, until formal approval had been given to the proposals and a date fixed for their realisation.

The remainder of July passed with no very startling occurrences. In the south the German withdrawal from the Soissons salient and the Marne continued steadily, with the French and Americans on their heels; but it was a methodical retreat, which would bring about a substantial shortening of the German line, and so release divisions to rest and refit, which might conceivably become available for a fresh assault elsewhere.

But there was still no sign of any such design upon that always tender spot, the Allied junction at Villers-Bretonneux. On the contrary, my second division still continued to make free with the enemy's advanced patrols, and in a very brilliant little infantry operation by the 7th Brigade captured the "Mound", a long spoilbank beside the railway at a point about a mile east of the town, which dominated the landscape in every direction. The ardour of his troops was only enhanced when they heard that General Rosenthal himself, while reconnoitring from the Mound, had been sniped at and had received a nasty wound in the arm.

The enemy attempted nothing in the way of infantry retaliation. But whenever he had been thoroughly angered, he treated my front to a liberal drenching of mustard gas, fired by his artillery. His supplies of mustard gas shell seemed inexhaustible, and he would frequently expend as many as 10,000 of them in a single night upon the half-ruined town of Villers-Bretonneux or on the Bois l'Abbé and other woods which he suspected were sheltering my reserve infantry.

These gas attacks were annoying and troublesome in the extreme. During the actual bombardments, troops wore their gas masks as a matter of course, but doffed them when the characteristic smell of the gas had disappeared. But it was warm weather, and as the sun rose, the poisonous liquid, which had spattered the ground over immense areas, would volatilise, and rise in sufficient volume still to attack all whose business took them to and fro across this ground. In this way hundreds of our men became incapacitated; although there were a few serious cases, most of the men would be fit to rejoin in two or three weeks. But this form of attack, and the constant dread of it, made life in the forward areas anything but endurable.

I was beset by quite another trepidation also. Prisoners captured during the German withdrawal from the Marne, which was then in progress, told tales of contemplated withdrawals on other fronts, and some even asserted that a withdrawal opposite my own front was being talked of. Judged by subsequent events, it is more than probable that these stories were stimulated by the many articles which were at that time appearing in the German newspapers from the pens of press strategists, who, in order to allay public anxiety, were representing these withdrawals as deliberate, and as a masterpiece of strategy, compelling the Allies to a costly pursuit over difficult and worthless ground.

Opposite Albert, signs that such a withdrawal was actually in progress also began to appear, although it subsequently transpired that, in its early stages, this procedure was merely prompted by a purely local consideration, namely, the desire of the enemy to improve his tactical position by abandoning the outposts, which he had been maintaining in the valley of the Ancre, and transferring them to the higher and better ground on the east of that river.

It was only natural that those of us who knew of the impending attack, and of the immense effort which its preparation would involve, felt nervous lest the enemy might forestall us by withdrawing his whole line to some methodically prepared position of defence in the rear, just as he had done once before in 1917 on so large a scale in the Bapaume region. It would probably have been a sound measure of military policy, but it would assuredly, at that juncture, have had as disastrous an effect upon the *morale* of the German people as his enforced withdrawal, which was soon to begin, actually produced not long after.

The order to prepare the attack, and fixing the date of it for August 8th, came in the closing days of July, and at once all was bustle and excitement in the Australian Corps. Commanders, staff officers, and Intelligence Service, the artillery, the Corps Flying Squadron, the map and photography sections spent busy days in reconnaissance, and toilsome nights in office work. The vast extent of the detailed work involved, particularly upon the administrative services, can only be appreciated by a study of the plan for the battle, which it fell to my lot, as Corps Commander, first to formulate, and then to expound to a series of conferences which were held at Bertangles on July 30th, and on August 2nd and 4th.

It is, therefore, perhaps appropriate that I should now attempt to repeat, in non-technical language, an exposition of the outlines of that plan.

Chapter 5

The Battle Plan

My plan for the impending battle involved the employment of four divisions in the actual assault, with one division in reserve. The reserve division was to be available for use in one of two ways; either as a reserve of fresh troops to exploit any successes gained upon the first day, or else to take over and hold defensively the ground won, if the assaulting divisions should have become too exhausted to be relied upon for successful resistance to a counter-attack in force.

The frontage allotted to the corps was 7,000 yards, and this extent of front accommodated itself naturally to the employment of two first-line divisions, each on a 3,500-yard front, each division having two brigades in the front line, with one brigade in reserve.

As four divisions were available to me for immediate use in the battle, I decided to undertake, for the first time in the war, on so comprehensive a scale, the tactical expedient of a "leapfrog" by divisions over each other.

This term had, long before, passed into the homely phraseology of the war, in order to describe a procedure by which one body of troops, having reached its objective, was there halted, as at a completed task, while a second body of troops, of similar order of importance, but under an entirely separate commander, advanced over the ground won, reached the foremost battle line, took over the tactical responsibility for the fighting front, and after a prescribed interval of time continued the advance to a further and more distant objective.

This conception of an advance by a process of "leapfrog" had been evolved early in 1917 in connection with a method of assault on successive lines of trenches. It was intended at the outset to be applied only to very small bodies of infantry, such as platoons. A normal battle plan for a company of infantry of four platoons was for the first two platoons to capture and hold the front line trench, while the next two following platoons would leap over this trench and over the troops who had gained it, and then pass beyond to the capture of the second, or support trench. The method was used, for the first time, on such a modest scale, at the Battle of Messines, in June, 1917, and later on in the same year was adopted for bodies as large even as battalions, in the fighting for the Broodseinde and Passchendaele Heights.

But on no previous occasion had such a principle been applied to whole divisions. It is true that at the Battle of Messines, the Fourth Australian Division passed through the New Zealand Division after the latter had completed the capture of the main Messines Ridge, but this was really exploitation, undertaken in order to take advantage of the temporary confusion of the enemy, and for the purpose of gaining ground upon the eastern slopes of the captured ridge. It was not a movement which was really part of the main assault, and it was confined to a single division.

On the present occasion my purpose was to carry out a clear and definite process of "leapfrogging", not only simultaneously by two divisions side by side, but also as an essential part of the time-table programme for the main battle, and before the exploitation stage of the fighting was timed to be reached. It was, undeniably, a daring proposal, involving very definite risks, enormously increasing the labour of preparation and the mass of detailed precautions which had to be undertaken in order to obviate the possibility of great confusion.

The preparations necessary for a single division proposing to advance alone, to a prescribed distance, over country much of which was usually visible to us from our front line, are sufficiently complex, relating as they do, not only to the establishment of numerous protected headquarters for brigades and battalions, of miles upon miles of buried and ground cables, of dumps of all kinds of supplies, and of dressing stations and medical aid posts; but also to the disposition, in concealed positions, of all the assaulting units, down to the smallest of them, of infantry engineers and pioneers.

All these preparations assume a tenfold complexity when a second division has to make arrangements exactly similar in character, variety and extent, using exactly the same territory for the purpose and at the same time, and planning to advance over more distant country, entirely beyond visual range and preliminary reconnaissance.

The project also involved a much greater crowding of troops into the areas immediately behind our line of departure, and, therefore, enormously increased the risk of premature detection by the enemy, both from ground and from air observation, of unusual movement and of other symptoms which presaged the possibility of an attack by us. The plan also necessitated the closest possible co-ordination of effort, and mutual sympathy and understanding, between the commanders and staffs of the twin divisions having a common jurisdiction over one and the same area of preparation, and one and the same battle front. This was a degree of co-operation which could not have been looked for unless the personnel concerned had already established, from long and close association with each other, the most cordial personal relations.

And dominating all other difficulties were those involved in the proposal to execute this difficult and untried operation of a divisional leapfrog, not singly but in a duplex manner, necessitating the assurance of exactly similar simultaneous action, similarly timed in every stage, both before and during battle, by each of two separate pairs of divisions.

These threatening difficulties were surely formidable enough, but I knew that I could rely upon the good-will of the divisions towards each other, and upon the loyal support of them all. This seemed to me to justify the attempt, and to minimize the risks; having regard above all else to the results which I stood to gain if the operation could be executed as planned.

On no previous occasion in the war had an attempt ever been made to effect a penetration into the enemy's defences at the first blow, and on the first day, greater than a mile or two. Rarely had any previous set-piece attack succeeded in reaching the enemy's line of field-guns. The result had been that the bulk of his artillery had been withdrawn at his leisure, and his losses had been confined to a few hundred acres of shattered territory. But the task I had set myself was not only to reach, at the first onslaught, the whole of the enemy's artillery positions, but greatly to overrun them with a view to obliterating, by destruction or capture, the whole of his defensive organisations and the whole of the fighting resources which they contained, along the full extent of my corps front.

To achieve this object, I prepared my plans upon the basis of a total advance, on the first day, of not less than 9,000 yards. This was to be divided into three separate stages, as follows:

Phase A—Set-piece attack with barrage,	3,000 yards
Phase B—Open-warfare advance,	4,500 yards
Phase C—Exploitation,	1,500 yards
Total distance to final objective,	9,000 yards

The opening phase involved no novel or unusual features so far as the infantry were concerned, and was conceived on lines with which the fighting of 1917 had familiarised me, modified further by the accumulated experience gained from earlier mistakes in the technical details of such an enterprise. The recent Battle of Hamel became the model for this phase, the conditions of that battle being now reproduced on a much enlarged scale.

But there was one very important feature which distinguished the present undertaking from the Battles of Messines and Broodseinde, and that was in regard to the frontage allotted for attack to a single division. At Messines, the divisional battle front was 2,000 yards; in the third Battle of Ypres it differed but little from the same standard. For the present battle, I adopted a battle front of two miles for each assaulting division, or a mile for each of the four assaulting brigades.

This innovation seemed to me to be justified by four principal factors. The first of these was that the weather, which was dry, and the state of the ground, which was hard, made the "going" easy and the stress upon the infantry comparatively light. Next, the condition of the enemy's defensive works was undeveloped and stagnant, as clearly disclosed by the air photographs which the Corps Air Squadron produced in great numbers on every fine day.

No doubt this was due to the encroachments we had made on his forward works during the fighting at Hamel and in the remaining weeks of July. Thirdly, the powerful assistance anticipated from a contingent of four battalions of tanks which General Rawlinson had arranged to place under my orders led me to estimate that I might greatly reduce the number of men per yard of front. Lastly, the plan was justified by the known distribution of the enemy's infantry and guns along the frontage under attack. For all these reasons, I felt prepared to impose on the infantry a task which, computed solely upon the factor of frontage, was more than twice that demanded by me on any previous occasion.

At the same time, so extended a frontage involved the employment of a much higher ratio of barrage artillery to the number of battalions of infantry actually engaged. Success depended more upon the efficiency of the fire power of the barrage than upon any other factor, and I could not afford to incur any risk by weakening the density of the barrage. For this reason, I adhered to the standard which previous experience of several major battles and many minor raids had shown to be adequate for covering the assaulting infantry, and for keeping down the enemy's fire. This standard never fluctuated widely from one field-gun per twenty yards of front, and involved the employment, on this occasion, of some 432 field-guns in the barrage alone. This result could not have been achieved if the Fourth Army authorities had not seen their way to place at my disposal five additional brigades of field artillery over and above the thirteen Australian brigades which formed a permanent part of the whole artillery of the corps.

Phase A, as already stated, involved a penetration of 3,000 yards, and the objective line for this phase, which came to be known as the "green" line (from the colour employed to delineate it upon all the fighting maps propounded by the corps), was chosen, after an exhaustive study of all aeroplane photographs, and of the results of numerous observations, by many diverse means, of the locations of the enemy's artillery, so as to make certain that during this phase the whole mass of the enemy's forward artillery would be overrun, and captured or put out of action.

The green line was, in fact, located along the crest of the spur running north-easterly from Lamotte-en-Santerre in the direction of Cerisy-Gailly, with the object of carrying the battle well to the east of the Cerisy valley, in which large numbers of the enemy's guns had been definitely located. This would give us, by the capture of this valley, suitable concealed positions in which the infantry destined for Phase B could rest for a short "breather"; and would land the infantry of the original assault in a position from which they could detect and forestall any attempt on the part of the enemy to launch a counter-attack before the time for the opening of Phase B had arrived.

The task of executing Phase A of the battle fell to the Second and Third Australian Divisions, in that order from south to north, the southern flank of the Second Division resting upon the main railway line from Amiens to Péronne, and being there in contact with the Canadian Corps, under General Currie. The northern flank of the Third Division rested on the River Somme, and was there in contact with the Third British Corps under General Butler, while the interdivisional boundary was at the southern edge of the Bois-d'Accroche.

These two divisions were the line divisions during the period immediately preceding the battle, and had been holding the line each with two brigades in line and one brigade in support. Three days prior to the battle, however, it was arranged that each division should hold its front with only one brigade, thereby making available two brigades each for the actual carrying out of Phase A of the attack. These assaulting brigades were the 7th, 3th, 9th and 11th, in that order from south to north, each brigade having its due allotment of tanks and machine-guns, etc.

The total estimated time for the completion of Phase A was to be 143 minutes after the opening of the barrage at "zero" hour; and there was then to be a pause of 100 minutes to allow time for the advance and deployment into battle order of the succeeding two divisions, who were to carry out the process of "leapfrogging" and to execute Phases B and C of the battle.

The planning of Phase B, or the advance from the "green" to the "red" line, involved a totally different tactical conception and the adoption of a type of warfare which had almost entirely disappeared from the Western theatre of war since those far-off days in the late autumn of 1914, when the German Army first dug itself in, in France and Belgium, and committed both combatants to the prolonged agony of over three years of stationary warfare. I allude to the moving battle, or as it is called in text-book language, "open warfare"; a type of fighting in which few of the British Forces formed since the original Expeditionary Force had any experience except on the manoeuvre ground under peace conditions—a disability which applied equally to the Australian troops. Confident, however, in their adaptability and in their power of initiative under novel conditions, I did not hesitate to prescribe, for this second phase of the battle, the adoption of the principles and methods of open warfare.

In two very important respects in particular, this type of fighting involved conditions to which the troops had not been accustomed, and under which they had no previous experience in battle. In trench warfare, and in a deliberate attack on entrenched defences, the positions of all headquarters, medical aid posts, supply dumps and signal stations remained fixed and immovable. The whole of the internal communications by telegraph and telephone could, therefore, be completely installed beforehand, down to the last detail, and the transmission of all messages, reports, orders and instructions, during the course of the battle, was rapid and assured. But in a moving battle no such comprehensive or stable signalling arrangements are possible, and reliance must be placed upon the much slower and much more uncertain methods of transmission by flag and lamp signalling, by dispatch riders, pigeons and runners.

Divisional Headquarters would, therefore, almost as soon as the battle commenced, fall out of touch with brigades, and they in turn with their battalions; information as to the actual situation at the fighting front would travel slowly, and would reach those responsible for making consequential decisions often long after an entire alteration in the situation had removed the need for action. Thus, a greatly enhanced responsibility would come to be imposed upon subordinate leaders to decide for themselves, without waiting for guidance or orders from higher authority, and to grasp the initiative by taking all possible action on the spot in the light of the circumstances and situation of the moment.

Again, the nature of the artillery action is, in the moving battle, fundamentally different from that which prevails during trench warfare. To begin with, only that portion of the artillery which is in the strictest sense mobile can participate to any extent in open warfare. The employment of artillery is, therefore, confined to a few and to the smaller natures of Ordnance, namely, the 18-pounder field-gun, the 4½-inch field howitzer and the 60-pounder, which are all horse drawn and which are capable of being moved off the roads and across all but the most broken country. Heavier guns, from 6-inch upwards, are in practice confined to roads, and are too slow and cumbersome to keep pace with the infantry. The artillery fire action is also intrinsically different, because the guns can be sighted directly upon their targets, while in trench warfare they are always laid by indirect methods, with the use of the map and compass, and without observation, at any rate by the crew of the gun, of the objects fired at.

The decision which I had to take of carrying out the second phase of this great battle on the principles of open warfare was, therefore, one which also involved a certain element of risk. But it was a risk which I felt justified in taking, in spite of the fact that the German High Command had more than once expressed itself in contemptuous terms of the capacity of any British troops successfully to undertake any operation of open warfare. My justification lay primarily in my confidence in the ability of the subordinate commanders and troops to work satisfactorily under these novel conditions—a confidence which the event abundantly justified. But I was placed in the position of having either to accept this risk, or else abandon altogether the project of a quite unprecedented penetration of enemy country to be completed on the first day. It would have been clearly impossible to continue the advance beyond the green line without an interval of at least forty-eight hours, which would have been necessary to enable the artillery to be re-disposed for barrage fire in forward positions and provided with the necessary supplies of ammunition for such a purpose.

The divisions which were told off to carry out the "leapfrog" enterprise and to execute Phase B of the battle were the Fifth Australian Division on the south and the Fourth Australian Division on the north, the outer flanks of the attack remaining as before, *i.e.*, the Péronne Railway on the south and the River Somme on the north. Each of these divisions was directed to deploy, on its own frontage, two infantry brigades. Its third brigade was to be kept intact and to advance during Phase B at some distance behind, as a support to the fighting line, and to be employed in the subsequent phase, if it were found that Phase B could be completed without calling upon this spare brigade. The actual dispositions of the brigades finally proposed by the respective divisional commanders and approved by me brought about the arrangement that the four first-line mobile infantry brigades were successively, from south to north, the 15th, 8th, 12th and 4th, while the 14th and 1st Brigades followed as supports in a second line.

To each of these infantry brigades I allotted a brigade of field artillery, to be employed under the direct orders of the infantry brigade commander, and, in addition, three artillery brigades as well as one battery of 60-pounders, to each divisional commander. As my resources in artillery were not unlimited, the twelve artillery brigades, so disposed of, were necessarily drawn from the original eighteen brigades which were to fire the covering artillery barrage for Phase A of the battle. The orders to that portion of the field artillery which was to become mobile in pursuance of this plan, accordingly, were that immediately upon the completion of their original tasks, by the capture of the green line, they were to "pull out of the barrage".

This meant, in effect, that all the teams, limbers, battery wagons, and ammunition wagons of these twelve brigades, waiting in their wagon lines far in rear, fully harnessed up and hooked in at the opening of the battle, had to advance during the progress of the first phase, so as to reach their guns just at the right time, but no earlier, to enable these guns to be limbered up, and the batteries to become completely mobile in order to join and advance with the infantry of the second phase.

This was an operation which required the greatest nicety in timing, and the greatest accuracy in execution. No Australian artillery had ever previously undertaken such an operation, except perhaps on the manoeuvre ground, and then only on the very limited scale of a brigade or two at a time. That this rapid transition from the completely stationary to the completely mobile battle was carried out, during the very crisis of a great engagement, without the slightest hitch, and with only the trifling loss of two or three gun horse teams from shell fire, reflects the very highest credit upon every officer and man of the Australian field artillery.

The open warfare infantry brigades were also to be provided, out of their own divisional resources, each with a company of engineers, a company of machine-guns, a field ambulance, and a detachment of pioneers, so that, in the most complete sense, they became a brigade group of all arms, capable of dealing, out of their own resources and on their own ground, with any situation that might arise during their advance of nearly three miles from the green to the red line. A detachment of nine tanks completed the fighting equipment of each of the four front line brigades destined to capture the red line.

I must now briefly describe the nature of Phase C, the third and last stage in this ambitious and complex battle programme. This phase was to consist of "exploitation", which implies that it was a provisional preparation, which was to be carried out only if complete success attended the two preceding phases. The objective of Phase C was the "blue" line, which I had located about one mile to the east of the red line, along a system of old French trenches extending from the river at a point near Méricourt, and running southerly to the railway at a point a little to the south-east of Harbonnières. This line gave promise of furnishing a good defensive position in which to deal with any possible counter-attack. It also gave a good line of departure for subsequent operations, and provided ideal artillery positions in a series of valleys, running parallel and a little to the west of the line itself.

The troops earmarked for this Exploitation Phase were the two second line brigades of the two divisions which were to capture the red line, namely, the 14th and 1st Brigades, and the orders to the divisional commanders were that if the red line was reached without mishap, without undue loss of time, and without involving the reserve brigades, but not otherwise, these reserve brigades were to push on with the utmost determination to secure and hold the blue line until such time as they could be reinforced.

Each of these exploitation brigades was equipped similarly to the red line brigades in all respects except that they were provided with a special contingent of 18 Mark V. (Star) Tanks of the very latest design. These differed from the Mark V. Tank employed at Hamel and in the other stages of the present operation, in that they were longer and had sufficient internal space to carry, as passengers, over and above their own crews, two complete infantry Lewis gun detachments each. It was expected that this infantry fire power, added to the fire power from the machine-guns carried by these 36 tanks themselves and operated by the tank crews, would go far to compensate for the somewhat attenuated line of probably tired infantry spread in two brigades over an ultimate frontage of over 10,000 yards.

No definite time-table was laid down for the closing phases of the battle, except for the regulation of the times when our heavy artillery should "lift off" designated targets—such as villages, farms, and known gun positions—and lengthen its range so as not to obstruct the further advance of our own infantry. But it was estimated that, from the opening of the battle, the green line would be reached in two and a half hours, the red line in six hours, and the blue line in eight hours. As the battle was to open at the first streak of dawn, it would, if all went well, be completed according to plan by about midday.

In every battle plan, whether great or small, it is necessary first of all to map out the whole of the intended action of the infantry, at any rate on the general lines indicated above. When that has been done the next step is to work backwards, and to test the feasibility of each body of infantry being able to reach its allotted point of departure, punctually, without undue stress on the troops, and without crossing or impeding the line of movement of any other body of infantry. It is often necessary to test minutely, by reference to calculations of time and space, more than one alternative plan for marshalling the infantry prior to battle, and for the successive movements, day by day, and from point to point, of every battalion engaged.

The present case was no exception, and, indeed, presented quite special difficulties. The whole of the area for a depth of many thousands of yards behind our then front line was open rolling country, devoid of any cover, and (except in the actual valley of the Somme) with every village, hamlet, farmhouse, factory and wood obliterated. The plan involved the assembly, in this confined area, fully exposed by day to the view of any inquisitive enemy aircraft, of no less than 45 infantry battalions, with all their paraphernalia of war; not to speak of our 600 guns of all calibres, their wagon lines, horse lines and motor parks, together with Engineers, Pioneers, Tanks, Medical and Supply Units amounting to tens of thousands of men and animals.

A new factor which, however, ultimately controlled the final decision which I had to make as to the nature of the dispositions prior to battle, lay in the consideration of the maximum distances which would have to be covered by the foot soldiers in such a far-flung battle. I had little difficulty in coming to the conclusion that the obvious and normal arrangement was on this occasion a totally wrong arrangement. If the assaulting brigades had been arranged, from front to rear, in their assembly areas prior to battle, in the same order as that in which they would have to come into action, this would have involved that the individual man, who was to be required to march and fight his way furthest into enemy country, and, therefore, was to be the last to enter the fight, would also be called upon to march furthest from his rearmost position of assembly before even reaching the battle zone. The maximum distance to be traversed on the day of battle by infantry would have amounted, according to such a plan, to over ten miles. While this is an easy day's march on a good road, under tranquil conditions, it would have been an altogether unreasonable demand upon any infantryman during the stress and nervous excitement of battle. It would have been courting a breakdown from over-fatigue, among the very troops upon whom I had to rely most to defend the captured territory against any serious enemy reaction.

I therefore adopted the not very obvious course of completely reversing the normal procedure, and of disposing the brigades in depth, from front to rear, in exactly the *reverse* of the order in which, in point of time, they would enter the battle.

The following represents, diagrammatically, the disposition of all twelve brigades after having been fully *deployed* in the actual course of the battle:

```
                    (4th Division)      |                   (5th Division)
                  4    —    12          |                 8    —    15
Direction of enemy.  North   1          Inter-Divisional          14        South
                    (3rd Division)      Boundary.          (2nd Division)
                  11   —    9           |                 5    —    7
                 ───────────────────────┼──────────────────────────────────
                                        |                        Our front line
                                        |                         before battle
                  10 (in our trenches)  |                 6 (in our trenches)
```

The next diagram shows how the twelve brigades were disposed while Phase A of the battle was in progress, and before the second Phase had begun:

```
                (3rd Division)          |              (2nd Division)
              11   —   9                |            5    —    7
             ───────────────────────────┼──────────────────────────────
                                        Inter-Divisional      Our front line
                                        Boundary.              before battle
              10 (in our trenches)      |            6 (in our trenches)
                (4th Division)          |              (5th Division)
              4    —    12              |            8    —    15
                     1                  |                  14
```

But the following diagram represents, in a similar manner, the order of disposition of the same brigades, in the territory under our own occupation, immediately *prior* to the battle:

```
                    (3rd Division)      |              (2nd Division)
                                        |                         Our front line
                  ──────────────────────┼──────────────────────── before battle.
                  10 (in our trenches)  Inter-Divisional  6 (in our trenches)
                    (4th Division)      Boundary.          (5th Division)
Direction of enemy. North  4   —   12   |              8    —    15    South
                           1            |                    14
                    (3rd Division)      |              (2nd Division)
                  11   —   9            |              5    —    7
```

A little consideration will show that this apparently paradoxical procedure brought about the desired result of more nearly equalising the stress upon the whole of the infantry engaged, in point, at least, of the maximum distance to be traversed in the day's operations. But it produced something else, also, of much greater concern, which was that the scheme involved a leapfrogging of divisions during the approach march into the battle, in addition to a second leapfrogging, to which I was already committed, to occur at a later stage during the battle itself.

Thus I was confronted with the dilemma that the only scheme of disposition which promised success for the subsequent battle was also that scheme which made the greatest possible demands upon the intelligence of the troops and the sympathetic, loyal and efficient co-operation of my own corps staff, and those of the commanders acting under me. Influenced once again by the confidence which I felt in my whole command, I did not hesitate to increase the complexity of the plans for the infantry action by calling upon the four divisions to execute a manoeuvre which is unique in the history of war, namely, a "double leapfrog", simultaneously carried out by two separate pairs of divisions, operating side by side. The first leap was to take place during the approach to the battle, the second during the progress of the battle itself.

This expedient, which I finally decided to adopt, in spite of the dangers involved in its complexity and in the absence of any precedent, was, however, as logical analysis and the event itself proved, the very keynote of the success of the entire project. The whole plan, thanks to an intelligent interpretation by all commanders and staffs concerned, worked like a well-oiled machine, with smoothness, precision and punctuality, and achieved to the fullest extent the advantages aimed at.

On the one hand, the stress upon the troops was reduced to a minimum. By the reduction of physical fatigue, it conserved the energies of whole divisions in a manner which permitted of their speedy re-employment in subsequent decisive operations. And on the other hand, by the great depth of penetration which it rendered possible, it ensured a victory which amounted to so crushing a blow to the enemy that its momentum hurled him into a retrograde movement, not only along the whole front under attack, but also for many miles on either flank. This recoil he was never able to arrest, as we followed up our victory by blow after blow delivered while he was still reeling from the effects of the first onslaught of August 8th. But, so far, I have written of the infantry plan only; and much remains to be told of the simultaneous action designed to be taken by all the other arms, which rendered possible and emphasised the success of the infantry. No one can rival me in my admiration for the transcendent military virtues

Tanks marching into Battle.

Morcourt Valley—the Australian attack swept across this on August 8th, 1918.

of the Australian infantryman, for his bravery, his battle discipline, his absolute reliability, his individual resource, his initiative and endurance.

But I had formed the theory that the true role of the infantry was not to expend itself upon heroic physical effort, nor to wither away under merciless machine-gun fire, nor to impale itself on hostile bayonets, nor to tear itself to pieces in hostile entanglements—(I am thinking of Pozières and Stormy Trench and Bullecourt, and other bloody fields)—but, on the contrary, to advance under the maximum possible protection of the maximum possible array of mechanical resources, in the form of guns, machine-guns, tanks, mortars and aeroplanes; to advance with as little impediment as possible; to be relieved as far as possible of the obligation to *fight* their way forward; to march, resolutely, regardless of the din and tumult of battle, to the appointed goal; and there to hold and defend the territory gained; and to gather in the form of prisoners, guns and stores, the fruits of victory.

It is my purpose, therefore, to emphasise particularly the extent to which this theory was realised in the battle under review, by the achievement of a great and decisive victory at a trifling cost. That result was due primarily to the very ample resources in mechanical aids which the foresight and confidence of the Fourth Army commander, General Rawlinson, entrusted to me; but it was due partly, also, to the manner in which those resources were employed. And that is why I shall attempt to describe the remainder of the corps plan.

CHAPTER 6

The Battle Plan (Continued)

Surprise has been, from time immemorial, one of the most potent weapons in the armoury of the tactician. It can be achieved not merely by doing that which the enemy least anticipates, but also by acting at a time when he least expects any action. It was a weapon which had been employed only rarely in the previous greater battles of this war. The offensive before Cambrai, planned by General Sir Julian Byng, and the Battle of Hamel, were rare exceptions to our general procedure of heralding the approach of an offensive by feverish and obvious activity on our part, and by a long sustained preliminary bombardment of the enemy's defences, designed to destroy his works and impair his *morael*.

The situation on the Fourth Army front, early in August, 1918, offered a rare opportunity for the employment of surprise tactics on the boldest scale. The incessant "nibbling" activities of the Australian troops during the preceding three months had been of such a consistent nature as to suggest that our resources were not equal to any greater effort upon such an extended front as we were then holding, from the Ancre down to and beyond Villers-Bretonneux. On the other hand, the passivity of the first French Army, to the south of the latter town, conveyed no suggestion of any offensive enterprise on the part of our Ally in this region.

The problem, therefore, was to convert an extensive front from a state of passive defence to a state of complete preparedness for an attack on the largest scale, and to keep the enemy—who, as always, was alert and observant both from the ground and from the air—in complete ignorance of every portion of these extensive preparations, until the very moment when the battle was to burst upon him. It was, of course, a question not merely of deceiving the enemy troops in their trenches immediately opposed to us, but also of arousing in the minds of the German High Command no suspicions which might have prompted them to hold in a state of readiness, or to put into motion towards the threatened zone, any of the reserve divisions forming part of their still considerable resources.

The following memorandum, which was issued to the whole of the senior commanders in the Australian Corps on August 1st, gives in outline some of the measures adopted to this end:

SECRECY.

1. The first essential to success is the maintenance of secrecy. The means to be adopted are as follows:

(i) No person is to be told or informed in any part or way until such time as the development of the plan demands action from him. This is the main principle and will be pursued throughout, down to the lowest formation.

(ii) Divisional Commanders will work out their reliefs in such a way as will ensure that the troops in the line know nothing of the proposed operation until the last possible moment. This will apply in particular to any troops who may be employed in the area south of the Amiens—Villers-Bretonneux railway.

2. In order to conceal the intention to carry out a large operation on this front the following plan has been adopted:

The Australian Corps has been relieved of one divisional sector by the Third Corps, and takes over a divisional sector from the French Corps. The object of this is to lead the enemy, and our own people, too, to believe that the action of the French in the Soissons salient has been so costly as to demand that further French troops had to be made available, and that this is the apparent cause of the extension of the Australian Corps front to the south.

3. (*a*) The idea is being circulated that the Canadian Corps is being brought to the south to take over the role of Reserve Corps at the junction of the British and French Armies in replacement of the 22nd Corps, which occupied that role until it was ordered to the Champagne front. In order that the enemy may be deceived as to the destination of the Canadian Corps in the event of his discovering that it has been withdrawn from the Arras front, Canadian wireless personnel has been sent to the Second Army area, (this was in Flanders and Belgium), where they have taken over certain wireless zones.

(*b*) To prevent the enemy from discovering the arrival of the Canadian Corps in this region, they will not take over from the 4th Australian Division until 'Y' night. This will necessitate a proportion of the troops of the Fourth Australian Division remaining in the line in this sector until 'Y' night. As the Fourth Australian Division will be required to participate in the attack it is proposed to distribute one brigade to hold the whole of the line from 'W' night onwards. This will enable the remaining two brigades to be withdrawn, given a day or two's rest, and allow of their part in the operation being fully explained to them. The place of these two brigades in rear of the line brigade will be taken over by Canadian divisions.

(*c*) In order to deceive our own troops as to the cause of the coming down here of the Canadians, a rumour is going abroad that the Canadian Corps is being brought down with the object of relieving the Australian Corps in the line. To most of the Australian Corps this would appear to be an obvious reason for their coming, as the idea has been mooted on former occasions. While it is not intended that this rumour should be promulgated, it is not desired that anyone should disclose the actual facts. This idea, together with the idea put forth in paragraph 3 (*a*), should do much to prevent the real facts from becoming known."

★★★★★★

Note: The secret was, indeed, so well kept, and the "camouflage" stories circulated proved so effective, that the King of the Belgians forwarded a strong protest to Marshal Foch because the Canadians were about to deliver an attack in his country, without his having been consulted or made aware of the plans;

and the Canadian Headquarters in London complained to the War Office that the Canadian Forces were being divided, and were being sent by detachments to different parts of the front, instead of being always kept together as the Canadian Government desired. It is said that even Mr. Lloyd George knew nothing of the intention to attack until late on the day before the battle.

★★★★★★

The references to "W", "X", "Y" and "Z" days and nights in the above memo, are to the successive days preceding Zero day—known briefly as "Z" day, on which the battle was to open. The actual *date* of "Z" day was kept a close secret by the army commander and the three corps commanders concerned, until a few days before the actual date; while the actual moment of assault, or "Zero" hour, was not determined or made known until noon on the day preceding the battle, after a close study of the conditions of visibility before and after break of day, on the three preceding mornings.

But these arrangements were directed only towards the prevention of a premature disclosure of our intention to attack to the enemy, to our own troops, and through them to the civilian public, and to enemy agents, whose presence among us had always to be reckoned with. It still remained to carry out our battle preparations in a manner which would preclude the possibility of detection by enemy aircraft, either through direct observation, or by the help of photography.

Accordingly I issued orders that all movements of troops and of transport of all descriptions, should take place only during the hours of darkness, whether in the forward or in the rear areas; and in order to keep an effective control over the faithful execution of these difficult orders, I arranged for relays of "police" aeroplanes, furnished by our No. 3 Squadron, to fly continuously, by day, over the whole of the corps area, in order to detect and report upon any observed unusual movement.

At the same time, the normal work on the construction of new lines of defence, covering Amiens, in my rear areas, which had been continuously in progress for many weeks and was still far from complete, was to continue, with a full display of activity; so that the enemy should be unable to infer, from a stoppage of such works, any change in our attitude.

Orders were also given to discourage the usual stream of officers who ordinarily visited our front trenches prior to an operation, and who often, thoughtlessly, made a great display of unusual activity, under the very noses of the enemy front line observers, by the flourishing of maps and field-glasses, and by bobbing up above our parapets to catch fleeting glimpses of the country to be fought over. Such reconnaissance, however desirable, was to be confined to a few senior commanders and staff officers. All subordinates were to rely upon the very large number of admirable photographs, taken regularly from the air, both vertically and obliquely, by the indefatigable Corps Air Squadron. These served excellently as a substitute for visual observation from the ground.

The prohibition against the movement of any transport in the daylight naturally very seriously hampered the freedom of action of the troops of all arms and services, but was felt in quite a special degree by the whole of the artillery. Over 600 guns of all natures had to be dragged to and emplaced in their battle positions, and there camouflaged, each gun involving the concurrent movement of a number of associated vehicles. A full supply of ammunition had to be collected from railhead, distributed by mechanical transport to great main dumps, and thence taken by horsed vehicles for distribution to the numerous actual gun-pits.

As the amount of ammunition to be held in readiness for the opening of the battle averaged 500 rounds per gun, it became necessary to handle a total of about 300,000 rounds of shells and a similar number of cartridges of all calibres, from 3½ to 12 inches, not to mention fuses and primers, or the immense bulk and weight of infantry and machine-gun ammunition, bombs, flares, rockets, and the like, for the supply of all of which the artillery was equally responsible. (The weight of supplies of all kinds exceeded 10,000 tons.) The great amount of movement involved in the handling and dumping of all these munitions, and the deterrent difficulties of carrying out all such work only during the short hours of darkness, must be left to the imagination.

The artillery was, however, confronted, for the first time, with a difficulty of quite a different nature. In the previous years of the war every gun, *after* being placed in its fighting pit or position, had to be carefully "registered", by firing a series of rounds at previously identified reference points, and noting the errors in line or range due to the instrumental error of the gun, which error varied with the gradual wearing-out of the gun barrel. By these means, battery commanders were enabled to compute the necessary corrections to be applied to any given gun, at any one time or place, so as to ensure that the gun would fire true to the task set.

Such registration naturally involved, for a large number of guns, a very considerable volume of artillery fire, the extent of which would speedily disclose to the enemy the presence of a largely increased mass of artillery, and would inevitably lead him to the conclusion that some mischief was afoot. Fortunately, however, the rapid evolution during the war of scientific methods had by this juncture placed at my disposal a means of ascertaining the instrumental error of the guns on a testing ground located many miles behind the battle zone. This method was known as "calibration", and consisted of the firing of the gun through a series of wired screens, placed successively at known distances from the muzzle of the gun. The whole elements of the flight of the projectile could then be accurately determined by recording the intervals of time between its passage through the respective screens. From these data could be deduced the muzzle velocity, the jump, the droop and the lateral error of each gun.

Simple and obvious as was the principle of such an experiment, the merit of the new process of calibration lay in the remarkable rapidity and accuracy with which the electric and photographic mechanism employed made the necessary delicate time observations, correct to small fractions of a second, and automatically deduced the mathematical results required.

The calibration hut, in which this mechanism was housed, became one of the show spots to which visitors to the corps area were taken to be overawed by the scientific methods of our gunners. In the early days of August, the calibration range of the Australian Corps was a scene of feverish activity. All day long, battery after battery of guns could be seen route-marching to the testing ground, going through the performance of firing six rounds per gun, and then route-marching back again the same night to its allotted battle position. So rapid was the procedure that long before he had reached his destination the battery commander had received the full error sheet of every one of his guns, and by means of it was enabled to go into action whenever required without any previous registration whatever. This great advance in the art of gunnery contributed in the most direct manner to the result that when these 600 guns opened their tornado of fire upon the enemy at daybreak on August 8th, the very presence in this area of most of them remained totally unsuspected.

The manner of the employment of the ponderous mass of heavy artillery at my disposal will be referred to later. The action of that portion of the field artillery which was to become mobile in the concluding phases of the battle has already been dealt with. It remains only to describe, in outline, the arrangements made for the normal barrage fire of the field artillery during the first phase.

It has been my invariable practice to reduce the barrage plan to the simplest possible elements, avoiding in every direction the over-elaboration so frequently encountered. By following these principles not only is the actual preparatory work of the artillery greatly reduced in bulk and simplified in quality, but also the liability to mistake and to erratic shooting of individual batteries or guns, and consequent risks of damage to our own infantry, are greatly diminished.

These advantages are bought at the small price of calling upon the infantry to undertake, before the battle, such rectifications and adjustments of our front line as would accommodate themselves to a straight and simple barrage line. This is in sharp contrast to the much more usual procedure which prevailed (and persisted in other corps to the end of the war) of complicating the barrage enormously in an attempt to make it conform to the tortuous configuration of our infantry front line.

For the present battle it was accordingly arranged that the barrage should open on a line which was *dead straight* for the whole 7,000 yards of our front, and the infantry tape lines, (see Chapter 3), which were to mark the alignment of the infantry at the moment of launching the assault, were to be laid exactly 200 yards in rear of this artillery "start line". The barrage was to advance, in exactly parallel lines, 100 yards at a time, at equal rates along the whole frontage. These rates were 100 yards every 3 minutes, for the first 24 minutes, and thereafter 100 yards every 4 minutes, until the conclusion of the time-table at 143 minutes after Zero. By such a simple plan every one of the 432 field guns engaged was given a task of uniform character.

Great as was the care necessary to conceal all artillery preparations, it required still greater thought and consideration to keep entirely secret the presence behind the battle front of some 160 tanks, and particularly to conceal their approach march into the battle. To both combatants, the arrival of a tank, or anything that could be mistaken on an air photograph for a tank, had for long been regarded as a sure indication of coming trouble. And, therefore, imputing to the enemy the same keenness to detect, in good time, the presence of tanks, and the same nervousness which we had been accustomed to feel when prisoners' tales of the coming into the war of enormous hordes of German monsters had been crystallized by the reports of some excited observer into a definite suspicion that the fateful hour had arrived, I considered it wise to repeat on a much elaborated scale all the precautions of secrecy first employed for this purpose at Hamel.

It is quite easy to detect from an air photograph the broad, corrugated track made by a tank, if the ground be soft and muddy enough to record such an impression. Consequently, tanks were forbidden to move across ploughed fields or marshy land, and were confined to hard surface. They moved only in small bodies, and only at night, and were carefully stabled, during the daylight, in the midst of village ruins, or under the deep shade of woods and thickets. Thus, by daily stages, and by cautious bounds, each tank or group of tanks ultimately reached its appointed assembly ground, from which it was to make its last leap into the thick of the battle, where it would arrive precisely at Zero hour.

But that last leap was just the whole difficulty. For the tank is a noisy brute, and it was just as imperative to make him inaudible as to make him invisible. By a fortunate chance, the noise and buzz made by the powerful petrol engines of a tank are so similar to those of the engines of a large-sized bombing plane, as for example of the Handley-Page type, especially if the latter be flying at a comparatively low altitude, that from a little distance off it is quite impossible to distinguish the one sound from the other.

It was therefore possible to adopt the conjurer's trick of directing the special attention of the observer to those things which do not particularly matter, in order to distract his attention from other things which really do matter very much. In other words, a flight of high-power bombing planes was kept flying backwards and forwards over the battle front during the whole of that very hour, just before dawn, during which our 160 tanks were loudly and fussily buzzing their way forward, along carefully reconnoitred routes, marked by special black and white tapes, across that last mile of country which brought them up level with the infantry at the precise moment when the great battle was ushered in by the belching forth of a volcano of artillery fire.

The subterfuge succeeded to perfection, as was obvious to observers and confirmed by the subsequent narratives of prisoners. The German trench garrisons and trench observers were fully occupied in listening to the hum of the bombing planes, in watching their threatened visitation for their customary "egg" dropping performances, in engaging them with rifle fire, and in holding themselves in readiness to duck for cover should they come too near. They never suspected for a moment that this was merely a new stratagem of "noise camouflage", and that the real danger was stalking steadily and relentlessly towards them over the whole front, upon the surface of the ground, instead of in the air.

But the trick would not have succeeded so well, or would perhaps have failed altogether, if the employment of those planes had been confined to the morning of the battle. Such an unusual demonstration might have aroused vague suspicions sufficient to justify a "stand to arms" and a preparedness for some further activity on our part. And what we had most to fear was the danger of "giving the show away" in the last ten minutes. For it would have taken much less than that time for nervous German trench sentries, by the firing of signal rockets, to bring down upon our front line trenches, crowded as they were with expectant fighters, a murderous fire from the German artillery.

Consequently, the puzzled enemy was treated to the spectacle of an early morning promenade by these same bombing planes on every morning, for an hour before dawn, during several mornings preceding the actual battle day. Doubtless the first morning's exhibition of such apparently aimless air activity in the darkness really startled him. After two or three repetitions, it merely earned his contempt. By the time the actual date arrived he treated it as negligible. All prisoners interrogated subsequently agreed that neither the presence nor the noisy approach of so mighty a *phalanx* of tanks had been in the least suspected up to the very moment when they plunged into view out of the darkness, just as day was breaking.

The force of tanks placed at my disposal for the purposes of this battle comprised the 2nd, 8th and 13th Tank Battalions, commanded respectively by Lieut.-Colonels Bryce, Bingham and Lyon, all under the 5th Tank Brigade, commanded by Brigadier-General Courage. All these tanks were of the Mark V. type, as used at Hamel; but there were also attached to the same brigade a battalion of Mark V. (Star) Tanks, of still later design, under Lieut.-Colonel Ramsay-Fairfax, and also a full Company of 24 Carrying Tanks, under Major Partington. These Carrying Tanks were not employed in fighting, but were of wonderful utility in the rapid transport of stores of all descriptions across the battle zone; and in carrying the wounded out of the battle on their return journey. I am confident that each of these tanks was capable of doing the work of at least 200 men, with an almost complete immunity from casualty.

There were thus available to me 168 tanks in all, and their dispositions have been already indicated in sufficient detail in Chapter 5. It was a definite feature of the whole plan of battle that the combined tank and infantry tactics which had proved so successful in the Hamel operation, and which have been described in Chapter 2, were to be employed and exploited to their utmost. Each tank became thereby definitely associated with a specified body of infantry, and acted during the actual battle under the immediate orders of the commander of that body: the working rule was "one tank, one company".

To this was added the second working principle of "one tank, one task", which rules meant, in their practical application, that no individual tank was to be relied upon to serve more than one body of infantry, nor to carry out more than one phase of the battle. Elementary as this may sound, it involved this striking advantage that, in the event of any one tank becoming disabled, its loss would impair no portion of the battle plan other than that fraction of it to which that tank had been allotted.

Thus, the whole of the infantry operating in Phases B and C of the battle had each their own adequate equipment of tanks, which would be certain to be available to them, even if the whole of the tanks employed during Phase A had been knocked out. At the same time clear orders were issued, and due arrangements were made, that all tanks which survived Phase A, and whose crews were not by then too exhausted, were to rally (during the 100 minutes' pause on the green line) in order to co-operate in the succeeding phases of the fight.

There was still another unit, coming under the jurisdiction of the Tank Corps, which proved of wonderful utility to me, and which deserved quite special mention. This was the 17th Armoured Car Battalion, organised into two companies of eight cars each. Each car carried one forward and one rear Hotchkiss gun. It was heavily armoured, and the crew operating the guns, as also the car driver, were protected from all except direct hits by artillery. The cars had a speed of 20 miles per hour, either, forwards or backwards. The battalion was under the command of Lieut.-Colonel E.J. Carter, an officer of the British cavalry. I allotted 12 cars to the use of the 5th Australian Division, under Major-General Hobbs, who would be likely to find specially useful employment for them, in scouring the network of roads beyond his final objective; and retained four cars in corps reserve for a special reconnaissance enterprise.

Full of promise of usefulness as were the speed and armament of these cars, they suffered from one serious disability. Their top hamper was so heavy compared to their light chassis that they could not be relied upon to travel without premature breakdown across country, or indeed on anything but moderately good roads. Now, such roads were certainly available, as was evident from aeroplane photographs, in the enemy's back country, after a zone for a mile or two immediately behind his front line was passed; but all the subsidiary roads in that zone had been practically obliterated by shell-craters, and even the great main road from Villers-Bretonneux to Saint Quentin, which is a Roman Road and substantially constructed throughout, was known to have been cut up and traversed by numerous trenches both on our side and on the enemy's side of "No Man's Land". There was also every expectation that the few remaining trees which flanked this great road would be felled by our bombardment, and some of them would surely fall across and obstruct the roadway.

That road was, however, the only possible outlet into enemy country for the armoured cars, and I resolved upon a special programme, and the allotment of a special body of troops for its execution. The object was to ensure that the cars could be taken across the impracticable and obstructed stretch of roadway already described, and launched at the enemy at its eastern extremity, at the earliest possible moment of time. Then, before the numerous enemy corps and Divisional Headquarters and all their rear organisation had time to get clear intelligence of what was happening at the front, or to recover from the first shock of surprise, these armoured cars would fall upon them, and, travelling hither and thither at great speed, would spread death, destruction and confusion in all directions.

A whole battalion of pioneers, and detachments of other technical troops, with an adequate amount of road-repairing material, were got ready, under the direct orders of my chief engineer, to carry out this special task. All trenches in that portion of the road lying within our own zone of occupation were bridged or filled in and all obstructions cleared away before the day of the battle. But as to the more distant stretch of the road, still in the hands of the enemy, elaborate preparations were made, by a careful and detailed distribution of tasks to small gangs of men, and by a fully worked-out time-table. The plan was that from the moment of the opening of the battle, this road repair work was to commence, and its advance was to synchronise with the advance of the artillery barrage and infantry skirmishing line.

A pilot armoured car was to follow the working gangs in order to test the sufficiency of the repair work, and arrangements were made for sending back signals to the remainder of the cars, lying waiting in readiness in the shelter of Villers-Bretonneux. It was planned that the first two miles of road would, by these means, be cleared and repaired to a sufficient width, within four hours after the opening of the battle.

I am tempted to anticipate the narrative of the battle by saying that the whole plan worked out with complete success to the last detail. The cars got through punctually to time, and the story of their subsequent adventures, as told later, reads like a romance. As indicating the importance which I attached to this little enterprise, which in magnitude was quite a small "side-show", but which in its results had the most far-reaching consequence, I reproduce below the full text (omitting merely formal portions) of one of the several orders issued by me on this subject:

Australian Corps,
7th August, 1918.

1. The detachment of the 17th Armoured Car Battalion held in Corps Reserve (2 sections each of 2 cars), will be employed on the special duty of long distance reconnaissance on "Z" day.

2. These sections will be sent forward under the orders of the C.O., 17th Armoured Car Battalion, passing the green line as soon as practicable after Zero plus four hours, and proceeding eastward, following the lifts of our heavy artillery bombardment, so as to pass the blue line at or after Zero plus five hours.

3. The area to be reconnoitred lies in the bend of the Somme, north of the Villers-Bretonneux—Chaulnes Railway; but the old Somme battlefield lying N.E. of Chaulnes need not be entered.

4. Information is required as to presence, distribution and movement of enemy supporting and reserve troops, and his defensive organisations within this area.

5. While the primary function of this detachment is to reconnoitre and not to fight, except defensively, advantage should be taken of every opportunity to damage the enemy's telephonic and telegraphic communications.

6. The following information as to enemy organisations is thought to be reliable:

Vauvillers	Billets and Detraining point.
Proyart	Divisional H.Q. and billets.
Chuignolles	Divisional H.Q. and billets.
Framerville	Corps H.Q.

Rainecourt	Billets.
Cappy	Aerodrome and dumps.
Foucaucourt	Corps H.Q., dump, billets.
Chaulnes	Important railway junction.
Ommiécourt	Dumps.
Fontaine	Aerodrome, Div. H.Q. and dump.

The heavy artillery of the corps was divided, for this battle as normally, into two distinct groups, of which the one, or Bombardment Group, was to devote its energies to destructive attack, throughout the course of the battle, upon known enemy centres of resistance, suspected headquarters, and telephone or telegraph exchanges, villages believed to be housing support and reserve troops, railway junctions and the like. The selection of all such targets depended upon a judicious choice of many tempting objectives disclosed by the very comprehensive records of the highly efficient intelligence officers belonging to my Heavy Artillery Headquarters. After that selection was made, all that remained was to draw up a time-table for the action of all bombardment guns which would ensure that they would lift off any given target just before our own infantry would be likely to reach it, and then to apply their fire to a more distant locality.

The second group of heavy guns was known as the Counter-battery Group, and was at all times under the direction of a special staff, especially skilled in all the scientific means at our disposal for determining the position and distribution of the enemy's artillery, and in the methods and artifices for silencing or totally destroying it. Just as it was the special role of the tanks to deal with the enemy machine-guns, so it was the special role of our Counter-battery Artillery to deal with the enemy's field and heavy guns and howitzers. These—the guns and the machine-guns—were the only things that troubled us; because, for the German soldier individually, our Australian infantryman is and always has been more than a match.

Very special care was, therefore, devoted to the whole of the arrangements, first for carefully ascertaining beforehand the actual or probable position of every enemy gun that could be brought to bear on our infantry, and then for allocating as many heavy guns as could be spared, each with a task appropriate to its range and hitting-power, to the destruction or suppression of the selected target. For it served the immediate purpose of eliminating the causes of molestation to our advancing infantry equally well, whether the enemy gun was merely

Dug-outs at Froissy-Beacon—being "mopped up" during battle.

Péronne—barricade in main street.

silenced by a sustained fire of shrapnel or high explosives which drove off the gun detachment, or by a flood of gas which compelled them to put on their gas masks, or whether it was actually destroyed by a direct hit and rendered permanently useless.

The days before the battle were of supreme interest in this particular aspect. Each day I visited the Counter-battery staff officer, in his modest shanty, hidden away in the interior of a leafy wood, where in constant touch, by telephone, with all balloons, observers and sound-ranging stations, and surrounded by an imposing array of maps, studded with pins of many shapes and colours, he made his daily report to me of the enemy gun positions definitely identified or located, or found to have been vacated. And here again there was an opportunity for the display of a modest little stratagem. Having suspected or verified the fact that the enemy had altered the location of any given battery, leaving the empty gun pits as a tempting bait to us, fruitlessly to expend our energies and ammunition upon them—it would have been the worst of folly to prove to him that he had failed to fool us, by engaging his battery in its new position.

On the contrary, we deliberately allowed ourselves to be fooled; and for several days before the great battle we intentionally committed the stupid error of methodically engaging all his empty gun positions. No doubt the German gunners laughed consumedly as they watched, from a safe distance, our wasted efforts; but they did not, doubtless, laugh quite so heartily when at dawn on the great day, the whole weight of our attack from over a hundred of my heaviest Counter-battery guns fells upon them in the new positions, which they believed that we had failed to detect.

The Intelligence Service of the corps was an extensive and highly organised department, whose jurisdiction extended throughout all the divisions, brigades and battalions. Its routine work comprised the collection and collation of the daily flow of information from a large staff of observers in the forward zone, from the interrogation of prisoners, from the examination of documents and maps, and from neighbouring corps and armies. Before and during battle, however, a greatly added burden fell upon the shoulders of the intelligence staff.

Closely associated with this branch of the staff work were two activities of quite special interest. The Australian Corps organised a Topographical Section, manned by expert draftsmen and lithographers, who compiled and printed all the maps required throughout the whole corps, and it was their business to keep all battle maps, barrage maps and topographical data recorded and corrected up to date. This alone proved a heavy task when pace had to be kept with a rapid advance. At such times the maps prepared on one day became obsolete two or three days later.

The issue of such maps was not confined to commanders and staffs. For all important operations, large numbers of handy sectional maps were struck off, so that they could be placed in the hands even of the subordinate officers and non-commissioned officers. These maps not only enabled the most junior leaders to study their objectives and tasks in detail before every battle, but also became a convenient vehicle for sending back reports as to the positions reached or occupied by front-line troops or detached parties. On occasions as many as five thousand of such maps would be struck off for the use of the troops, in a single operation.

There was also a branch of the Intelligence Staff attached to the No. 3 Australian Air Squadron. Its special business was to print and distribute large numbers of photographs, both vertical and oblique, taken from the air over the territory to be captured—showing trenches, wire, roads, hedges and many other features of paramount interest to the troops. Thousands of such photographs were distributed before every battle.

The important considerations, in regard both to maps and photographs, were that on the one hand, they were of priceless value to all who understood how to read and use them, and on the other hand, the event proved that their issue was in no sense labour in vain, for the keen interest taken, even by the private soldiers, in these facilities contributed powerfully to the success and precision with which all battle orders were carried out, and this more than repaid us for the additional trouble involved. It was inspiriting to me to see, on the eve of every great battle, as I made my round of the troops, numerous small groups of men gathered around their sergeant or corporal, eagerly discussing these maps and the photographs and the things they disclosed, the lie of the land, the wire, the trenches, the probable machine-gun posts, the dug-outs and the suspected enemy strong points.

My account of the details prepared for the battle of August 8th is not nearly complete; but the demands of space forbid any more informative reference to numerous other essential ingredients of the plan than a mere recital of some of them. Thus, for example, it was necessary to decide the action of all machine-guns, both those used collectively under corps control, and those left to be handled by the divisions; the employment of smoke tactics, by the use of smoke screens created both by mortars from the ground and by phosphorus bombs dropped from the air; the use to be made of all the technical troops (engineers and pioneers) in bridging, road and railway repairs and field fortifications; the arrangements for the medical evacuation of the wounded, and for the collection and safe-keeping of the anticipated haul of prisoners, the synchronisation of watches throughout the whole command, so that action should occur punctually at a common clock time; and last, but not least, the establishment of the machinery of liaison internally between all the numerous formations of the Australian Corps, and also externally with my flank corps, the Canadians, under Currie, on my right, and the British Third Corps, under Butler, on my left.

Such, in outline, were my battle plans and my preparations for what I hoped would prove an operation of decisive influence upon the future of the campaign. The immediate results, which could be estimated on the spot and at the time, and the admissions of Ludendorff, which came to light only many months afterwards, combine to show that I was not mistaken.

Chapter 7
The Chase Begins

The preliminary movements of divisions were duly carried out without special difficulty. The Fifth Australian Division was relieved on August 1st by a division of the Third Corps, in that part of the corps front which lay north of the Somme, and passed into Corps Reserve, in a rear area, there to undergo training with tanks, and to prepare itself for the work which it had to do.

The Fourth Australian Division, from Corps Reserve, took over the French front, as far south as the Amiens-Roye road on August 2nd, and on the next night took over from the Second Australian Division all that part of its front which lay south of the railway, thus disposing itself upon what was ultimately to become the battle front of the Canadian Corps.

On the same night, the Second and Third Divisions, who had thus been left in sole occupation of the sector which was to be the Australian Corps battle front, carried out a readjustment of their own mutual boundary, which would place each of these two divisions upon its own proper battle front.

On the night of August 4th, the Second and Third Divisions rearranged their defensive dispositions so that each of them deployed only a single brigade for the passive defence of its front, and withdrew to its rear area its remaining two brigades, who were thus afforded three clear days to complete their internal preparations.

The Canadian Corps commenced to arrive, and on August 4th two Canadian brigades relieved two brigades of the Fourth Division, thereby releasing them so that they also might commence to prepare for the battle. It was originally intended that the last brigade of the Fourth Division should also be relieved by Canadians on August 6th, when an untoward incident happened, which caused considerable alarm and speculation; and it led to a modification of this part of the plan.

The 13th Australian Brigade (of the Fourth Division) was on August 4th spread out upon a front of over six thousand yards. It had no option but to leave the greater part of the front-line trenches unoccupied, and to defend its area with a series of small, but isolated, posts. On that night, one of these posts, in the vicinity of the road to Roye, (see Map J), was raided by the enemy, and the whole of its occupants, comprising a sergeant and four or five men, were surrounded and taken prisoner.

It was an unusual display of enterprise on the part of the enemy, at this point of time and in this locality. Whether it had been inspired by sneering criticisms from behind his line of the nature which have been quoted, or whether signs of unusual movement or a changed attitude on the part of our trench garrison had instigated a suspicion that something was happening which required investigation, could only be surmised. But the fact remained that five Australians had been taken, at a place several miles south of the southernmost point hitherto occupied by "the English".

The side-stepping of the Australian Corps southwards had thereby become known to the enemy, and it was necessary to estimate the deductions which he would be likely to draw from that discovery. Much depended upon the behaviour of these prisoners. Would they talk? and, if so, what did they know? That Australian captives would not volunteer information likely to imperil the lives of their comrades, might be taken for granted, but German intelligence officers had means at their disposal to draw from prisoners, unwittingly, anything they might know.

We could only hope, under the circumstances, that these men really did know nothing of our intention to attack; and that, if they had become aware of the presence of Canadian troops in the rear areas, they would believe the story which we had sedulously spread, that the

Canadians were merely coming to relieve the Australian Corps, so that it might have a long rest after its heroic labours.

Not many weeks afterwards it was my good fortune to capture a German Headquarters, in which were found Intelligence Reports containing a narrative of this very incident. The importance of the capture of these men had been recognised, and they had been taken far behind the lines for an exhaustive examination. But, despite all efforts of the German Intelligence Staff, they had refused to disclose anything whatever but their names and units—which they were bound to do under the rules of war. The report went on to praise their soldierly bearing and loyal reticence, and held up these brave Australians as a model to be followed by their own men, adding that such a demeanour could only earn the respect of an enemy.

The alarm which this untoward happening created on our side of the line led to a determination to redouble our precautions. The army commander proposed, and I agreed, that the relief of the 13th Brigade by Canadians, *prior* to the eve of the battle, was out of the question, as being too risky. It was decided that the 13th Brigade must remain in the line until the very last. This decision deprived General Maclagan of one of his three brigades, and as it would be asking too much of the Fourth Division to carry out the role which had been allotted to it in the battle, with only two brigades, I decided that the only thing to be done was to transfer to the Fourth Division, temporarily, one of the brigades of the First Division, which was to arrive from the north in the course of the next three days.

Urgent telegrams were therefore despatched to accelerate the arrival of one of the brigades of the First Division. In due course the First Australian Brigade (Mackay) arrived by four special trains on the night of August 6th, in sufficient time to enable it to take its place in General Maclagan's order of battle, in substitution for the 13th Brigade. The 13th Brigade was destined to have some further stirring adventures before it again joined its own division.

The day preceding the great battle arrived all too soon. The prospect of an advance had sent a thrill through all ranks and expectation became tense. The use of the telephone had been ordered to be restricted, especially in the forward areas; for it was known that the enemy was in possession of listening apparatus, similar to our own, by which conversations on the telephone could be tapped, and unguarded references to the impending operations could be overheard.

Final inspections had, therefore, to be made, and final injunctions administered, by commanders and staffs traversing long distances over the extensive corps area by motor car and horse, and even on foot. A strange and ominous quiet pervaded the scene; it was only when the explosion of a stray enemy shell would cause hundreds of heads to peer out from trenches, gun-pits and underground shelters, that one became aware that the whole country was really packed thick with a teeming population carefully hidden away.

Later in the afternoon of that last day came another note of alarm. To the Fourth and Fifth Australian Divisions had been allotted eighteen Store and Carrying Tanks. These had been brought the night before, into a small plantation lying about half a mile to the north of Villers-Bretonneux, loaded to their utmost capacity with battle stores of all descriptions: reserves of food and water, rifle ammunition, and a large reserve of Stokes Mortar bombs; also considerable supplies of petrol, to satisfy the ravenous appetites of the tanks themselves.

This locality, suddenly became the object of the closest attention by the enemy's artillery. He began to deluge it with such a volume of fire that in less than half an hour a great conflagration had been started, which did not subside until fifteen of the tanks and all their valuable cargo had been reduced to irretrievable ruin.

Had some unusually keen enemy observer perceived the presence of tanks in our area, and would that knowledge have disclosed to him our jealously guarded secret? Fortunately, my artillery commander, Brigadier-General Coxen, making his last rounds of the battery positions, was an eyewitness of the whole occurrence, and was able to reassure me. A chance shell—the last of a dozen fired entirely at random into our area—fell into the very centre of this group of tanks, and set fire to some of the petrol. The resulting cloud of smoke became a signal to the enemy that something was burning which our men would probably attempt to salve; and in consonance with an entirely correct artillery procedure, he at once concentrated a heavy fire upon the spot.

That incident is typical of the perturbations through which all responsible commanders have to pass on such occasions. The occurrence was explained as accidental, and implied no premature discovery by the enemy. Nothing remained but to repair the damage, and make special arrangements to replenish the stores which these divisions had lost.

On the forenoon of the day before the battle, the following message was promulgated to all the troops:

Corps Headquarters,

August 7th, 1918.

To the Soldiers of the Australian Army Corps.

For the first time in the history of this corps, all five Australian divisions will tomorrow engage in the largest and most important battle operation ever undertaken by the corps.

They will be supported by an exceptionally powerful artillery, and by tanks and aeroplanes on a scale never previously attempted. The full resources of our sister dominion, the Canadian Corps, will also operate on our right, while two British divisions will guard our left flank.

The many successful offensives which the brigades and battalions of this corps have so brilliantly executed during the past four months have been but the prelude to, and the preparation for, this greatest and culminating effort.

Because of the completeness of our plans and dispositions, of the magnitude of the operations, of the number of troops employed, and of the depth to which we intend to overrun the enemy's positions, this battle will be one of the most memorable of the whole war; and there can be no doubt that, by capturing our objectives, we shall inflict blows upon the enemy which will make him stagger, and will bring the end appreciably nearer.

I entertain no sort of doubt that every Australian soldier will worthily rise to so great an occasion, and that every man, imbued with the spirit of victory, will, in spite of every difficulty that may confront him, be animated by no other resolve than grim determination to see through to a clean finish, whatever his task may be.

The work to be done tomorrow will perhaps make heavy demands upon the endurance and staying powers of many of you; but I am confident that, in spite of excitement, fatigue, and physical strain, every man will carry on to the utmost of his powers until his goal is won; for the sake of Australia, the Empire and our cause.

I earnestly wish every soldier of the corps the best of good fortune, and a glorious and decisive victory, the story of which will re-echo throughout the world, and will live for ever in the history of our homeland.

John Monash,
Lieut.-General.
Cmdg. Australian Corps.

Not many days afterwards a copy of this order fell into the hands of the enemy, and the use he tried to make of it, to his own grave discomfiture, as the event proved, is an interesting story which will be told in due course.

Zero hour was fixed for twenty minutes past four, on the morning of August 8th. It needs a pen more facile than I can command to describe, and an imagination more vivid to realise the stupendous import of the last ten minutes. In black darkness, a hundred thousand infantry, deployed over twelve miles of front, are standing grimly, silently, expectantly, in readiness to advance, or are already crawling stealthily forward to get within eighty yards of the line on which the barrage will fall; all feel to make sure that their bayonets are firmly locked, or to set their steel helmets firmly on their heads; company and platoon commanders, their whistles ready to hand, are nervously glancing at their luminous watches, waiting for minute after minute to go by—and giving a last look over their commands—ensuring that their runners are by their sides, their observers alert, and that the officers detailed to control direction have their compasses set and ready.

Carrying parties shoulder their burdens, and adjust the straps; pioneers grasp their picks and shovels; engineers take up their stores of explosives and primers and fuses; machine and Lewis gunners whisper for the last time to the carriers of their magazines and belt boxes to be sure and follow up. The Stokes Mortar carrier slings his heavy load, and his loading numbers fumble to see that their haversacks of cartridges are handy. Overhead drone the aeroplanes, and from the rear, in swelling chorus, the buzzing and clamour of the tanks grows every moment louder and louder. Scores of telegraph operators sit by their instruments with their message forms and registers ready to hand, bracing themselves for the rush of signal traffic which will set in a few moments later; dozens of staff officers spread their maps in readiness, to record with coloured pencils the stream of expected information. In hundreds of pits, the guns are already run up, loaded and laid on their opening lines of fire; the sergeant is checking the range for the last time; the layer stands silently with the lanyard in his hand. The section officer, watch on wrist, counts the last seconds: "A minute to go"—"Thirty seconds"—"Ten seconds"—"Fire".

And, suddenly, with a mighty roar, more than a thousand guns begin the symphony. A great illumination lights up the Eastern horizon; and instantly the whole complex organisation, extending far back to areas almost beyond earshot of the guns, begins to move forward; every man, every unit, every vehicle and every tank on their appointed tasks and to their designated goals; sweeping onward relentlessly and irresistibly. Viewed from a high vantage point and in the glimmer of the breaking day, a great artillery barrage surely surpasses in dynamic splendour any other manifestation of collective human effort.

The artillery barrage dominates the battle, and the landscape. The field is speedily covered with a cloak of dust, and smoke and spume, making impossible any detailed observation, at the time, of the course of the battle as a whole. The story can only be indifferently pieced together, long after, by an attempted compilation of the reports of a hundred different participants, whose narratives are usually much impaired by personal bias, by the nervous excitement of the moment, and by an all too limited range of vision. That is why no comprehensive account yet exists of some of the major battles of the war, and why those partial narratives hitherto produced are so often in conflict.

In so great a battle as this, only the broad facts and tangible results can be placed on record without danger of controversy. The whole immense operation proceeded according to plan in every detail, with a single exception, to which I must specially refer later on. The first phase, controlled as it was by the barrage timetable, necessarily ended punctually, and with the whole of the green line objective in our hands. This success gave us possession of nearly all the enemy's guns, so that his artillery retaliation speedily died down.

The captures in this phase were considerable, and few of the garrisons of the enemy's forward offensive zone escaped destruction or capture. The Second and Third Divisions had a comparative "walk over", and they had come to a halt, with their tasks completed, before 7 a.m.

The "open warfare" phase commenced at twenty minutes past eight, and both the red and the blue lines were captured in succession half-an-hour ahead of scheduled time. This capture covered the whole length of my front except the extreme left, where a half-expected difficulty arose, but one which exercised no influence upon the day's success.

The Canadians, on my right, had a similar story to tell; they had driven far into the enemy's defences, exactly as planned. In spite of the difficulties of observation, the recurrence of a ground mist of the same nature as we had experienced at Hamel, and the long distances over which messages and reports had to travel—the stream of information which reached me, by telegraph, telephone, pigeon and aeroplane was so full and ample that I was not left for a moment out of touch with the situation. The "inwards" messages are, naturally, far too voluminous for reproduction; but a brief selection from the many "outwards" messages telegraphed during that day to the Fourth Army Headquarters, and which, on a point of responsibility, I made it an invariable rule to draft myself, will give some indication of the course of events as they became known:

Sent at 7 a.m.: Everything going well at 6.45 a.m. Heavy ground mist facilitating our advance, but delaying information. Infantry and tanks got away punctually. Our attack was a complete surprise. Gailly Village and Accroche Wood captured. Enemy artillery has ceased along my whole front. Flanks Corps apparently doing well.

Sent at 8.30 a.m.: Although not definitely confirmed, no doubt that our first objective green line captured along whole corps front including Gailly, Warfusee, Lamotte and whole Cerisy Valley. Many guns and prisoners taken. Infantry and artillery for second phase moving up to green line.

Sent at 10.55 a.m.: Fifteenth Battalion has captured Cerisy with 300 prisoners. Advance to red line going well.

Sent at 11.10 a.m.: Have taken Morcourt and Bayonvillers and many additional prisoners and guns. We are nearing our second objective and have reached it in places. My cavalry brigade has passed across our red line. We are now advancing to our final objective blue line.

Sent at 12.15 p.m.: Hobbs has captured Harbonnières and reached blue line final objective on his whole front.

Sent at 1.15 p.m.: Australian flag hoisted over Harbonnières at midday today. Should be glad if chief would cable this to our governor-general on behalf of Australian Corps.

Sent at 2.5 p.m.: Total Australian casualties through dressing stations up to 12 noon under 600. Prisoners actually counted exceed 4,000. Many more coming in.

Sent at 4.40 p.m.: Captured enemy Corps H.Q. near Framerville shortly after noon today. (This was the 51st German Corps).

Sent at 8 p.m.: Corps captures will greatly exceed 6,000 prisoners, 100 guns, including heavy and railway guns, thousands of machine-guns, a railway train, and hundreds of vehicles and teams of regimental transport. Total casualties for whole corps will not exceed 1,200.

The vital information, which it is imperative for the corps commander to have accurately and rapidly delivered throughout the course of a battle, is that relating to the actual position, at any given moment of time, of our front line troops; showing the locations which they have reached, and whether they are stationary, advancing or retiring. For it has to be remembered that the whole artillery resources of the corps were pooled and kept under his own hand; and it was imperative that any changes in the artillery action or employment must be quickly made, so as to extend the utmost help to any infantry which might get into difficulties.

Thus, for example, the failure of any body of infantry to enter and pass beyond a wood or a village, would be a sure indication that such locality was still held in strength by the enemy, and it would be appropriate to "switch" artillery fire upon it, in order to drive him out. But such a proceeding would be anything but prudent if the information on which such action was to be based were already an hour old.

Transmission of messages from the front line troops to the nearest telephone terminal is usually slow and uncertain, and the retransmission of such messages, in succession, by battalions, brigades and divisions only prolongs the delay. The normal process is in consequence far too dilatory for the exigencies of actual battle control.

A vastly superior method had therefore to be devised, and recourse was had to the use of aeroplanes. The No. 3 Australian Squadron soon acquired great proficiency in this work. They were equipped with two-seater planes, carrying both pilot and observer, and the work was called "Contact Patrol."

The "plane" flying quite low, usually at not more than 500 feet, the observer would mark down by conventional signs on a map the actual positions of our infantry, of enemy infantry or other facts of prime importance, and he often had time to scribble a few informative notes also. The "plane" then flew back at top speed to Corps H.Q., and the map, with or without an added report, was dropped in the middle of an adjacent field, wrapped in a weighted streamer of many colours. It was then brought by cyclists into the Staff Office.

Relays of Contact planes were on such service all day on every battle day, and although it was a hazardous duty few planes were lost. The total time which elapsed between the making of the observation at the front line and the arrival of the information in the hands of the Corps Staff was seldom more than ten minutes.

There can be no doubt that the whole operation was a complete surprise both to the troops opposed to us and to the German High Command. It became abundantly clear, in the following days, that no proper arrangements existed for rapidly reinforcing this part of the front in the event of an attack by us, but that these had to be extemporised after the event. This discovery points to the conclusion that the enemy had once again come to regard the British Army as a negligible quantity, a mistake for which he paid an even heavier price than when he made it in the early days of the war.

As an indication that even the divisions in the line whose duty it primarily was to know, had no suspicions of an impending attack, comes the story of a German medical officer who was captured in his pyjamas in Warfusee village, and who confessed that being awakened by our bombardment and thinking it was merely a raid, he left his dugout to see what was afoot, and thought he must be still dreaming when he saw our pioneers a few hundred feet away, busily at work repairing the main road.

There was only one blemish in the whole day's operations. Not serious in relation to the whole, it nevertheless gravely hampered the work of the left brigade of the Fourth Division. In short, the Third Corps Infantry failed to reach their ultimate objective line, and the enemy remained in possession of the Chipilly Spur and of all the advantages which that possession conferred upon him.

The advance of my left flank, from the green to the red line, along the margin of the plateau bordering the Somme, was left exposed to his full view, while the river valley itself remained under the domination of his rifle fire, at quite moderate ranges. But worse than all, a battery of his field artillery emplaced just above the village of Chipilly remained in action, and one after another, six of the nine tanks which had been allotted to the 4th Brigade were put out of action by direct hits from these guns.

The possibility was one which had been considered and measures to meet it were promptly taken. Maclagan, whose right brigade in due course reached the blue line according to programme, making in its progress a splendid haul of prisoners and guns, took immediate steps to "refuse" his left flank, *i.e.*, to bend it back towards Morcourt, and to establish, with a reserve battalion, a flank defence along the river, facing north from Cerisy to Morcourt.

Both these villages were, however, successfully captured, and "mopped up", which meant that all the enemy and machine-guns lurking in them were accounted for. But the river valley was not captured, and became, until the situation was ultimately cleared up, a kind of No Man's Land between the enemy still holding the Chipilly Spur on the north, and the Fourth Division on the south of the river.

The ultimate conquest of the Chipilly Bend forms no part of that day's story. What were the reasons for the failure of the Third Corps to complete its allotted task may have been the subject of internal inquiry, but the result of any such was not made known. The official report for the day was to the effect that the enemy on this front had resisted strongly, that fighting had been fierce, and that no progress could be made. But one is compelled to recognise that such language was often an euphemistic method of describing faulty Staff co-ordination, or faulty local leadership. There would be no justification, however, for questioning the bravery of the troops themselves.

It has already been foreshadowed that the experiences on that day of the contingent of sixteen armoured motorcars under Lieutenant-Colonel Carter would form sensational reading, and the story of August 8th would not be complete without at least a brief reference to their exploits.

It was nearly midnight when Carter, with a staff officer, got back to Corps H.Q. to render their report. They were scarcely recognisable, covered as they were from head to feet, with grime and grease. They had had a busy time. The substance of what they had to tell was taken down at the time almost *verbatim*, and reads as follows:

> Got armoured cars through to Warfusee-Abancourt. When we reached the other side of No Man's Land we found that the road was good but a number of trees (large and small) had been shot down and lay right across it in places. Obstacles removed by chopping up the smaller trees and hauling off the big ones by means of a tank. Pioneers helped us to clear the road all the way down. We did not come up to our advancing troops until they were almost near the Red Line. When we got past our leading infantry, we came upon quite a number of Huns and dealt with them. Had then to wait a little on account of our barrage, but went through a light barrage. When we got to Blue Line, we detached three sections to run down to Framerville.
>
> When they got there, they found all the Boche horse transport and many lorries drawn up in the main road ready to move off. Head of column tried to bolt in one direction and other vehicles in another. Complete confusion. Our men killed the lot (using 3,000 rounds) and left them there; four staff officers on horseback shot also. The cars then ran down to the east side of Harbonnières, on the south-east road to Vauvillers, and met

there a number of steam wagons; fired into their boilers causing an impassable block.

Had a lot of good shooting around Vauvillers. Then came back to main road. Two sections of cars went on to Foucaucourt and came in contact with a Boche gun in a wood north-east of Foucaucourt. This gun blew the wheels off one car and also hit three others. However, three of the cars were got away. Two other cars went to Proyart and found a lot of troops billeted there having lunch in the houses. Our cars shot through the windows into the houses, killing quite a lot of the enemy.

Another section went towards Chuignolles and found it full of German soldiers. Our cars shot them. Found rest billets and old trenches also with troops in them. Engaged them. Had quite a battle there. Extent of damage not known, but considerable. Cars then came back to main road. We were then well in advance of Blue Line. Everything was now perfectly quiet—no shell-fire of any kind.

I went a quarter of a mile beyond La Flaque. There was a big dump there, and Huns kept continually coming out and surrendering, and we brought quite a lot of them back as prisoners. It was then about 10.30 a.m. A party of Hun prisoners was detailed to tow back my disabled car. I saw no sign of any wired system anywhere. Old overgrown trenches but no organised trench system. I proceeded to some rising ground near Framerville. Did not go into Framerville, but could see that the roofs of the houses were intact. Saw no trace of any organised system of defence of any kind and no troops. My people saw no formed bodies of troops of any kind during the day coming towards us, but very large numbers of fugitives hastening in the opposite direction. Engaged as many of them as could be reached from the roads. I saw, from the hill, open country with a certain amount of vegetation on it.

The consternation and disorganisation caused by the sudden onslaught of these cars, at places fully ten miles behind the enemy's front line of that morning, may be left to the imagination. It was a feat of daring and resolute performance, which deserves to be remembered.

Throughout the whole day, surrenders by the enemy, particularly of troops in rear or reserve positions, were on a wholesale scale. The total number of live prisoners actually counted up to nightfall in the

The Burning Villages—east of Péronne.

Dummy Tank Manufacture.

divisional and corps prisoner-of-war cages exceeded 8,000 and the Canadians had gathered in at least as many more.

The Australian Corps also captured 173 guns capable of being hauled away, not counting those which had been blown to pieces. These captures included two "railway" guns, one of 9-inch and the other of 11.2-inch bore. The latter was an imposing affair. The gun itself rested on two great bogie carriages, each on eight axles; it was provided with a whole train of railway trucks fitted some to carry its giant ammunition, others as workshops, and others as living quarters for the gun detachment. The outfit was completed by a locomotive to haul the gun forward to its daily task of shelling Amiens, and hauling it back to its garage when its ugly work was done.

The captures of machine-guns and of trench mortars of all types and sizes were on so extensive a scale that no attempt was ever made to make even an approximate count of them. They were ultimately collected into numerous dumps, and German prisoners were employed for many weeks in cleaning and oiling them for transport to Australia as trophies of war.

But the booty comprised a large and varied assortment of many other kinds of warlike stores. The huge dumps of engineering material at Rosières and La Flaque served all the needs of the corps for the remainder of the war. There were horses, wagons, lorries and tractors by the hundred, including field searchlights, mobile pharmacies, motor ambulances, travelling kitchens, mess carts, limbers, and ammunition wagons and there were literally hundreds of thousands of rounds of artillery ammunition scattered all over the captured territory in dumps both large and small.

For the next two days all roads leading from the battle area back towards the army cage at Poulainville, where railway trains were waiting to receive them, were congested with column after column of German prisoners, roughly organised into companies—tangible evidences to the civilians of the district, as to our own troops, that a great victory had been won.

The tactical value of the victory was immense, and has never yet been fully appreciated by the public of the Empire, perhaps because our censorship at the time strove to conceal the intention to follow it up immediately with further attacks. But no better testimony is needed than that of Ludendorff himself, who calls it Germany's "black day", after which he himself gave up all hope of a German victory.

Ludendorff in his *Memoirs*, republished in the *Times* of August

22nd, 1919, writes:

August 8th was the black day of the German Army in the history of the war. This was the worst experience I had to go through.... Early on August 8th, in a dense fog that had been rendered still thicker by artificial means, the British, mainly with Australian and Canadian divisions, and French, attacked between Albert and Moreuil with strong squadrons of tanks, but for the rest with no great superiority. They broke between the Somme and the Luce deep into our front. The divisions in line allowed themselves to be completely overwhelmed. divisional staffs were surprised in their headquarters by enemy tanks (*sic*, our armoured cars were meant).... The exhausted (*sic*) divisions that had been relieved a few days earlier and that were lying in the region south-west of Péronne were immediately alarmed and set in motion by the commander-in-chief of the Second Army.

At the same time, he brought forward towards the breach all available troops. The Rupprecht Army Group dispatched reserves thither by train. The 18th Army threw its own reserves directly into the battle from the south-east.... On an order from me, the 9th Army too, although itself in danger, had to contribute. Days of course elapsed before the troops from a further distance could reach the spot.... It was a very gloomy situation.... Six or seven divisions that were quite fairly to be described as effective had been completely battered.... The situation was uncommonly serious. If they continued to attack with even comparative vigour, we should no longer be able to maintain ourselves west of the Somme.... The wastage of the Second Army had been very great.

Heavy toll had also been taken of the reserves which had been thrown in.... Owing to the deficit created our losses had reached such proportions that the Supreme Command was faced with the necessity of having to disband a series of divisions, in order to furnish drafts.... The enemy had also captured documentary material of inestimable value to him.... The general staff officer whom I had dispatched to the battlefield on August 8th, gave me such an account that I was deeply confounded.... August 8th made things clear for both army commands, both for the German and for that of the enemy.

A hole had been driven on a width of nearly twelve miles, right through the German defence, and had blotted out, at one blow, the whole of the military resources which it had contained. The obligation which was thereby cast upon the enemy to throw into the gap troops and guns hastily collected from every part of his front, imposed upon him also an increased vulnerability at every other point which had to be so denuded.

It was no part of our programme to rest content upon our oars, and allow the enemy time to collect himself at leisure. The resources of the Australian Corps had suffered scarcely any impairment as the result of that glorious day. Such small losses as had been incurred were more than counter-balanced by the elation of these volunteer troops at this further demonstration of their moral and physical superiority over the professional soldiers of a militarist enemy nation. On that very day all necessary measures were taken to maintain the battle without pause. But, in order not to interrupt the continuity of the story of subsequent developments, it will be convenient to mention, in this place, two events which cannot be dissociated from the great battle, and which will be memorable to those who participated in them.

The first was an accidental meeting together of a number of the most distinguished figures in the war. On August 11th, the commander-in-chief was to come to congratulate the corps and to thank the troops through their commanders. I called the divisional generals together at the Red Château at Villers-Bretonneux to meet him that afternoon. In the meantime, General Rawlinson invited his corps commanders to meet him in the same village for a battle conference, and chose the same hour and a spot in the open, under a spreading beech, where his generals sat informally around the maps spread upon the grass. At this meeting were Rawlinson, Currie, Kavanagh, Godley, myself, Montgomery and Budworth. The field marshal, with Laurence, the chief of his general staff, on their way to the Red Château, soon arrived. Shortly after Sir Henry Wilson, happening to pass in his car, also joined the party; and not many moments afterwards there arrived, again entirely without previous arrangement, Clemenceau and his Finance Minister Klotz.

Villers-Bretonneux, only three days before reeking with gas and unapproachable, and now delivered from its bondage, was the lodestone which had attracted the individual members of this remarkable assemblage; and the more serious business in hand was perforce postponed while Rawlinson, Currie and I had to listen to the generous felicitations of all these great war leaders.

The second event was the visit of His Majesty the King, on August 12th, to Bertangles, when he conferred on me the honour of knighthood, in the presence of selected detachments of five hundred of the men who had fought in the battle, a hundred from each of my five divisions. A representative collection of guns and other war trophies had been hauled in from the battlefield to line the avenues by which the king approached. His Majesty was particularly interested in the German transport horses, expressing the hope that they would soon learn the Australian language; a pleasantry which he well remembered when I had the honour of an audience with him, on the anniversary of that very day.

Chapter 8
Exploitation

The Fourth British Army had opened the great Allied counter-offensive with a brilliant stroke. It remained to see in what fashion the Allied High Command would proceed to exploit the victory. Would the Fourth Army be called upon, with added resources, at once to thrust due east, with the object of drawing upon itself the German reserves, and dealing with them as they arrived; or would blows now be delivered on other fronts with a view to keeping those reserves dispersed?

The immediate decision, communicated to me by the army commander on the afternoon of August 8th, was that, while the whole situation was being considered, and troop movements were in progress to enable the necessary concentrations to be made elsewhere, the Fourth Army would continue its advance forthwith; but that, instead of driving due east, the thrust was to be made in a south-easterly direction.

The object was to aim at Roye, and either by the capture of that important railway centre, or at least by the threat of its capture, to precipitate a withdrawal by the enemy from the great salient which he had in his April and May advances pressed into the French front opposite Moreuil and Montdidier, a salient which could be kept supplied by that railway alone.

The Australian Corps front on the evening of August 8th lay roughly on a north and south line, just east of Méricourt and just west of Vauvillers. But the Canadian Corps front bent back sharply from the latter point in a south-westerly direction. The Canadians were, therefore, to advance between the railway and the Amiens-Roye road to the general line Lihons-Le Quesnoy. The role of the Australian Corps was to make a defensive flank to this advance, by pivoting its left on the Somme in the vicinity of Méricourt, but advancing its right along the railway, in the direction of Lihons.

It was a decision which was unpalatable to me, for it condemned me to leaving the whole of the great bend of the Somme, on which lay Bray, Péronne and Brie, in the undisturbed possession of the enemy; and in view of the reports sent in from the front and confirmed later by the armoured cars, it appeared to me that the resumption of a vigorous advance due east next day would give us, without fighting, possession, or at least command, of the whole of this bend; while if we allowed the enemy to take breath and recover from his shock, he would probably have time to rally the fugitives, and turn again to face us.

This same great bend of the river had been the scene of two years of sedentary warfare, in 1915 and 1916, when the French and German artillery had converted it into a barren wilderness. It was, in its eastern part, scored with trenches, and bristled with wire entanglements in every direction; it was devoid of villages, woods, or any kind of shelter—a forbidding expanse of devastation.

But between our front lines of that day and the western edge of this wilderness, there still lay a belt of some six or seven miles of practically unharmed country over which the retreat of our Fifth Army in March had carried them without much fighting. I should have welcomed an order to push on the next morning, in open warfare formation, to gain possession of the whole of this belt, and force the enemy to make any attempt to reorganise his line on the inhospitable ground which lay beyond.

The order stood, however; and instructions were issued for the First Australian Division to be drawn into the fight, and to take upon themselves the task of conforming to the advance of the Canadians along the railway. The first phase of this advance was to have been carried out at 11 a.m. on August 9th by the First Division passing through the right brigade of the Fifth Division.

The 1st Brigade of the First Australian Division had, as already related, arrived from the North in time to participate in the fighting of the day before; but the remaining two brigades arrived so late, and had to perform so long a march from their detraining station near Amiens to our now greatly advanced battle front, that it soon became evident that they could not arrive at the line of departure in time to synchronize with the Canadian advance.

In consequence, the Fifth Division was instructed to detail its right line brigade to begin this duty; and in due course the 15th Brigade carried out the first part of the task and advanced our line to include the capture of Vauvillers, an operation which was successfully completed by midday.

It will be remembered that the Second and Third Divisions had been given a task for the previous day which was limited in time, though not in difficulty, and that this task had been completed, as it proved with very little stress, by 7 a.m. These divisions had thus had a whole day in which to rest and reorganise. The Second Division was therefore placed under orders to participate in the advance of August 9th.

In due course, the First Division arrived at our fighting front, and that afternoon both the First and Second Divisions advanced in battle order, the former passing through the right brigade of the Fifth Division, and the latter through its left brigade. This operation carried our front line in this part of the field to the foot of the Lihons Hill, and gave us complete possession of the village of Framerville. It also incidentally released the Fifth Division from further line duty.

The opposition met with during this day's operations varied considerably along the battle front, which extended in this part of the field over about 6,000 yards. The Lihons Ridge was found to be strongly held, and much fire both from field guns and machine-guns was encountered. It was evident that, overnight, the enemy had succeeded in organising sufficient troops for the local defence of this important point.

Upon the front of the Second Division, however, there was little opposition and the enemy gave up Framerville almost without a struggle. Three battalions of tanks co-operated in the day's fighting, but several of them were disabled by direct fire from Lihons. The task assigned to the corps for that day was, none the less, carried out in its entirety, and by nightfall contact had been made with the Second Canadian Division on the railway about a mile east of Rosières.

The situation on the left flank of the Australian Corps was, however, anything but satisfactory. The Chipilly Spur was still in the hands of the enemy, all the efforts over-night on the part of the 58th Division (Third Corps) to dislodge them having failed. General Butler, the Corps Commander, in pursuance of arrangements come to some days before, was to proceed on sick leave, as he had for some time been far from well; and General Godley (my former chief of the 22nd Corps) was temporarily to take his place. I therefore persuaded the army commander to avail himself of this change to allow me to take in hand the situation at Chipilly, and to give me, for this purpose, a limited jurisdiction over the north bank of the Somme. This was merely getting in the thin edge of the wedge; and not many hours later, I found myself where I had so strongly desired to be from the first, namely, astride of the Somme valley.

Accordingly, the 13th Australian Brigade, after a day's rest from the anxious duty of acting as a screen for the Canadians on the eve of the main battle, were told off to deal with the Chipilly Spur. Before, however, they could reach the locality, and in the late afternoon of August 9th, the 131st American Regiment (of Bell's Division), which was still under the orders of the Third Corps, very gallantly advanced in broad daylight and took possession practically of the whole spur.

In the meantime, the 13th Brigade arrived, sending a battalion across the Somme at Cerisy, and, joining the Americans, helped to clear up the whole situation. This made my left flank more secure, and enabled Maclagan to withdraw the defensive flank which he had deployed along the river from Cerisy to Morcourt. That night I took over the 131st American Regiment from the Third Corps, attached it, as a temporary measure, to the Fourth Division, and placed Maclagan in charge of the newly captured front, which extended north of the river as far as the Corbie—Bray road.

The day ended with divisions in the line from south to north in the following order, *viz.*:—First, Second and Fourth, the last named having been augmented by an American regiment, having had its own 13th Brigade restored to it, and having in exchange yielded up to the First Division the 1st Brigade of the latter.

The Fourth Division had had comparatively much the worst of it, up to this stage, of any of my divisions, and I felt that they were due for a short rest. Accordingly, I issued orders that same night for the Third Division, which, like the Second, had been resting since the previous forenoon, to relieve the Fourth Division on that part of the front which lay between the Somme and the main St. Quentin road on the following day, but for the time being leaving the newly captured ground north of the Somme still in Maclagan's hands.

After an examination of the ground and a study of the situation, the opportunity for a further immediate local operation, certain to gain valuable tactical ground, and likely also to yield a good number of prisoners, presented itself to me. A further attraction was that it would permit of a useful advance of my left flank on the south of the Somme. This project, being of some tactical interest, demands a short explanatory reference to the terrain.

The River Somme, from Cerisy as far east as Péronne, flows in a tortuous valley which describes a succession of bends, almost uniform in size and regular in disposition. These bends face with their bases alternately north and south, and average a depth of two miles, by a width across the base of about a mile and a half. Each came to be known to us by the name of one of the villages which reposed in its folds, such as Chipilly, Etinehem, Bray, Cappy, Feuillères, and Ommiécourt; all these have become names to be remembered in the subsequent conquest of this part of the Somme valley.

The valley itself is in this region a mile broad; its sides are steep and often precipitous, and the adjoining plateaus rise some 200 feet above its bed. Through this valley winds, in ordered curves, the canal for barge traffic; it is flanked by vast stretches of backwaters and heavily grassed morasses, in which the river loses itself. The valley can be traversed only by the few bridges and the lock gates of the canal, and the causeways leading to them from either bank.

It would be difficult country for a fight on a general scale, but ideal for guerilla warfare. The whole succession of villages clinging to the sides of the valley were in the hands of the enemy, and in use by him for the housing and shelter of his troops. To attack and overcome them one by one, by fighting up the winding valley, would have been a costly business. But it suggested itself that they might all be won by a species of investment.

Taking any one of these U-shaped bends singly, by drawing a cordon across its base, the whole of any enemy forces who might be occupying the bend would be denied escape from it, except by *crossing* the river into the adjacent bend. But if a semi-cordon had been simultaneously drawn across the base of that next bend also, even that loophole would be closed, and moreover such troops as inhabited the second bend would find themselves surrounded also.

Immediately before my left flank lay the Méricourt bend on the south of the river and the Etinehem bend to the north of it. Both were held by the enemy, doubtless fugitives from the great battle, who had sought food, water and underground shelter in the numerous dugouts which honeycombed the sides of the valley. The design was to capture the whole of these with little effort. It was a good plan, and only an unforeseen accident prevented its full realisation.

Early on the morning of the 10th, I summoned a conference at Maclagan's Headquarters in Corbie, which was attended by the commanders and certain brigadiers of the Third and Fourth Divisions. It was arranged that on the north of the river, the 13th Brigade would that night get astride of the Etinehem Spur on the north, while simultaneously the 10th Brigade, by making a side sweep skirting Proyart, would advance our line till its left rested on the river a mile east of Méricourt.

Columns were to move along defined routes, leaving the objectives well to the flanks, and then to encircle the enemy positions. Each column was to be accompanied by tanks and was to move in an easterly direction and then wheel in towards the Somme. Although tanks had never previously been used at night, as their utility was uncertain, it was thought that the effect of the noise they made would lead to the speedy collapse of the defence.

The plan succeeded to perfection on the north of the river, and the Etinehem spur and village with all its defenders fell to us almost without a blow. Four tanks amused themselves by racing up and down the main Corbie—Bray road at top speed, and the clamour they made cleared the path for the marching infantry.

On the south, however, just after nightfall, a sudden onslaught by a flight of enemy bombing planes, threw the head of the 10th Brigade column into confusion, and its commander was killed. Two of the tanks were also disabled by direct hits from artillery. This delayed the progress of the operation, and the next day broke with the task uncompleted. The 9th and 11th Brigades were, however, at once sent up to reinforce, and during the following day all three brigades completed the operation by possessing themselves of the villages of Méricourt and Proyart and the woods adjoining the river.

This series of local operations yielded some 300 prisoners, and entirely cleared up the confused and unsatisfactory situation which had existed on my left flank, as the aftermath of the Chipilly Spur failure of the first day. It also brought my line up more square to the Somme, and so somewhat shortened my already expanding front. But my left flank was at last quite secure.

I must now turn to the extreme right flank, which was, on this same day, also the scene of very severe fighting. I have related the progress of the First Division to the foot of the Lihons Ridge the night before. On August 10th and 11th the advance was continued by the First and Second Divisions in sympathy with the advance of the Canadian Corps on the south of the railway. There were only a few tanks left available to assist in this advance; and the resistance of the enemy in the neighbourhood of Lihons had stiffened considerably.

The devastated area had already been reached by us in this part of the field, and the terrain was a labyrinth of old trenches, and a sea of shell-holes; the remains of old wire entanglements spread in every direction, and the whole area had been covered by a rank growth of thistles and brambles. It furnished numerous harbours for machine-guns, and it was country over which it was difficult to preserve the semblance of an organised battle formation during an advance.

The enemy fought hard and determinedly to retain Lihons, and in some parts of the line the battle swayed to and fro. But before the morning was well advanced, we had taken possession of the whole of the Lihons Knoll, of Auger Wood, and of the villages of Lihons and Rainecourt, while the Canadians had passed through Chilly just south of the railway. All that afternoon the enemy made repeated counter-attacks, particularly directed against Lihons and Rainecourt; but they were all successfully driven off by rifle and machine-gun fire without the loss of any ground.

It was a great feat to the credit of the First Australian Division, and ranks among its best performances during the war. Some 20 field-guns and hundreds of machine-guns were captured. Such a battle, with such results, would, in 1917, have been placarded as a victory of the first magnitude. Now, with the new standards set up by the great battle of August 8th, it was reckoned merely as a local skirmish.

General Currie, operating on my right, had had a similar experience of slow, although definite, progress, against hourly stiffening opposition, and the fighting by the methods of open warfare was growing daily more costly. The enemy had recovered from his first surprise, our resources in tanks had been greatly diminished, and much of our heavy artillery had not yet had time to get into its forward positions. In other words, the possibility of further cheap exploitation of the success of August 8th had come to an end.

It was decided, therefore, to recommend to the army commander that a temporary halt should be called on the line thus reached, and that rested troops should be brought up to relieve the line divisions. He concurred and decided that we should prepare for the delivery on August 15th of another combined "set-piece" blow, which would have the probable effect of again putting the enemy on the run, so that the moving battle could be resumed.

This plan was never actually carried into effect, for reasons which did not at once appear. But it transpired later that General Currie had made very strong private representations to the Fourth Army against the plan. He questioned the wisdom of expending the resources of the Canadian Corps upon an attempt to repeat, over such broken country, covered as it was with entanglements and other obstacles, the great success of August 8th. He urged that the Canadian Corps should be transferred back to the Arras district—which they knew so well. It was country lending itself admirably to operations requiring careful organisation, which none understood better than Currie and his admirable staff.

It was an issue in which I was not greatly concerned, for my share in the proposed operation of August 15th was to be quite subsidiary. It was to consist merely in once again advancing my right flank, in sympathy with the Canadian advance, as far as to include Chaulnes Hill and the very important railway junction at that town. In ignorance of the fact that the matter was under discussion, I prepared complete plans for the co-operation of the Australian Corps, and detailed the Fourth and Fifth Australian Divisions to carry them out. Fortunately, before any actual executive action had been initiated, orders came that the project was to be abandoned.

It soon became known that still larger questions were being discussed. The British front, which in July reached south as far only as Villers-Bretonneux, had now been extended to the latitude of Roye. The field marshal was urging reduction, so as to liberate divisions for offensive operations elsewhere, and Marshal Foch agreed that, as by the elimination of the Soissons salient the French front had been shortened, this could be done. In due course confidential announcements were made that, as soon as it could be arranged, the Canadians would be withdrawn from the line, and their places taken by French troops. This would once again make my corps the south flank corps of the British Army, and I would junction with the French on the Lihons Hill.

The halt thus called gave me breathing time to consider a thorough re-organisation of my whole corps front. This had, by August 12th, again grown to a total length of over 16,000 yards. This increase had been the result, firstly, of my having, as narrated, taken over ground to the north of the Somme, secondly, by reason of the fact that during the advances of the last four days my right had hugged the railway, while my left had continued to rest on the Somme, two lines which were rapidly diverging from each other, and thirdly, because my front line now lay sharply oblique to my general line of advance.

Even with a fifth Division, which I now had at my disposal, a front of 16,000 yards was far too attenuated for corps operations on the grand scale, and even for more localised operations, by one or two divisions at a time, there was little opportunity to provide the troops with adequate intervals of rest. I therefore strongly urged upon General Rawlinson either a shortening of my front, or a further increase in my resources.

He chose the latter alternative, and on August 12th placed under my orders, provisionally, the 17th British Division (Major-General P.R. Robertson), coupled with the condition that while it might be employed as a line division, it was not to be used for offensive operations. The reason, confidentially given, was that it was shortly to be employed in a large scale offensive in course of preparation by the Third British Army.

It was, for me, a most opportune measure of relief from a difficult situation; for the Third Australian Division was now also badly in need of a rest. Prior to the great advance, it had been longest of any of the divisions in the line, and had subsequently had a hard time in fighting its way forward from Méricourt to Proyart. It was therefore relieved in the line on August 13th by the 17th Division and went into Corps Reserve.

On the same day I put into effect a project of organisation which the necessities of the case forced upon me. North of the river stood the 13th Australian Brigade, and the 131st American Regiment, both still under the command of General Maclagan, the remainder of whose division was resting, and this division might be required at short notice for operations at a totally different part of the front. (I had, in fact, earmarked it for the proposed attack on August 15th to which I have referred.)

To overcome this anomalous position, I decided to constitute, for a brief period, an independent force, composed of the two units north of the river which I have named, to appoint to the command of it Brigadier-General Wisdom (of the 7th Brigade), and to supply him with a nucleus staff, some artillery, and supply and signal services. It became, in fact, to all intents and purposes, an additional division with a headquarters directly responsible to me.

This force received the name of "Liaison Force" and continued in existence for about eight days. Its functions were to keep tactical touch and liaison with the Third Corps, to protect my left flank by guarding the Etinehem spur from recapture, and to act as a kind of loose link between the two corps, advancing its northern or its southern flanks, or both, in sympathy with any forward movement to be made by either corps. While, during its existence as a separate force,

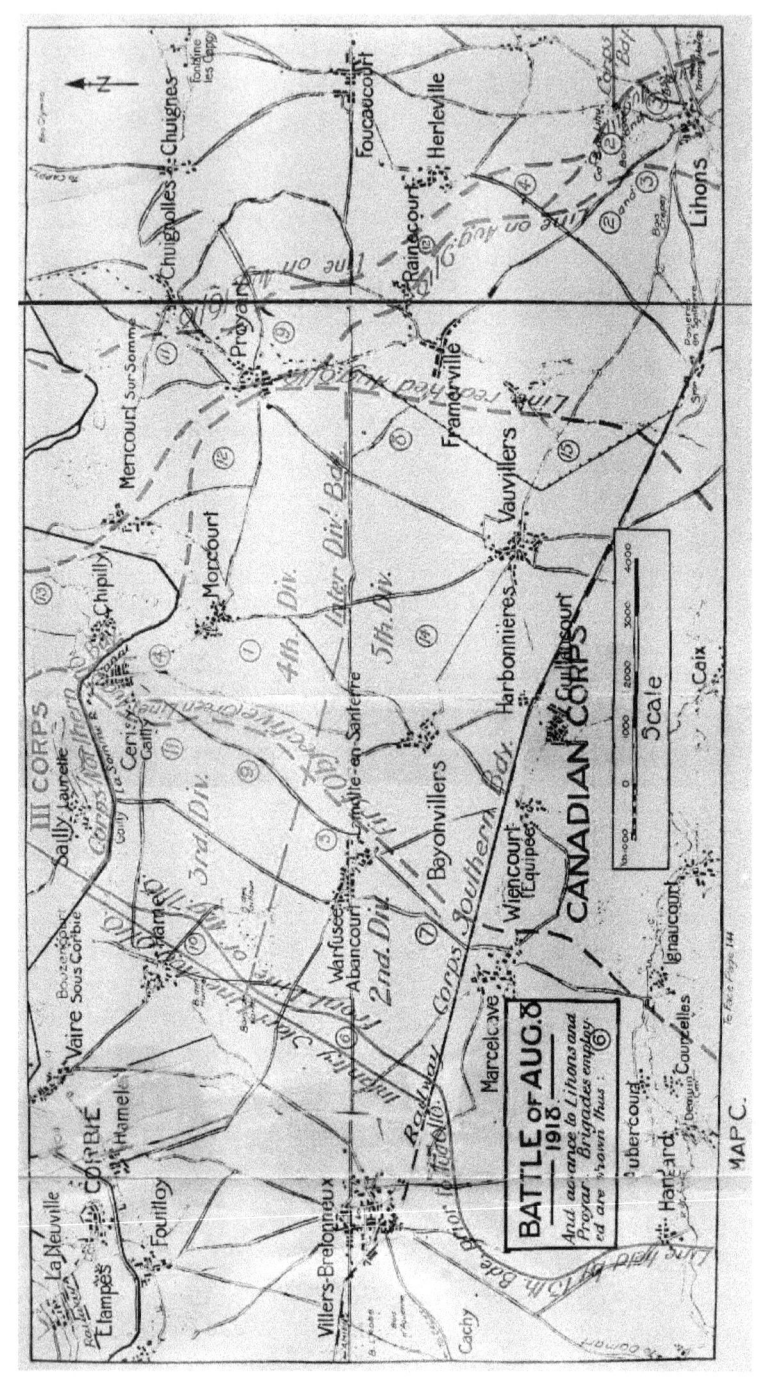

no operations of first magnitude took place, yet the Liaison Force served me well in the very useful function of a custodian of my tactical ownership of the Somme valley, an ownership which I succeeded in retaining to the immense advantage of the operations of the corps less than three weeks later.

By August 13th, therefore, my responsibilities included the control of seven separate divisions as well as all the corps troops, and army troops attached. The next week was occupied in local operations by the front line divisions to straighten our front, and to dispose of a number of strong points, small woods, and village ruins which, so long as they were in enemy hands, were a source of annoyance to us. The attitude of the enemy was alert but not aggressive, and an important point was that he showed every desire to stand his ground, and to contest our further advance. There was as yet no indication of any comprehensive withdrawal out of the great river bend. Each day brought its useful toll of prisoners, all of whom, however, corroborated the view that the enemy meant to hold on, and that the troops opposing us were more than a mere rear-guard intended to delay our advance.

The period from August 13th to 20th was also occupied in carrying out a number of inter-divisional reliefs—events of merely technical interest to the student of military history, but imposing an immense amount of detailed work upon the staff of the corps and upon the commanders and staffs of the divisions concerned. It was my own special responsibility, and one which I could not delegate, to decide the date of the relief of each division and by which other division it should be relieved. Such decisions involved a close inquiry into, and a just and humane appreciation of the condition of the troops, almost from hour to hour every day, a duty in the discharge of which I was able to rely upon the loyal help of the divisional commanders and brigadiers.

The time that had elapsed since last they had rested, the marching they had since done, the fighting they had undertaken and its nature, the mental and physical stress which they had undergone, and the probable nature and date of their future employment were all factors which had to be weighed carefully, and set against the advantages or disadvantages of cutting short the period of rest of the troops who were available to relieve them. It was a function which had to be exercised, at all times, with the greatest circumspection, and the strictest justice; for troops are very ready to acquire the impression that they are being called upon to do more than their fair share.

An actual inter-divisional relief usually occupied two nights and the intervening day. Incoming units, both fighting and technical, had to be shown all over the sector, to be taught the dispositions and the exact situation in front of us; maps, orders and photographs had to be explained and handed over; stores and dumps had to be inventoried and receipts passed; while on the other hand the outgoing troops expected to find their billets, offices, stables, wagon lines, bathing-places and entertainment rooms in the rear area all allocated and ready for their occupation.

Each such mutual relief meant the movement of upwards of 20,000 men, and separate roads had to be allotted for their use. Frequently in so large a corps as this, two such inter-divisional reliefs would synchronize or overlap, and the danger of congestion and the Staff work necessary to avoid it would be thereby more than doubled. And all this work would have to go on smoothly even if the corps front were in the throes of an actual battle at the time.

Although much of the routine of such reliefs, which had become almost a ritual during the preceding years of trench warfare, was now scrapped, it is a matter of pride to the Australian Corps and its divisions, that all such relief operations, even amid all the stress of these busy fighting months of August and September, were, until the end, carried out with precision, freedom from irritating hitches, and a minimum of stress on the troops.

The decisions which had to be given regarding the times and alternations of these divisional reliefs became from now on really of basic importance, and affected the main framework of the whole of my future plans. It was no longer merely a question of earmarking certain divisions for a specified single operation; but of planning, many days ahead, the rotation in which the divisions were to be employed in a continuous series of operations. I regarded it as a fundamental principle to employ whenever possible absolutely fresh and rested troops for an operation of any magnitude or importance. To carry such a principle into effect involved the necessity of making the best surmise that was possible as to the course of events a week or even two weeks ahead.

As I shall endeavour to make clear in the course of the following pages, the really outstanding and exceptional features of the work of the corps in its last sixty days were the sustained vigour of its fighting, and the unbroken continuity of its collective effort. Those results would clearly depend more on the manner in which the resources in troops were manipulated than upon any other factor. Each division had to be kept employed until the last ounce of effort, consistent with speedy recovery, had been yielded, and each division had to rest a sufficient time to enable it fully to recover its spirit and tone, and yet had to be ready by the time it was wanted.

The fulfilment of such conditions involved, as a little reflection will show, a great deal more than a mere mechanical rotation of employment; for the problem was, always to have available an adequate supply of sufficiently rested troops for a prospective demand which, although varying always in accordance with the changing situation, had nevertheless to be predicted or conjectured.

August 21st found our front line much about the same as that of August 13th, although generally more advanced and straightened out. The corps frontage was still over 16,000 yards, and upon the completion of the series of reliefs to which I have alluded the dispositions of the corps were as follows: The Fourth Australian Division from Lihons to just south of Herleville, the 32nd British Division opposite Herleville, the Fifth Australian Division in front of Proyart, and the Third Australian Division on the north of the river. The First and Second Divisions were in Corps Reserve, the former having by then had a good rest from its Lihons fighting. The Liaison Force had been broken up; and the 32nd British Division (Major-General T.S. Lambert) had joined my command in substitution for the 17th Division, which had been withdrawn to join the Third Army.

Such was the situation of the Australian Corps, when on August 21st the short period of comparative inactivity came to a close, and it was destined soon to go forward to further decisive events. On the previous day the French opened a great attack in the south, which yielded 10,000 prisoners on the first day, and on the day in question the Third British Army delivered north of Albert the attack which had been expected for some days. Thus, the enemy would have his hands full in endeavouring to parry those fresh blows; and the time seemed appropriate for another stroke on the front of the Fourth Army.

Chapter 9

Chuignes

Allusion has been made to the great bend which occurs in the course of the River Somme. It is indeed a geographical circumstance which must be borne in mind, if the phraseology current at this epoch in the war is to be clearly comprehended.

The river flows in an almost due northerly direction from the neighbourhood of Roye as far as Péronne, and then bends quite sharply, at that locality, in a western direction, past Bray, Corbie and Amiens, towards the sea, beyond Abbeville. In the story of the fighting of the period from March to August we have been concerned only with that portion of the river valley which ran parallel to our line of advance; but interest will henceforth focus itself largely upon that other reach of the Somme which runs on a north and south line, upstream, from the town of Péronne.

This latter stretch of the river lies squarely athwart the direction in which the corps had been advancing, and the obstacle to that advance which the river would presently constitute was continued in a northerly direction from Péronne by an unfinished work of a great canalisation scheme to be called the "Canal du Nord". This canal was already wide and deep, and formed a tactical obstacle of some significance, for the excavations incidental to this project had been almost completed before the war.

The "line of the Somme", as it was understood in the tactical discussions of the period now to be dealt with, meant, in short, the line formed by that part of the river which lay upstream (*i.e.*, to the south of Péronne), and the continuation northwards of that line by the Canal du Nord. Both features being military obstacles, they and the highlands to the east of them together afforded an eminently suitable continuous line on which the enemy might, if he were permitted to do so, establish himself in a defensive attitude in order to bar our eastward progress.

The autumn was upon us; not more than another eight or nine weeks of campaigning weather could be relied upon. A quite definite possibility existed that the enemy might be able to put forth so powerful an effort to contest our further advance, inch by inch, that he would gain sufficient time to prepare the line of the Somme for a stout defence, and hold us up until the arrival of winter compelled a suspension of large operations.

There were at that time, indeed, some who contended that as we had apparently succeeded in putting an end to the German offensive we should rest content with the year's work; that our soundest strategy would be to permit the enemy to take up such a line of defence; and then quietly to wait over the winter until 1919 for the full development of the American effort, now only in its inception.

So far, the enemy had given no indication of any readiness to undertake a precipitate withdrawal from the great bend west of the Somme. On the contrary, his resistance had stiffened to such an extent that little further progress was to be hoped for from the methods of open warfare which I had employed since August 8th.

If, however, another powerful blow could be delivered, to be followed by energetic exploitation, it was quite possible that the enemy might be hustled across the Somme, that this might be achieved at such a rate that I could gain a firm footing on the east bank, and that thereby the value to him of the line of the Somme, as a winter defence, might be destroyed.

This was the very project on which I now embarked. The First Division was in Corps Reserve, had rested and was fresh. The 32nd Division had only just come into the line. By handing over a substantial sector to the French, my frontage south of the Somme was about to be shortened to 7,000 yards, a very suitable front for a deliberate attack by two divisions.

I held a conference at Fouilloy, near Corbie, in the afternoon of August 21st to announce the plan, and to settle all details with the commanders and services concerned. The infantry assault was to be entrusted to Glasgow and Lambert, attacking side by side; but the former had allotted to him much the larger share of the battle front, at the northern end, the corollary role of the 32nd Division being to seize Herleville and carry our line just to the east of it.

The date of the attack was fixed for August 23rd, and the Second and Fifth Divisions were warned to be in readiness to come into the line a day or two after the battle, in order to commence immediately the process of keeping the enemy on the run, and hustling him clean out of the river bend and across the line of the Somme.

The conference of that day was of special interest, in that I had to deal with two divisions which had not participated in any of those Corps Conferences, previously held, which had initiated a fully organised corps operation. The commanders and staffs were strangers to each other and, some of them, to me and my staff. Nearly all of them were yet unfamiliar with the special methods of the corps. The conference was therefore a lengthy one, for many problems of tactical mechanism, which had been settled in connection with the preceding Battles of Hamel and August 8th, had to be reopened and elucidated.

These regular battle conferences were in the Australian Corps an innovation from the time the command of it devolved upon me. They proved a powerful instrument for the moulding of a uniformity of tactical thought and method throughout the command. They brought together men who met face to face but seldom, and they permitted of an exhaustive and educative interchange of views. They led to a development of "team-work" of a very high order of efficiency.

The work of preparing for, and the actual conduct of, these conferences was always a very arduous business; but they more than repaid me for the effort they entailed. They served two paramount purposes. They enabled me to apply the requisite driving force to all subordinates collectively, instead of individually, and thereby created a responsive spirit which was competitive. In addition, each commander or service had the advantage not only of receiving instructions regarding his own action, but also of hearing in full detail the instructions conveyed to his colleagues. He knew, not merely what his colleagues had to do, but also knew that they had been told what to do; and he had an opportunity of considering the effect of their action on his own.

The senior representative of the heavy artillery, Tank and Air Services invariably attended, and listened to all the points discussed with the divisions, and the divisional commanders heard all matters arranged with these services. In this way, each arm acquired in the most direct manner a steadily expanding knowledge of the technology of all the other arms.

My reason for emphasising these matters in the present context is that, on this particular occasion, an attempt was to be made to carry out a major corps operation at little more than thirty-six hours' notice; and the division which was to have assigned to it the principal role was still in Corps Reserve and a day's march from the battle front.

That, in spite of these handicaps, the battle proved brilliantly successful is a testimony to the valuable part which these corps conferences played in securing rapid and efficiently co-ordinated action; a result which would, I am confident, have been unattainable under the stated conditions by the mere issue of formal written orders.

Although only two out of the seven divisions of the corps were to participate in this operation, it was my intention to employ, for the full assistance of the infantry, the whole resources of the corps in artillery, tanks and aircraft. That was a principle which I always regarded as fundamental, and one from which I never permitted any exception to be made, although the pressure upon me to rest a substantial portion of these ancillary services was always very great.

The general plan for the battle ran briefly as follows. The 32nd Division would attack with one infantry brigade, under a barrage, on a frontage of 1,000 yards; the capture of the village of Herleville, which was still strongly held, being its principal objective.

The 1st Australian Division would attack on a frontage of 4,500

The Canal and Tunnel at Bellicourt—looking north.

The Hindenburg Line—a characteristic belt of sunken wire.

yards, with two brigades in line, and one brigade in reserve. The attack would be carried out in three phases.

The first phase was a normal assault, under an artillery barrage, and with the assistance of tanks, to a predetermined line, which would carry us beyond the Chuignes Valley; the second phase was in the nature of exploitation by the two line brigades, but was expressly limited to a maximum distance of 1,000 yards beyond the main first objective.

The third phase was to be contingent upon the complete success of the preceding phases, and would consist of an advance by the Reserve Brigade for a further exploitation of success, by the seizure of the whole of the Cappy bend of the river, including the towering hill close to the Somme Canal known as Froissy Beacon.

All arrangements for the forthcoming battle having thus been completed, the First Division duly relieved the Fifth Division on the night of August 21st, and hastened forward its preparations for the attack, which had been fixed for 4.45 a.m. on August 23rd.

In the meantime, the first attack which any British Army other than the Fourth had made since August 8th was at last launched on August 21st along the whole front of the Third British Army, northwards from Albert.

It has come to be an article of faith that the whole of the successive stages of the great closing offensive of the war had been the subject of most careful timing, and of minute organisation on the part of the Allied High Command, and of our own G.H.Q. Much eulogistic writing has been devoted to an attempted analysis of the comprehensive and far-reaching plans which resulted in the delivery of blow upon blow, in a prescribed order of time and for the achievement of definite strategical or tactical ends.

All who played any part in these great events well know that it was nothing of the kind; that nothing in the nature of a detailed time-table to control so vast a field of effort was possible. All commanders, and the most exalted of them in a higher degree even than those wielding lesser forces, became opportunists, and bent their energies, not to the realisation of a great general plan for a succession of timed attacks, but upon the problem of hitting whenever and wherever an opportunity offered, and the means were ready to hand.

In these matters it was the force of circumstances which controlled the sequence of events, and nothing else. An elaborate time-table controlled by definite dates and sequences for the successive engagement of a series of armies would have been quite impossible of realisation. Even a corps commander had difficulty in forecasting within a day or two when he would be ready to launch an attack on any given part of the front. For an army commander it was a matter of a week or even two.

All attempted time-tables were controlled by our artillery requirements; both the assembling of the necessary guns—often drawn from distant fronts—and the accumulating of the requisite "head" of ammunition to see a battle through, were processes whose duration could only be very roughly forecasted.

The dumping, in the gun pits and in ammunition stores, of the necessary 500 or 600 rounds per gun meant days of labour in collection and distribution on the part of the railways and motor lorries. The breakdown of a few motor lorries at a critical time, or the dropping of a single bomb upon an important railway junction, were disturbing factors quite sufficient to have arrested the flow of ammunition, and to have postponed, indefinitely, any programme based upon its prompt delivery.

It will be obvious, therefore, that no reliance could be placed, days or weeks beforehand, upon a given attack taking place on a given day; therefore, no plans could be made which depended upon such attacks taking place in a predetermined sequence.

Shortly put, therefore, the decisions of the high command were confined to questions such as where an attack should be made, in what direction, and by what forces. The date was always a matter of uncertainty, and the only control that could be exercised was by postponement, and never by acceleration.

For the greater part of the offensive period it was therefore necessarily left to the commanders of the armies to conform to a general policy of attack, the time and method being left to their own decision or recommendation. And they, in turn, relied upon their corps commanders to seize the initiative in the pursuit of such a policy. Naturally, the army at all times made every effort to secure co-ordinated action by its several corps; but it rarely happened that more than one corps at a time carried through the main effort—the other corps performing subsidiary roles. The great battle of September 29th to October 1st, which completed the final rupture of the Hindenburg line, was, however, a signal exception to this rule.

The attack by the Third British Army on August 21st is a case which illustrates the delays inseparable from battle preparations. The project of such an attack had already been mooted on August 11th, when General Byng (Third Army) paid me a visit to discuss my battle plan of August 8th, and I gathered on that occasion that he hoped to begin within four or five days. The event showed that the operation actually took ten days to materialise. No criticism is suggested. The conditions of transport of troops and munitions doubtless made its earlier realisation quite impossible.

The attack coming when it did, however, considerably eased the situation of the Fourth Army, upon whose front Ludendorff had flung all his available reserves, drawn from all parts of the German front, in his endeavours to bring the Australians and Canadians to a halt.

He was now suddenly confronted with the prospect of another "breakthrough" in a different part of his line, and the German people had been taught by their press correspondents to believe that a "breakthrough" was the one thing most to be resisted by the German Supreme Command, and the one thing impossible of achievement by us.

There can be no doubt, therefore, that the success of the Third Army on August 21st, although not comparable in its results with the battle of August 8th, did materially assist the prospects of my own success in the operations upon which I was then embarking.

The immediate effect of it was already felt the very next day. For the Third Corps, which was still the left flank corps of the Fourth Army, and which had made very little progress since August 8th, was enabled to advance its line a little past Albert and Meaulte.

The Third Australian Division, which, it will be remembered, had taken over the front and the role of the now disbanded Liaison Force, participated, by arrangement, in this attack and, swinging up its left, brought my front line, north of the river, square to the Somme Valley, and just to the forward slopes of the high plateau overlooking Bray and La Neuville. The Third Pioneer Battalion at once got to work on restoring the broken crossings over the Somme, to the south of Bray, and put out a series of advanced posts upon the left bank of the river, which gave us practical control of the great island on which stands La Neuville.

Meanwhile, on the left flank of the 9th Brigade, which had carried out the Third Divisional attack, there was serious trouble. The enemy counter-attacked in the late afternoon. The 9th Brigade stood firm; but the 47th Division (of the Third Corps) yielded ground, leaving the flank of the 9th Brigade in the air. A chalk pit, which we had seized, formed a welcome redoubt which enabled the 33rd Battalion to hang on for sufficiently long to permit of the 34th Battalion coming up to form a defensive flank, facing north.

In this way the gallant 9th Brigade (Goddard) was able to retain the whole of its gains of that day; but the risk of an immediate further advance was too great while the situation to the north remained obscure and unsatisfactory. The capture of the village of Bray, which was still strongly held by the enemy, had, therefore, to be postponed, although it had been part of my plan to capture it that same day as a measure of precaution, seeing that I calculated upon being able the next day to advance my line south of the Somme to a point well to the east of Bray.

The great attack by the First Division supported by the 32nd Division, which has come to be known as the Battle of Chuignes, was launched at dawn on August 23rd, and was an unqualified success.

The main valley of the Somme in this region is flanked by a number of tributary valleys, which run generally in a north and south direction, extending back from the river four or five miles. They are broad, with heavily-wooded sides, and harbour a number of villages, such as Proyart, Chuignolles, Herleville and Chuignes, which cluster on their slopes.

One such valley, larger and longer than any of those which, in our previous advances, we had yet crossed, lay before our front line of that morning, and square across our path. It ran from Herleville, northwards, past Chuignes, to join the Somme in the Bray bend. It was the most easterly of all the tributary valleys to which I have referred, and it was also the last piece of habitable country before the devastated area of 1916 was reached, just a mile to the east of it.

The valley afforded excellent cover for the enemy's guns, and the expectation was that some of them would be overrun by our attack. It was also ideal country for machine-gun defence, for the numerous woods, hedges and copses afforded excellent cover, and had in all probability been amply fortified with barbed wire. It was a formidable proposition to attack such a position on such a frontage with only two brigades.

The 2nd Brigade (Heane) attacked on the right, the 1st Brigade (Mackay) on the left, and the first phase was completed to timetable, with the green objective line, located on the east side of the long valley, in our possession. The only temporary hitch in the advance along the whole front was at Robert Wood, where the enemy held out, and had to be completely enveloped from both flanks before surrendering.

Then came the second phase, and no difficulty was experienced in advancing our line 1,000 yards east of the green line, nor in establishing there a firm line of outposts for the night.

The third phase presented a great deal more difficulty than I had anticipated. It was to have been undertaken by the 3rd Brigade (Bennett) pushing without delay through the 1st Brigade, and advancing in open warfare formation north-easterly towards Cappy, for the seizure of Hill 90, overlooking that village and on the south-west of it, and terminating at its northern extremity in the high bluff of Froissy Beacon.

There was, however, some unexplained delay in the initiation of this advance, and it was not until about 2 o'clock that the 3rd Brigade moved forward to the assault of the long slope of the Chuignes Valley, which still lay before them in this part of the field. The enemy, under the impression that our attack had spent itself, had occupied the plateau in great strength, and at first little progress could be made.

Mobile artillery was, however, promptly pushed up, and this proved of great assistance to the infantry. Garenne Wood, on the top of the plateau, into which large numbers of the enemy had withdrawn, proved a difficult obstacle, and incapable of capture by frontal attack. It, too, was conquered by enveloping tactics, and with its fall the resistance of the enemy rapidly subsided, and the 3rd Brigade had the satisfaction of hunting the fugitives clean off the plateau into the Cappy Valley.

The whole of this phase of the battle was an especially fine piece of work on the part of the regimental officers. It was open warfare of the most complete character, and the victory was won by excellent battle control on the part of the battalion commanders, by splendid co-operation between the four battalions of the brigade, and by intelligent and gallant leadership on the part of the company and platoon commanders.

Beset as I had been by many anxieties during the early afternoon as to how the Third Brigade would fare in the difficult task which had been given it, rendered more difficult by the delay of which I have spoken, I had the satisfaction that night of contemplating a victory far greater than I had calculated upon.

For the 32nd Division had successfully captured Herleville, and the First Division had seized the whole country for a depth of 1½ miles up to a line extending from Herleville to the western edge of Cappy. The whole Chuignes Valley was ours. By its capture the enemy had been despoiled of all habitable areas, and had been relegated to a waste of broken and ruined country between us and the line of the Somme.

We took that day 21 guns and over 3,100 prisoners from ten different regiments. The slaughter of the enemy in the tangled valleys was considerable, for our infantry are always vigorous bayonet fighters. They received much assistance from the tanks in disposing of the numerous machine-gun detachments which held their ground to the last.

It was a smashing blow, and far exceeded in its results any previous record in my experience, having regard to the number of troops engaged. Its immediate result, the same night, was the capture of Bray by the Third Division, north of the river, thus completing the work of that division which the failure of the 47th Division on their left the day before had compelled them to leave unfinished. The 40th Battalion took 200 prisoners, with trifling loss to themselves.

A more remote result, which made itself apparent in the next few days, was that it compelled the enemy to abandon all hope of retaining a hold of any country west of the line of the Somme; it impelled him at last to an evacuation of the great bend of the river, a process which he began in a very few days.

Such was the Battle of Chuignes. Much of the success of this brilliant engagement was due to the personality of the divisional commander, Major-General Glasgow. He had commenced his career in the war as a major of light horse, and had participated in the earliest stages of the fighting on the Gallipoli Peninsula.

Speedily gaining promotion during that campaign, his outstanding merits as a leader gained him an appointment to the command of the 13th Brigade, when the latter was formed in Egypt in the spring of 1916. For two years he led that brigade through all its arduous experiences on the Somme, at Messines and in the third Battle of Ypres.

This fine record was but the prelude to the history-making performances of the 13th Brigade in 1918 at Dernancourt and Villers-Bretonneux, and Glasgow seemed easily the most promising, among all the brigadiers of that time, as a prospective divisional commander: a judgment which fully justified itself. Of strong though not heavy build and of energetic demeanour, Glasgow succeeded not so much by exceptional mental gifts, or by tactical skill of any very high order, as by his personal driving force and determination, which impressed themselves upon all his subordinates. He always got where he wanted to get—was consistently loyal to the Australian ideal, and intensely proud of the Australian soldier.

The number of prisoners captured on this day, and the total numbers of the enemy encountered in the course of an advance which was relatively small, pointed to a disposition of troops which was unusual on the part of the enemy.

According to the principles so strongly emphasized by Ludendorff, in instructions which he had issued, and copies of which duly fell into my hands, there was to be, in his scheme of defensive tactics, a "forefield" relatively lightly held by outposts and machine-guns. The main line of resistance was to be well in rear, and there the main concentration of troops was to be effected.

Why had this dictum been so widely disregarded on this occasion? It was a question worthy of close inquiry, and two German battalion commanders who were captured by us on that day supplied the answer. Reference has already been made to the message which I issued to the corps on the eve of the great opening battle; and to the fact that a copy of this message had fallen into the hands of the enemy, probably by the capture of an officer in the close fighting which took place at Lihons on August 9th and 10th. In due course the substance of this message was published in the German wireless news, and in the German press of the time, but cleverly mistranslated to convey a colouring desirable for the German public.

It so happened that not long before the opening of our offensive I had, at the request of the authorities, sent to Australia a recruiting cable, which appealed to the Australian public for a maintenance of supplies of fighting men.

★★★★★★

The cablegram in question was dated July 13th, and was in the following terms:

"Since the opening of the German offensive in March every division of the Australian Army in France has been engaged and always with decisive success. The men of Australia, wherever and whenever they have entered this mighty conflict, have invariably brought the enemy to a standstill, and have made him pay dearly for each futile attempt to pass them on the roads to Amiens and to the Channel ports. Their reputation as skilful, disciplined and gallant soldiers has never stood higher throughout the Empire than it does today. Those who are privileged to lead in battle such splendid men are animated with a pride and admiration which is tempered only by concern at their waning numbers.

"Already some battalions which have made historic traditions have ceased to exist as fighting units, and others must follow unless the Australian nation stands by us and sees to it that our ranks are kept filled. We refuse to believe that the men and women of Australia will suffer their famous divisions to decay, or that the young manhood still remaining in our homeland

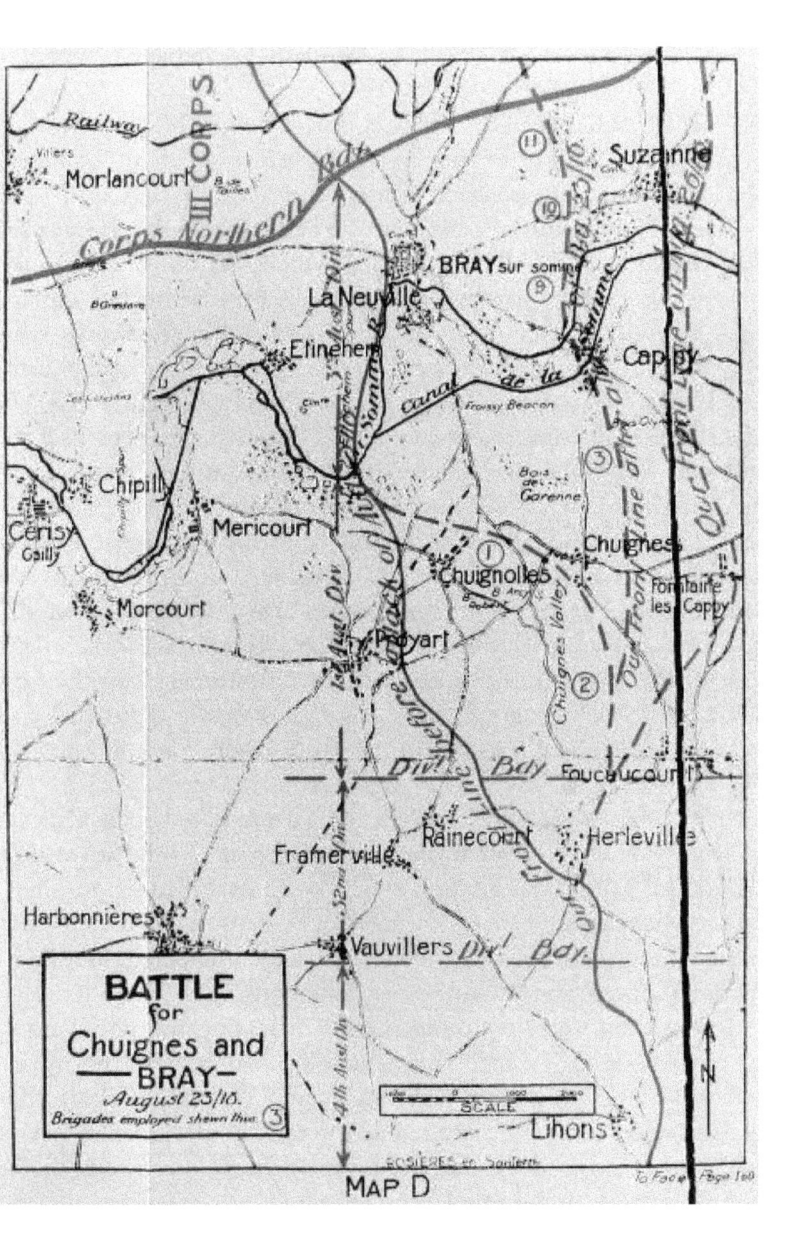

will not wish to share in the renown of their brothers in France. Nothing matters now but to see this job through to the end, and we appeal to every man to come, and come quickly, to help in our work, and to share in our glorious endeavour.

"Monash, Lieutenant-General."

★★★★★★

That the full text of this cable also became speedily known to the enemy is a testimony to the far-flung alertness of their Intelligence Service. It, also, was published in their press.

Basing their editorial comments on this material, the *Berliner Tageblatt* of August 17th, 1918, a copy of which I captured, and another journal whose name was not ascertainable, because in the copy captured the title had been torn off, both indulged in arguments, which were long, and intended to be convincing, to prove to the German people that I had promised my troops a "breakthrough"; that I had failed, and that, admittedly, the "proud" Australian Corps had been shattered, had come to the end of its resources and was no longer to be taken into calculation as an instrument of attack by the "English".

It was perfectly legitimate, if clumsy, propaganda. But it was a curious example of a propaganda which recoiled upon the heads of its propounders. The battalion commanders, who, like all German officers whom we captured, were always voluble in excuses for their defeat, pleaded that they had been deceived by the utterances of their own journals into believing that the Australian offensive effort had come to an end, once and for all, and that no further attack by this corps was possible.

It was this belief which, they said, had prompted their respective divisions (for each of them represented a separate one) to disregard Ludendorff's prescription; their divisional generals had felt justified in availing themselves of the very excellent living quarters which existed in the Chuignes Valley, near the German front line of August 22nd, to quarter all their support and reserve battalions.

It was there that we found them—increasing the population of the front zone far beyond that which we had been accustomed to find. Was there ever a more diverting example of a propaganda which recoiled upon those who uttered it? Intended to deceive the German public, it ended in deceiving the German front line troops, to their own lamentable undoing.

Among the captures of the Battle of Chuignes, which, as usual, comprised a large and varied assortment of warlike stores, including another great dump of engineering materials near Froissy Beacon, and two complete railway trains, was the monster naval gun of 15-inch bore, which had been so systematically bombarding the city of Amiens, and had wrought such havoc among its buildings and monuments.

It was first reached by the 3rd Australian Battalion (1st Brigade) during a bayonet charge which cleared Arcy Wood, in the shelter of which the giant gun had been erected. An imposing amount of labour had been expended upon its installation, and the most cursory examination of the effort involved was sufficient to make it evident that the enemy entertained no expectation of ever being hurled back from the region which it dominated.

The gun with its carriage, platform and concrete foundations weighed over 500 tons. It was a naval gun, obviously of the type in use on the German Dreadnoughts, and never intended by its original designers for use on land. It had a range of over twenty-four miles, fired a projectile weighing nearly a ton, and the barrel was seventy feet long. It had been installed with the elaborate completeness of German methods. A double railway track, several miles long, had been built to the site, for the transport of the gun and its parts. It was electrically trained and elevated. Its ammunition was handled and loaded by mechanical means. The adjacent hillside had been tunnelled to receive the operating machinery, and the supplies of shells, cartridges and fuses.

The gun and its mounting, when captured, were found to have been completely disabled. A heavy charge of explosive had burst the chamber of the gun, and had torn off the projecting muzzle end, which lay with its nose helplessly buried in the mud. The giant carriage had been burst asunder, and over acres all around was strewn the debris of the explosion.

For some time, some of my gunner experts favoured the theory that the gun had burst accidentally, but the view which ultimately prevailed was that the demolition had been intentional. Many months afterwards, the full story of the gun and its performances was elicited from a prisoner who had belonged to the No. 4 (German) Heavy Artillery Regiment, and it was circumstantial enough to be credible.

The story is worthy of repetition, not only because no authentic account of this wonderful trophy has yet been published, but also because the history of this gun curiously illuminates the enemy's plans, intentions and expectations between the dates of his onslaught in March and his recoil in August.

The substance of the story is as follows: The gun came from

Krupp's. Work on the position was started early in April, 1918—only a few days after the site had fallen into the enemy's hands. It was completed and ready for action on the morning of June 2nd. Its maximum firing capacity was twenty-eight rounds per day. It fired continuously until June 28th. By this time the original gun was worn out, having fired over 350 rounds at Amiens. A new piece was ordered from Krupp's. It arrived on August 7th, and was ready to fire by 7 p.m. It fired its first round on August 8th at 2 a.m. and kept on firing till August 9th, firing thirty-five rounds in all. At 7 a.m. on August 9th, all hands were ordered to remove everything that was portable and of value. Demolition charges were laid and fired about 9 a.m. on August 9th. The crew returned to Krupp's.

It is to be inferred from this narrative that the enemy's defeat at Hamel on July 4th did not deter him from his enterprise of replacing the original worn gun, but that after August 8th, he quite definitely accepted the certainty that he would be allowed no time to remove the gun intact, and so he destroyed it in order that we might not be able to use it against him.

This is the largest single trophy of war won by any commander during the war, and it was a matter of great regret to me that the cost of its transportation to Australia was prohibitive. The gun, as it stands, was, therefore, fenced in, and it has been formally presented to the City of Amiens as a souvenir of the Australian Army Corps.

So long as any Australian soldiers remained in France, this spot was a Mecca to which thousands of pilgrims wandered; and soon there was, over the whole of the immense structure, not one square inch upon which the "diggers" had not inscribed their names and sentiments. There, in the shade of Arcy Wood, the great ruin rests, a memorial alike of the sufferings of Amiens and of the great Australian victory of Chuignes.

CHAPTER 10

Pursuit

The design which I had formed after the battle of August 8th of driving the enemy completely out of the bend of the Somme—but which I was obliged to abandon for the time being because of the decision of the Fourth Army to thrust in a south-easterly direction—was now about to be realised. The effect of the Battle of Chuignes, following so closely upon the advance of the Third Army two days before, made it probable that the enemy would decide upon a definite withdrawal to the line of the Somme.

It now became my object to ensure, if he should attempt to do so, firstly, that his withdrawal should be more precipitate than would be agreeable to him, and, secondly, that when he reached that line he should be accorded no breathing time to establish upon it a firm defence from which he could hold us at bay for the remainder of the fine weather.

The French Army took over from me on the night of the 23rd August the whole of that portion of my front which still extended south of Lihons. General Nollet, commander of the 36th French Corps (34th and 35th French Divisions), became my southern neighbour, displacing my Fourth Division, and also a Canadian Division, for whose sector I had become responsible since the departure of General Currie, a few days before.

During these redispositions, probably induced to do so by evidences patent to him that large troop movements were in progress, the enemy carried out a very heavy gas bombardment and maintained it for some hours over the whole of the front which was being taken over by the French.

The wind blowing from the south, the gas, which was unusually dense, drifted over the whole areas both of the Fourth Australian and the 32nd British Divisions, and caused a large number of gas casualties, which weakened the available garrisons of these sectors.

The Second and Fifth Divisions were brought up on the night of August 26th to relieve the First Division, which had worthily earned a rest, and by these redispositions my whole frontage, which, in spite of the reduction effected, still exceeded nine miles, was organised to be held by four divisions, counting from south to north as follows: 32nd Division, Fifth Division, Second Division and Third Division, the latter lying north of the River Somme.

The First and Fourth Divisions were each sent back, the former to a pleasant reach of the Somme near Chipilly, and the latter to the neighbourhood of Amiens, there to have a long rest and to recuperate after their strenuous labours. These two divisions were, I had resolved, to be kept in reserve for any *tour de force*, the need for which might arise later. This disposition was based on intuition rather than on reasoning; but the event proved that it was a fortunate decision; for, at a juncture, three weeks later, when a great opportunity presented itself, these two divisions, then fully rested, proved of priceless value.

The Third Division held my front north of the Somme, and their presence there ensured my unchallenged tactical control of that important river valley. Numerous crossings had been systematically destroyed by the enemy, as he was being driven back from bend to bend, and as systematically repaired by my indefatigable engineer and pioneer services, as fast as the ground passed under our control.

Reconstruction of bridges and culverts is as tedious a business as their demolition is expeditious. A charge of gun-cotton, placed in the right spot, a primer, a short length of fuse, or an electric lead to a press button are all that are needed, and a single sapper standing by with a match, to be lighted at the last moment, can do all that is necessary to provide three days' work for a whole company of engineers.

Nevertheless, the control of the river valley was of inestimable advantage, for it enabled me to carry out a policy of continuous and rapid repair. Consequently, during the whole of our subsequent advance, every means of traversing the valley from south to north, which had been tampered with, was soon restored, as fast as my infantry had made good their advance beyond the ruined crossing.

This facility was to have an important bearing upon my freedom of action, not many days later, when the corps came head on to the north and south stretch of the Somme, and found every bridge gone. That circumstance alone would have proved an irretrievable misfortune, if I had not had already available numerous restored crossings upon the east and west reach of the river. For by that means, my ability to pass troops and guns rapidly from one bank of the Somme to the other remained unimpaired.

Before leaving the line, the First Division had captured Cappy and advanced its line on the right to the western outskirts of Foucaucourt, while the Third Division had possessed itself of Suzanne. This was the situation when, on the night of August 26th, the Second and Fifth Divisions came into the line. Conferences with the four line divisions were held both on the 25th and 26th August, in order to ensure co-ordinate action for the process of hustling the enemy across the Somme.

I was, at this stage, sorely perplexed by the uncertain attitude of the Fourth Army. I was all for pushing on energetically, and received General Rawlinson's approval to do so on August 24th; but on the very next day he enunciated a diametrically opposite policy, which greatly embarrassed me.

The gist of the army attitude on the 25th may be thus expressed. The presence of a new German division, the 41st, of whom we had taken many prisoners in Cappy, pointed to an intention on the part of the enemy to reinforce. This negatived any intention to undertake a withdrawal. This conclusion justified a revision of the Fourth Army policy. The army had done its fair share; it had drawn in upon its front all the loose German reserves. Its resources in tanks had been depleted, and it would take a month to replace them. Other armies would now take up the burden, and the Fourth Army would now mark time, and await events elsewhere. There was no object in hastening the enemy's evacuation of the bad ground in the bend of the Somme, or in our taking possession of it. There was a possibility of the French taking over more frontage from us, and the Australian Corps front might in consequence be reduced to a three-division front, with three divisions in Corps Reserve.

The course of events, in the next seven days, convinced me that the results which were then achieved were totally unexpected by the Fourth Army, and very vitally influenced the whole subsequent course of the campaign. In point of fact, Lord Rawlinson quite frankly conceded to me as much in express terms a week later. The appreciation made at the time was doubtless an intentionally conservative one, but it did not take into account the reserve of striking power which remained in the Australian Corps, even after the past eighteen days of continuous fighting, and even without the assistance of the tanks.

There was only one saving clause in the army attitude, and this fortunately gave all the loophole necessary for the continued activity which I desired to pursue. It was this: "Touch must be kept with the enemy." This was of course a mere formality of tactics, and was intended as no more than such. But it was sufficient to justify an aggressive policy on my part.

As the result of my redispositions, completed by the night of August 27th, and of my conferences with the line divisions, each division stood on that morning on a single brigade front, with its two remaining brigades arranged in depth behind it. My orders were that in the event of the enemy giving way, the line brigade was to push on energetically, and was to be kept in the line until it had reached the limits of its endurance. The other two brigades were to follow up more leisurely, but to be prepared, each in turn, to relieve the line brigade.

I had calculated that, by this method, each brigade should be able to function for at least two days on the frontage allotted; and that, therefore, the present line divisions could continue for at least six days; and if the stress upon the troops had not been severe, they could carry out a second rotation of brigades for a second tour of six days. The calculation was, in general terms, fully realised; and all of the four line divisions of that day did actually carry on for twelve days, and two of them for an additional six days.

The artillery resources of the corps were throughout the whole of this period fully maintained at the standard of the early days of August. I still had at my disposal eighteen brigades of field artillery; and so was able to allot four brigades of artillery to each line division, while keeping two in Corps Reserve.

Early on the morning of August 27th, a policy of vigorous patrolling all along our front was initiated. At several points, enemy posts which were known to have been strongly held the night before were found to be now unoccupied. Although reports varied along my front, they so fully confirmed my anticipations, that without waiting to make any reference to the army, I ordered an immediate general advance along my whole front.

There followed a merry and exciting three days of pursuit; for the enemy was really on the run, and by nightfall on August 29th, not a German who was not a prisoner remained west of the Somme between Péronne and Brie.

In previous years, during the enemy's retreat from Bapaume to the Hindenburg Line, we had had experience of his methods of withdrawal. Then they were deliberate, and his rear-guards so methodically and resolutely held up the British advance, that the enemy had been able not only to remove from the evacuated area every particle of his warlike stores, which were of any value, but also to carry out a systematic devastation of the whole area, even to the felling of all the fruit trees, and the tearing up of all the railways for miles.

The present withdrawal was of a very different character. To begin with, it had been forced upon him by the Battle of Chuignes, and he had to undertake it precipitately and without adequate preparation. Secondly, he had an impassable river behind him, which could be crossed only at three points, Brie, Eterpigny, and Péronne. Thirdly, he had in front of him a corps flushed with its recent victories, while he had been suffering a succession of defeats and heavy losses.

Nevertheless, he put up a good fight, and employed well-considered tactics. The German Machine-gun Corps was much the best of all his services. The manner in which the machine-gunners stood their ground, serving their guns to the very last, and defying even the Juggernaut menace of the tanks, won the unstinted admiration of our men. During these three days of retreat the enemy used his machine-guns to the best advantage, and they constituted the only obstacle to our rapid advance.

These tactics were not unexpected by me, and I had an answer ready. Defying the whole traditions of artillery tactics in open warfare, I insisted upon two somewhat startling innovations. The first was to break up battery control, by detaching even sections (two guns), to come under the direct orders of infantry commanders for the purpose of engaging with direct fire any machine-gun nest which was holding them up.

The second was to insist that all batteries should carry 20 *per cent,* of smoke shell. This elicited a storm of protest from the gunners. Every shell carried which was not a high explosive or shrapnel shell meant a shell less of destructive power, and, therefore, a shell wasted. That had been the Gunnery School doctrine. But I imagine that the test made at this epoch of the liberal use of smoke shell against machine-guns will lead to a revision of that doctrine.

Smoke shell proved of inestimable value in blinding the German machine-gunners. A few rounds judiciously placed screened the approach of our infantry, and many a machine-gun post was thereby rushed by us from the flanks or even from the rear. General Hobbs (Fifth Division) and General Rosenthal (Second Division), both of whom had formerly been gunners, proved the strongest advocates for these smoke tactics.

By such means an energetic and successful pursuit was launched and maintained. By the night of August 27th, our line already lay to the east of the villages of Vermandovillers, Foucaucourt (on the main road) and Fontaine. We also mastered the whole of the Cappy bend, including the crossings of the Somme at Eclusier. The Fifth Division had a particularly hard fight at Foueaucourt, which did not fall to us until we had subjected it to a considerable bombardment. Tivoli Wood was the chief obstacle encountered that day by the Second Division. The advance of the 32nd Division also progressed smoothly.

During August 28th our advance was continued methodically, and by that night the corps front had reached the line Genermont-Berry-en-Santerre-Estrées-Frise.

On August 29th the line of the Somme was reached, and all three Divisions south of the Somme stood upon the high ground sloping down to the Somme, with the river in sight from opposite Cléry, past Péronne and as far south as St. Christ.

In the meantime, the Third Division north of the Somme had marched forward, in sympathetic step with the southern advance, successively seizing Suzanne, Vaux, Curlu, Hem and Cléry. The Third Corps on my left had followed up the general advance, though always lagging a little in rear, thus keeping my left flank secure; and beyond the Third Corps, the Third Army was approaching the line of the Canal du Nord, which lay, as explained, in prolongation of the south-north course of the Somme.

The war correspondents of this time were given to representing the progress of the Australian Corps during these three days as a leisurely advance, regulated in its pace by the speed of the retiring enemy. But it was nothing of the kind.

On the contrary, it was his withdrawal which was regulated by the speed of our advance. There was not a foot of ground which was not contested by all the effort which the enemy was able to put forth. It is quite true that his withdrawal was intentional; but it is not true that it was conducted at the deliberate rate which was necessary to enable him to withdraw in good order.

He was compelled to fight all the time and to withdraw in disorder. He was forced to abandon guns and huge quantities of stores. The amount of derelict artillery ammunition found scattered over the whole of this considerable area alone reached hundreds of thousands of rounds, distributed in hundreds of dumps and depots, as well as scores of tons of empty artillery cartridge-cases, the brass of which had become of priceless value to the enemy.

Regimental and even Divisional Headquarters were abandoned as they stood, with all their furniture and mess equipment left intact. Signal wire and telephone equipment remained installed in all directions, hospitals and dressing-stations were left to their fate. The advance yielded to us over 600 prisoners, some half-dozen field-guns, and large numbers of smaller weapons.

The last two days of the advance led us across a maze of trenches and the debris of the 1916 campaign. The weather was unfavourable, there was much rain and an entire absence of any kind of shelter. As a result, the line brigades had to put forth all their powers of endurance and reached the Somme in a very tired condition.

In the meantime, my air squadron had an exceptionally busy time. Contact patrols were maintained throughout every hour of daylight. Difficult as it was to identify the positions reached by our leading troops during an organised battle, where their approximate positions and ultimate objective lines were known beforehand, it was doubly so when no guide whatever existed as to the probable extent of each day's advance, or as to the amount of resistance likely to be encountered at different parts of the front.

Yet it was just under these circumstances that rapid and reliable information as to the progress of the various elements of our front line troops was more important than ever, and no means for obtaining such information was so expeditious as the Contact Aeroplane.

To assist the air observer in identifying our troops, the latter were provided with flares, of colours which were varied from time to time in order to minimize the risk of imitation by the enemy. The method of their employment, whether singly or in pairs, or three at a time, was also frequently varied.

These flares on being lit gave out a dense cloud of coloured smoke, easily distinguishable from a moderate height. The contact plane, which would carry coloured streamers so that the infantry could identify it as flying on that particular duty, would, when ready to observe, blow its horn and thereupon the foremost infantry would light their flares.

It was a method of inter-communication between air and ground, which, after a little practice, came to be well understood and intelligently carried out. By its means a divisional or brigade commander was kept accurately informed, with great promptitude, of the progress of each of his front line units, in relation to the various woods, ruined mills, and other obstacles which lay spread across their path.

But the Air Force had another interesting duty, which was to watch the roads leading back from the enemy's front line to his rear areas. During tranquil times little movement could ever be seen on the enemy's roads in the hours of daylight, for the very good reason that he took care to carry out all his transportation to and from his front zone under cover of darkness.

Now, however, his needs pressed sorely upon him; and our air reports, from this time onwards, became almost monotonous in their iteration of the fact that large columns of transport were to be seen moving back in an easterly direction. These were his retiring batteries or his convoys of wagons carrying such stores as he was able to salve.

Occasionally, too, came reports of convoys, which looked like motor lorries or buses, moving hurriedly westward towards the German front. These were generally diagnosed by us as reinforcements which were being continually hurried forward to replace his human wastage, which was considerable both by direct losses from death, wounds and capture and by reason of the fatigue of such a strenuous and nerve-racking retreat.

All this movement in the enemy's rearward areas was a legitimate object of interest to my artillery. But, unfortunately, most of it lay well beyond the range of my lighter ordnance. The mobile field artillery was effective at no greater range than about four miles. The longer range 60-pounders found it a formidable task to traverse such broken country, while the still heavier tractor-drawn 6-inch guns found it quite impossible.

The latter, and all the heavy and super-heavy guns and howitzers were tied down to the roads, and it proved a tremendous business to advance them in sufficient time and numbers to make their influence felt upon the present situation. I have nothing but praise for the admirable manner in which Brigadier-General Fraser and his Heavy Artillery Headquarters carried out the forward moves of the whole of his extensive artillery equipment and organisation from August 8th onwards to August 23rd. But the rapid advance of the battle line during the last week of August left the great bulk of heavy artillery far behind.

This was not entirely or even appreciably a question of the rate of movement of the great lumbering steam or motor-drawn heavy guns. They could quite easily march their eight or ten miles a day if they could have a clear road upon which to do it. But it was this question of roads that dominated the whole situation during this period, and subsequently until the end of the campaign of the corps.

The construction and upkeep of roads throughout the corps area had been, even in the days of stationary warfare, a difficult problem. At a time like the present, when the battle was moving forward from day to day, it became one of the first magnitude.

The rate of our advance was controlled almost as much by the speed with which main and secondary roads could be made practicable for traffic as by the degree of resistance offered by the enemy. Obstacles had to be removed, the debris of war cleared to one side, shell holes solidly filled in, craters of mine explosions bridged or circumvented, culverts repaired and drains freed of obstructions.

The road surfaces, speedily deteriorating under the strain and wear of heavy motor lorry traffic, had to be kept constantly under repair. The transportation of the necessary road stone for this purpose alone, imposed a heavy burden upon the roads and impeded other urgent traffic. The amount of road construction and reconstruction actually in hand within the corps area, at any one time, far exceeded that normally required in peace time for any great city district.

The traffic on the roads was always of the most dense and varied character. For the proper maintenance and supply of a large army corps at least three good main roads, leading back to our sources of supply, would have been no more than adequate; but I seldom had at my disposal more than one such main road, which had often to be shared with an adjoining corps.

There was ever an endless stream of traffic, labouring slowly along in both directions. On such a road as that leading east from Amiens towards the battle front, the congestion was always extreme. Ammunition lorries, regimental horsed transport, motor dispatch riders, marching infantry, long strings of horses and mules going to and from water, traction engines, convoy after convoy of motorbuses, supply wagons, mess carts, signal motor tenders, complete batteries of artillery, motor tractors, tanks, Staff motorcars and gangs of *coolie* labourers surged steadily forward, in an amazing jumble, with never a moment's pause.

Such were some of the difficulties with which I was beset in the rear of my battle line. They were negligible compared with those which now loomed in front of it.

The reach of the Somme which runs northerly from Ham past Brie to Péronne and there turns westerly, differs entirely in its topographical features from that picturesque Somme Valley along both of whose banks the corps had been fighting its way forward. The steep banks have disappeared, and for a mile or so on either side the ground slopes gently towards the river bed.

The river itself is not less than 1,000 yards wide, being, in fact, a broad marsh, studded with islets which are overgrown with rushes, while the stream of the river threads its way in numerous channels between them. The marsh itself is no more than waist-deep, but the flowing water is too deep to be waded.

Along the western side of this marsh runs the canalised river, or, as it is here known, the Somme Canal, flowing between masonry-lined banks. The construction of a crossing of such a marsh was, even in peace time, a troublesome business. It meant, to begin with, a causeway solidly founded upon a firm masonry bed sunk deep into the mud of the valley bed. The canal itself and each rivulet required its separate bridge, in spans varying from thirty to sixty feet.

What, therefore, came to be known as the Brie Bridge, situated on the line of the main road from Amiens to St. Quentin, really consisted of no less than eight separate bridges disposed at irregular intervals along the line of the causeway, between the western and eastern banks of the valley. The demolition of even the smallest of these eight bridges would render the whole causeway unusable, and would prohibit all traffic.

There exists an almost exactly similar arrangement of bridges at St. Christ, about two miles to the south of Brie, but no other traffic crossing to the north of Brie until Péronne is reached. There, both the main road and the railway, which cross side by side, are provided with large span lattice girder bridges, over the main canal, while the marsh has been reclaimed where the town has encroached upon it. The river overflow is led through the town in several smaller canals or drains, all of them liberally bridged where crossed by roads and streets.

The Péronne bridges are, therefore, no less indispensable, and no less easily rendered useless than those at Brie. Should such crossings be denied to me, it would be just possible to pass infantry across the valley, by night, by wading and swimming, or by the use of rafts, always provided that no opposition were to be met with. But to pass tanks or heavy guns, or even vehicles of the lightest description across the marsh, would have been quite impossible.

The Somme threatened, therefore, to be a most formidable obstacle to my further advance. It was incumbent upon me to assume that at the very least one of each series of bridges would be demolished by the enemy in his retreat. It would have been criminal folly on his part were it to have been otherwise; and I had had previous evidence of the efficiency of his engineer services.

Reconnaissances pushed out on the night of August 29th speedily verified the assumption that some at least of the bridges had been wrecked. It was ultimately ascertained that every single bridge in every one of the crossings named had been methodically and systematically blown to pieces.

There was only one tactical method by which such an obstacle could be forced by a frontal operation. By bringing up sufficient artillery to dominate the enemy's defences on the east bank of the river valley, it might have been possible to pass across sufficient infantry to establish a wide bridge-head, behind which the ruined crossings could be restored, probably under enemy artillery fire. But it would have been a costly enterprise, and fraught with every prospect of failure, should the enemy be prepared to put up any sort of a fight to prevent it.

The value to me of the possession of the whole of the Somme Valley from Cléry westwards, and the rapid repair of the bridges therein which I had been able to effect, will now become apparent. For it permitted the crystallising into action of a project for dealing with the

Final Instructions to the Platoon – an incident of the battle of August 8th, 1918. The platoon is waiting to advance to Phase B of the battle

An Armoured Car – disabled near Bony, during the battle of September 29th, 1918.

present situation, which had been vaguely forming in my mind ever since the day when I took over the Chipilly Spur.

This was the plan of turning the line of the Somme from the north, instead of forcing it by direct assault from the west. It may be argued that such a plan would have been equally practicable, even if the left flank of the Australian Corps had hitherto remained and now still lay south of the Somme, instead of well to the north of it. In that case other corps on the north would have carried out that identical plan, which ultimately did achieve this important and decisive result.

I very much doubt it.

I had also had some experience of the futility of relying too much upon the sympathetic action of flank corps, who usually had their hands full enough with their own problems, and had little time to devote to the needs of their neighbours. It would, moreover, have been disagreeable and inexpedient in the extreme to seek a right of way through the territory over which another corps held jurisdiction. Corps commanders were inclined to be jealous of any encroachment upon their frontiers, or upon the tactical problems in front of them.

Moreover, I wanted, more than anything else, that this should be an exclusively Australian achievement.

The situation being as it was, I possessed freedom of action, elbow room, and control not only of all the territory which I should require to use, but also of all the Somme crossings west of Cléry.

The strategic object in view was to make the line of the Somme useless to the enemy as a defensive line, and thereby render probable his immediate further enforced retreat to the Hindenburg Line.

The tactical process by which this was to be achieved was to be an attack upon and the seizure of the key position of the whole line, the dominating hill of Mont St. Quentin. But the paramount consideration was that the attack must be delivered *without delay* and that the enemy should not be allowed a single hour longer than necessary to establish himself upon that hill.

Often since those days, wondering at the success which came to the Australian Corps at Mont St. Quentin, I have tried justly to estimate the causes which won us that success. And I have always come back to the same conclusion, that it was due firstly and chiefly to the wonderful gallantry of the men who participated, secondly to the rapidity with which our plans were put into action, and thirdly to the sheer daring of the attempt.

Mont St. Quentin lies a mile north of Péronne. It stands as a sentinel guarding the northern and western approaches to the town, a bastion of solid defence against any advance from the west designed to encircle it. The paintings and drawings of many artists who have visited the historic spot will familiarise the world with its gentle contours.

Viewed from the west, from the vantage point of the high ground near Biaches in the very angle of the bend of the river, Mont St. Quentin constitutes no striking feature in the landscape. But standing upon the hill itself one speedily realises how fully its possession dominates the whole of the approaches to it.

So placed that both stretches of the river can from it be commanded by fire, and giving full and uninterrupted observation over all the country to the west and north and south of it, the hill is ringed around with line upon line of wire entanglements, and its forward slopes are glacis-like and bare of almost any cover.

Estimated by the eye of an expert in tactics, it would surely be reckoned as completely impregnable to the assault, unaided by tanks, of any infantry that should attempt it.

It was the seizure, by a sudden attack, of this tactical key that was the kernel of the plan which now had to be evolved. The capture of the town of Péronne was consequential upon it, though little less formidable a task. The effect of both captures would be completely to turn the whole line of the Somme to the south, and the line of the Canal du Nord; to open a wide gate through which the remainder of the Fourth and Third Armies could pour, so as to roll up the enemy's line in both directions.

In view of the historical importance of the occasion, and the controversies which have already risen regarding the genesis of the conception of these plans, I make no apology for reproducing, *in extenso*, a literal copy of the notes used at the conference which I held in the late afternoon of August 29th at the Headquarters of the Fifth Division, then situated in a group of bare sheds—but recently vacated by the enemy—on the main east and west road, just south of Proyart. The conference was attended by Lambert (32nd Division), Hobbs (Fifth Division), Rosenthal (Second Division), and Gellibrand (Third Division). Neither "Tanks" nor "Heavy Artillery" attended as they could not, in any event, co-operate in the execution of the plan.

29. 8. 18.

Plan for Crossing the Somme

A. Alteration of Frontages.

Defensive Front: 32nd Division to take over on 30th from Fifth Division front as far north as Ferme Lamire, total 7,500 yards, to hold same defensively, place outposts on river line, demonstrate actively as if aiming to cross Somme; if no resistance, endeavour establish posts on far bank; otherwise demonstrate only. Use only one brigade; remainder of division to rest and refit.

Offensive Frontages: Fifth Division to extend along canal bank from Ferme Lamire to Biaches, frontage 4,000 yards. Second Division to extend from Biaches for 4,700 yards to bridge at Ommiécourt. Third Division: present front north of river.

B. Objectives.

All divisions to continue eastward advance. Each division to have an immediate and an ultimate objective, thus:

Third Division :	Immediate :	High ground north-east of Cléry.
	Ultimate :	Bouchavesnes Spur.
Second Division :	Immediate :	Bridge Head at Halle. If crossing there impossible then cross behind front of Third Division.
	Ultimate :	Mont St. Quentin.
Fifth Division :	Immediate :	Force crossing at Péronne Bridges ; if bridges gone, follow Second Division and aim at high ground south of Péronne.
	Ultimate :	Wooded spur east of Péronne.

Whic... lley, the other di... ry footing is established on immediate objective.

Second Division to lead the north-east movement.

Artillery to stand as at present allotted, but liable to re-allotment by me as operation develops.

The above brief notes require but little elucidation. It is to be remembered that at the time they were prepared, no definite information had yet been received as to the condition of any of the Somme crossings, because at that hour the river bank had not yet been reached, and fighting on the west bank of the Somme was still going on.

It has also to be remembered that these notes were only for my own guidance in verbally expounding the plan, and were not actually issued as written orders. Naturally many details, left unexpressed by the notes, were filled in during the conference. Moreover, I anticipated that the whole operation would be one of a nature in which I would have to intervene as the battle proceeded, in accordance with the varying situation from time to time, and this actually proved to be necessary.

It will be noted that on August 29th I had already reached the definite decision not to attempt to force the passage of the Somme south of Péronne; the 32nd Division was, however, instructed to make every demonstration of a desire to attempt it, the object being to divert the attention of the enemy from the real point of attack.

This was to be launched from the direction of Cléry. In preparation for it, the Second Division sent its reserve brigade, the 5th (Martin), to cross the river at Feuillères, on August 30th, to pass through the area and front of the Third Division, and secure a bridge head on the Cléry side of the river, opposite to the Ommiécourt bend. The object was to exploit the possibility of using the Ommiécourt crossing, and if it were found to be intact to use it for the purpose of crossing with the remaining two brigades that same night.

This move was successfully accomplished, although the 5th Brigade found portion of the village of Cléry still occupied, and that the trench systems to the east of it were still held in strength. After much skilful fighting, the brigade reached its allotted destination, with slight casualties, capturing seven machine-guns and 120 prisoners.

The bridge at Ommiécourt was found to be damaged, but repairable so as to be usable by infantry on foot, and this work was at once put in hand. The same night the re-arrangement of the fronts of all four divisions in the line was carried out, and all was in readiness for the daring attempt to break the line of the Somme.

During the afternoon of August 30th, General Rawlinson came to see me, and I unfolded to him the details of the operations contemplated and the arrangements made for the next day. I have already referred to the pleasant and attractive personality of this distinguished soldier. His qualities of broad outlook, searching insight, great sagacity, and strong determination, tempered by a wise restraint, never failed to impress me deeply. He always listened sympathetically, and responded convincingly. On this occasion he was pleased to be pleasantly satirical. "And so, you think you're going to take Mont St. Quentin with three battalions! What presumption! However, I don't think I ought to stop you! So, go ahead, and try!—and I wish you luck!"

Chapter 11
Mont St. Quentin and Péronne

From early dawn on Saturday, August 31st, until the evening of September 3rd, three divisions of the Australian Corps engaged in a heroic combat which will ever be memorable in Australian history.

At its conclusion we emerged complete masters of the situation. Mont St. Quentin, the Bouchavesnes spur, the large town of Péronne, and the high ground overlooking it from the east and north-east, were in our possession. A wide breach had been driven into the line of defence which the enemy had endeavoured to establish on the series of heights lying to the east of the Somme and of the Canal du Nord.

From the edges of this breach, the flanks of that portion of his line which were still intact were being threatened with envelopment. For him there was nothing for it, but finally to abandon the line of the Somme, and to resume his retreat helter-skelter to the hoped-for secure protection of the great Hindenburg Line.

The extraordinary character of this Australian feat of arms can best be appreciated by a realisation of the supreme efforts which the enemy put forward to prevent it. The shower of blows which he had received on the front of his Second Army from August 8th onwards, had wrought upon it a grievous disorganisation. The battered remnants of his line divisions had been reinforced from day to day by fresh units, scraped up from other parts of his front, and thrown into the fight as fast as they could be made available.

Sometimes they were complete divisions from reserve, often single reserve regiments of divisions already deeply involved, and sometimes even single battalions torn from other regiments—Pioneer battalions, units of the Labour Corps, Army Troops, Minenwerfer Companies had all been thrown in, indiscriminately.

This brought about a heterogeneous jumble of units, and of German nationalities, for Prussians, Bavarians, Saxons and Württembergers were captured side by side. The tactical control of such mixed forces, during a hasty and enforced retreat, and their daily maintenance, must have presented sore perplexities to the Headquarters of the German Second Army in those fateful days.

To meet the crisis with which Ludendorff was now confronted, he determined to throw in one of the finest of the reserve divisions still left at his disposal. The Second Prussian Guards Division was sent forward to occupy the key position of Mont St. Quentin, and to hold it at all costs. This famous division comprised among its units, the Kaiserin Augusta and the Kaiser Alexander Regiments, almost as famous in history and rich in tradition as are our own Grenadiers and Coldstreams. There is no doubt that this celebrated Division fought desperately to obey its instructions.

For the defence of Péronne, the enemy command went even further, and called for volunteers, forming with them a strong garrison of picked men drawn from many different line regiments, to man the ramparts which surround the town. Dozens of machine-guns were posted in vantage points from which the approaches could be swept.

All over the river flats lying in the angle of the Somme between Cléry, Mont St. Quentin and Péronne ran line upon line of barbed wire entanglements, a legacy from the 1916 fighting, and much of this was still intact, although breaches had been made in many places both by the French in 1917 and by the Germans themselves, to facilitate movement over the ground, during their respective re-occupations of this territory. The terrain, which was in greater part open, and exposed in every direction to full view from the heights, sloped gently upwards towards the commanding knoll. Cover was scarce, and the few ruins of brickfields and sugar refineries which dotted the landscape had also been garrisoned by the enemy as centres of resistance, designed to break up and dislocate any general attack.

Our infantry was deprived of the assistance of any tanks, for the heavy casualties which had been suffered by this arm made it imperative to allow the Tank Corps time for repairs, renewals and the training of fresh crews. Nor was any appreciable quantity of heavy artillery yet available, since the congested and dilapidated condition of the roads prevented the advance of all but a few of the lighter varieties of heavy guns. The fighting of these four days was, therefore, essentially a pure infantry combat, assisted only by such mobile artillery of lesser calibres as was available.

Such was the formidable nature of the task, and of the disabilities under which the Second, Third and Fifth Divisions approached it. That they overcame all obstacles, gained all their objectives, and captured nearly 2,000 prisoners, mainly from crack Prussian regiments, constitutes an achievement memorable in military annals and standing to the everlasting glory of the troops who took part in it.

★★★★★★

The following telegram, selected at random from the files of September 1st, indicates the extraordinary mixture of units

which the enemy had collected to defend this vital point:
"To Australian Corps Intelligence from 2nd Division—sent September 1st at 7 p.m. Identifications from prisoners examined since noon: 28th R.I.R.; 65th I.R.; 161st I.R.; 94th I.R.; 95th I.R.; 96th I.R.; Alexander Regt.; Augusta Regt.; 4th Bav. I.R.; 8th Bav. I.R.; 25th Bav. I.R.; 447th I.R.; 2nd G. Guard F.A.R.; 221st F.A.R.; 2nd Co. M.G. Corps; 67th Pioneer Co.; 23rd Army Troops; 102nd Pioneer Bn. of 2nd Guards Div.; 402nd M.W. Co.; 185th R.I.R. A pioneer of the 23rd Co. has been retained for 5th Aust. Div. to remove charges from bridges not yet blown. Prisoner 96th I.R. says regt. came up for counter-attack night 31-1 to retake Mt. St. Quentin, but counter-attack did not come off, owing to attack expected from us. All prisoners interrogated agree that line was to be held at all costs. Regiments are now considerably intermingled and disorganised."

(Note.—I.R.—Infanterie Regiment; R.I.R.—Reserve Infanterie Regiment; M.W. Co.—Minenwerfer Compagnie; Bav.—Bavarian.)

★★★★★★

It is difficult to write a connected and consecutive account of the details of the fighting which took place. The most that is possible in the brief space available is to indicate on general lines the successive stages of the battle. Indeed, a minute account of the action of each of the 35 battalions engaged would only prove wearisome and confusing. The best method of presenting a general picture of the course of the engagement is to follow the fortunes of each brigade in turn.

First in order of time, and of most importance in relation to its immediate results, was the action of the Second Division. It was the 5th Brigade (Martin) which Major-General Rosenthal had detailed to open the attack. The remaining two brigades of the divisions (6th and 7th) received orders to rest the troops as much as possible, but to be in readiness to move at the shortest notice. A Machine-gun Company (16 guns) was placed at the disposal of Brigadier-General Martin, while the artillery at the disposal of the division, comprising five brigades of field artillery and one brigade of heavy artillery, remained under the personal control of the divisional commander.

The attack opened with three battalions of the 5th Brigade in the first line, and one battalion in support. The total strength of the assaulting infantry of this whole brigade was on this day not more than

70 officers and 1,250 other ranks. The centre battalion was directed straight at the highest knoll of Mont St. Quentin, while the right battalion prolonged the line to the right. The left battalion had assigned to it as an immediate objective the ruins of the village of Feuillaucourt, from which it was hoped that a flank attack upon the Mount could be developed.

The advance began at 5 a.m. It was a dull morning and still quite dark. The two right battalions advanced with as much noise as possible, a ruse which secured the surrender of numbers of the enemy lying out in advanced outpost positions. A nest of seven machine-guns was rushed and captured without any loss to us.

At the appointed hour, our artillery opened on selected targets, the ranges being lengthened from moment to moment in sympathy with the advance of the infantry. Although during the advance a great deal of machine-gun fire was encountered, all went well. The centre and left battalions gained a footing respectively in Feuillaucourt and on the main hill, but the progress of the right battalion was arrested by heavy machine-gun fire from St. Denis. This was the site of a ruined sugar refinery, and lay on the main road between Péronne and Mont St. Quentin. It was a strong point that presented a great deal of difficulty and held out to the last.

The centre battalion had by 7 a.m. passed through the ruins of Mont St. Quentin village and had crossed the main road from Péronne to Bouchavesnes. It now had to receive the full brunt of a determined counter attack, at a moment when it was still disorganised and breathless from its difficult assault. The battalion was therefore withdrawn across the road and firmly established itself in an old trench system to the west of it.

In this position it beat off five successive counter attacks, inflicting most severe losses upon the enemy. The brigade maintained its position until nightfall. Its losses for the day were 380.

In the meantime, the 6th Brigade (Robertson) of the Second Division had been ordered to cross the Somme and move up behind the 5th Brigade, in readiness to carry on the attack, and obtain possession of the remainder of the main spur of Mont St. Quentin. As this brigade only entered into the fight at a later hour, I must revert to the events of the forenoon of August 31st.

It was about 8 a.m. that I was able to report to General Rawlinson, by telephone, that we had obtained a footing on Mont St. Quentin itself. He was at first totally incredulous, but soon generously congratulatory, proclaiming that the event was calculated to have a most important influence upon the immediate future course of the war. He expressed the hope that we should be able to hold on to all that we had gained.

To this task I now had to bend myself, and I found it necessary to put a severe strain upon the endurance and capacity of the troops. Great as had always been my concern in the pitched battles of the days recently passed to reduce to very definite limits the demands made upon the physical powers of the infantry soldier, a juncture had arrived and a situation had been created, which demanded the utmost rapidity in decision and action, and a relentless insistence upon prompt response by the troops.

The 5th Brigade had been thrust out nearly two miles beyond our general line. Its flanks were in the air. It was undoubtedly fatigued. Everything must be done and done promptly to render it adequate support, to take advantage of its success, and to ensure that its effort had not been in vain.

It will be remembered that the Fifth and Second Divisions had both been instructed to endeavour to secure a crossing over the river. Whichever division first succeeded was to accord right of way to its neighbour. No success had yet attended the efforts of the Fifth Division, the main Péronne bridges being still inaccessible from the south. The bridge sites were under the enemy's fire, which precluded the possibility of repair; and the approaches to them were also swept by machine-gun fire.

The Second Division, on the other hand, had during the past 48 hours succeeded in making the Feuillères bridge trafficable for guns and vehicles, and those at Buscourt and Ommiécourt for foot traffic. It transpired later that the enemy, rightly suspecting that I would attempt to use this latter crossing, kept it under heavy artillery fire all day.

As soon as I had formed a judgment on the situation, about 8.30 a.m. (August 31st), I issued instructions to General Hobbs immediately to put in motion his reserve brigade, the 14th (Stewart). He was to direct it towards the Ommiécourt crossing, and later in the day to pass it across the river and through the ground won that morning by the 5th Brigade, with a view to developing at the earliest possible moment an attack in a south-easterly direction upon the town of Péronne itself. The ultimate objective was still to be the high ground south and east of Péronne. His 8th Brigade was also to be held ready to move at the shortest notice.

It was a serious performance to demand, and it was fraught with many risks. There was no time to assemble responsible commanders concerned, separated as they were by long distances over bad and congested roads. In the absence of properly co-ordinated action, there was every chance of confusion, and cross-purposes, and even of collision of authority arising from the troops of one division passing over ground under the tactical control of another division.

But the only alternative was to do nothing and attempt nothing. That would have been the worst of bad generalship, and it was an occasion when risks must be taken.

The course of subsequent events fully demonstrated that the only true solution was the one chosen, for the whole of the defences of Péronne were thereby taken with a rush, while they were still being organised by the enemy. The delay of only a day or two would have meant that the capture of Péronne would have been many times more costly than it actually proved to be.

The 14th Brigade had before it a march of some seven miles to bring it into a position in which it could deploy for an attack on Péronne. Working according to text book such a march could have been accomplished in something under three hours. It took the brigade over ten hours. For the line of march lay across the very worst of the shell-torn, tangled country enclosed in the great bend of the Somme, and progress was most difficult and exhausting. Frequent halts were necessary to rest the men, and restore order to the struggling columns.

Discovering the impossibility of crossing the river at Ommiécourt, the brigade made a wide detour to cross by the newly established bridge at Buscourt. It arrived there just at the same time as the 7th Brigade (Wisdom), which Rosenthal had also directed to the same point for the same purpose. This occurrence illustrates the nature of the risks of a hastily developed tactical plan. However, the good sense of the commanders on the spot obviated any serious confusion and the 7th Brigade gave the 14th Brigade the right of way.

The 14th Brigade completed its march during the hours of falling darkness and, passing through Cléry, came up on the right of the 6th Brigade, in readiness for the combined attack by the two divisions at dawn on September 1st.

The night that followed was a stressful one for all commanders. Divisional generals had to co-ordinate all action between their brigadiers, and their artillery. The brigadiers in turn had afterwards to assemble their battalion commanders, and decide on detailed plans of action for each separate unit. Distances were long, the country was strange, roads were few and unfamiliar; so that it is not surprising that the last conferences did not break up until well into the small hours of September 1st. There was no sleep that night for any senior officer in the battle area.

September 1st was a day full of great happenings and bloody hand to hand fighting. The assault by the 6th Brigade passing over the line won the day before by the 5th Brigade carried it well over the crest of Mont St. Quentin, and confirmed for good and all our hold on that imperious fortress. Few prisoners were taken, for it was bayonet work over every inch of the advance, and the field was strewn all over with enemy dead. The impetus of the 6th Brigade assault carried our line 600 yards to the east of the summit of the knoll.

It is difficult to allocate, in due proportion, the credit for the capture of this important stronghold between the two gallant Brigades concerned. It is true that the 6th Brigade did on September 1st achieve the summit of the Mount; but it is equally true that it only completed what the 5th Brigade had so wonderfully begun the day before. No one will grudge to either of the two brigades their share of the honour that is due to both. The action of the Second Division on that day was completed by the bringing up of the 7th Brigade into a position of support behind the 6th Brigade, thereby relieving the 5th Brigade from further line duty.

Although the action of the individual brigades of all the three battle divisions must necessarily be narrated separately and with some attempt at a proper chronological sequence, yet it would be a mistake to suppose that their actions were independent of each other. On the contrary, they all operated as part of a comprehensive battle plan, which necessarily took full account of the interdependence of the course of events in different parts of the field.

Thus, the advance on this day of the 6th Brigade materially assisted the attack on Péronne by the 14th Brigade, while the progress of the latter removed much trouble from the southern flank of the 6th Brigade.

The men of the 14th Brigade that day had their mettle up to a degree which was astonishing. On the occasion of the great attack of August 8th, and ever since, it had been the cruel fate of this brigade to be the reserve unit of its division on every occasion when there was any serious fighting in hand. The brigade felt its position very keenly. As one company commander, who distinguished himself in that day's fighting, afterwards picturesquely put it: "You see! We'd been trying to buy a fight off the other fellows for a matter of three weeks. On that day we got what we'd been looking for, and we made the most of it."

******

Mr. Hughes, the Commonwealth Prime Minister, visited the battlefield of Mont St. Quentin, with a distinguished company, on September 14th. The officer in question, standing near the summit of the hill, was about to relate his experiences, and this was his preamble.

******

The 14th Brigade advanced to the assault at 6 a.m. concurrently with the eastern thrust of the 6th Brigade. One Battalion, with two others in support, was directed against St. Denis, while the fourth made a direct attack on Péronne. Many belts of wire had to be struggled through. There was much machine-gun fire, from front and flanks, and it looked as if further progress would be impossible. Nevertheless, this gallant brigade, by persistent effort, made itself master of the western half of Péronne.

The attack on St. Denis at first made very slow progress, the enemy holding out resolutely in the ruins of that hamlet, and in the adjacent brickfields. During the day, the 15th Brigade made spirited attempts to effect the crossing of the river, and to co-operate from the south.

The records of the events of these three days are confused and discontinuous. Many of the men who could have filled in the gaps of the story were unfortunately killed or evacuated as casualties. But from the mass of reports, the salient facts emerge clearly.

The 15th Brigade succeeded, on September 2nd, in putting a battalion across the river, and this assisted the 14th Brigade to "mop up" the remainder of the town of Péronne. Later the rest of the 15th Brigade and two battalions of the 8th Brigade (Tivey) were also drawn into the fighting. St. Denis and the brickfields fell to us during this period. Although the situation, from the point of view of the advance eastwards, remained almost stationary, it was a time of fierce local fighting. Many deeds of valour and sacrifice adorn the story.

It was late on September 3rd that the effects of this long-sustained struggle became apparent. The whole of Péronne and most of the high ground in its vicinity were, by then, definitely in our hands, and although the little suburb of Flamicourt held out determinedly for another day, the further resistance of the enemy began to fade away.

Doubtless the loss of Mont St. Quentin was a controlling factor in the decision which was forced upon him to undertake a retreat, for with that eminence in our possession, he could not have maintained himself for many days in the town, nor would its retention have been of any tactical value to him.

As an immediate result, the high ground of the Flamicourt Spur just south of Péronne fell into our hands on September 3rd, and the enemy outposts spread along the banks of the marsh in front of the 32nd Division sought safety from complete envelopment by a hasty withdrawal; a number of their isolated posts were, however, left unwarned of this retreat, so that these were, later on, captured by us from the rear.

I must now briefly turn to the doings of the Third Australian Division during these four epic days. Its three brigades (9th, 10th and 11th) daily performed prodigies of valour. The division carried our line, inexorably, up the Bouchavesnes spur in a north-easterly direction. The seizure of this very important ground not only powerfully aided but also strongly confirmed our seizure of Mont St. Quentin.

The division, having been given its general role, was necessarily left to a large extent to decide for itself its detailed action from day to day, seeing that it still had to perform the function, inevitable for a flank division, of a link with my neighbouring corps. Fortunately the arrival of a new, fresh division (the 74th) from the Eastern theatre of war, which came into the Third Corps and was promptly thrown in, enabled that corps to keep up fairly well with the general advance.

The British Third Army, too, was now beginning to make its pressure felt, and was approaching the line of the Canal du Nord over a wide front. The Third Division was therefore free to conform its forward movement to that of the rest of the Australian Corps; its energetic action gave me elbow room for the manoeuvring of so many brigades in the region of Cléry, and its capture of so much valuable ground east of the Canal du Nord served greatly to widen the breach.

By the night of September 3rd, the main tactical purposes on which the corps had been launched on August 29th had been achieved in their entirety. Their execution furnishes the finest example in the war of spirited and successful infantry action conducted by three whole divisions operating simultaneously side by side.

Lord Rawlinson has more than once referred to the operation as the finest single feat of the war. Inevitably the dramatic and unlooked for success of the Second Division in the rapid storming of the Mount enthrals the imagination and overshadows all the other noteworthy incidents of these pregnant days. But none will begrudge the

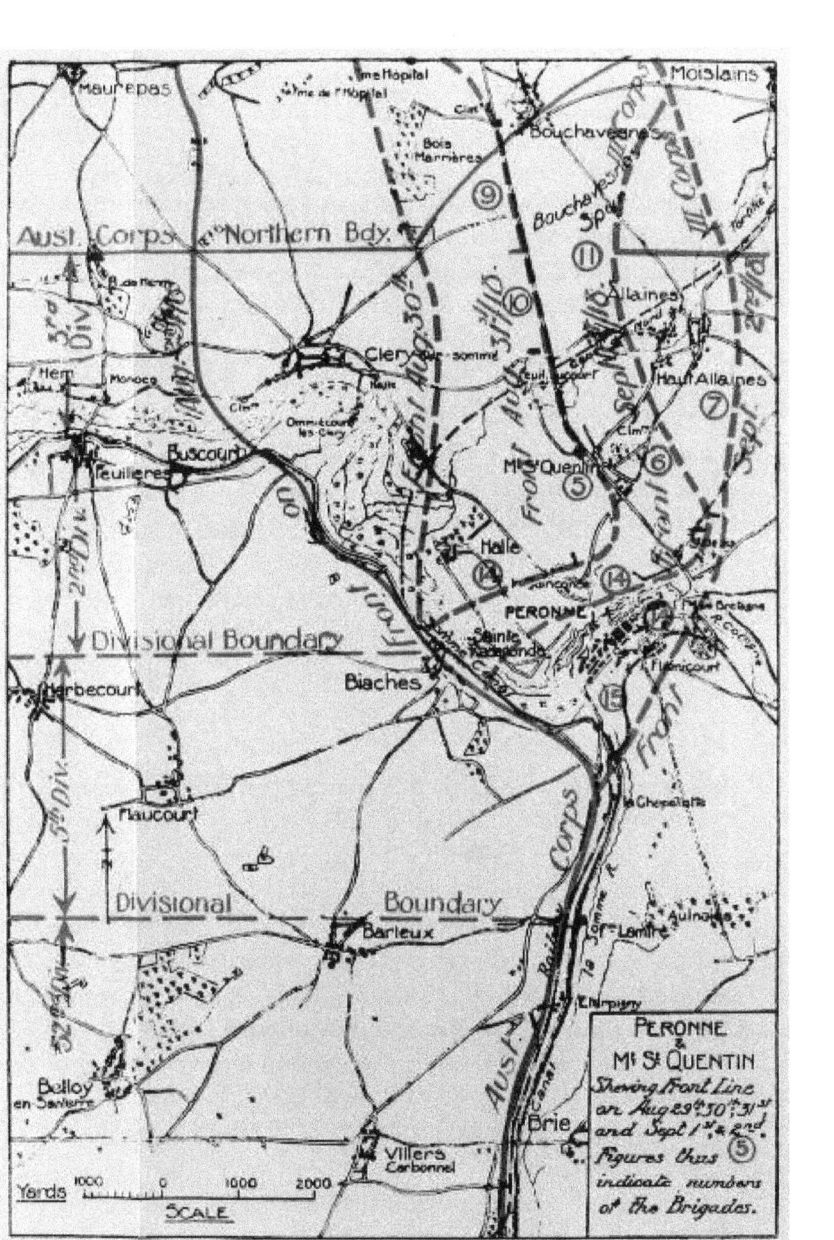

rain of congratulations which fell upon the head of Major-General Rosenthal. A massive man, whose build belies his extraordinary physical energy, he always was an egregious optimist, incapable of recognising the possibility of failure.

That is why he invariably succeeded in all that he undertook, and often embarked upon the apparently impossible. An architect before the war, he served for the first two years as an artillery officer, both as a brigade commander and as a general of divisional artillery. He gained his infantry experience as commander of the 9th Brigade, and so was well qualified by versatile service to assume the command of the Second Division. His leadership of the latter contributed in no small measure to the fame which it has won.

The text of the congratulatory message issued on this occasion by the Fourth Army read as follows:

> The capture of Mont St. Quentin by the Second Division is a feat of arms worthy of the highest praise. The natural strength of the position is immense, and the tactical value of it, in reference to Péronne and the whole system of the Somme defences, cannot be over-estimated. I am filled with admiration at the gallantry and surpassing daring of the Second Division in winning this important fortress, and I congratulate them with all my heart.
>
> Rawlinson.

I am concerned nevertheless that the fine performance of the Fifth Division should not be underrated. The circumstances under which General Hobbs was called upon to intervene in the battle, at very short notice, imposed upon him, personally, difficulties of no mean order. I am prepared to admit quite frankly that the demands which I had to make upon him, his staff and his division were severe.

Following upon four days of arduous pursuit, his troops were called upon to undertake a long and difficult march over a most broken country, to be followed by three days of intensive fighting of the most severe character.

General Hobbs was, first and foremost, a lover of the Australian soldiers, and their devoted servitor. He belonged to that type of citizen-soldier who, before the war, had spent long years in preparing himself for a day when his country would surely require his military services. Like several of the most successful of Australia's generals, he had specialised in artillery, and was, in fact, selected as the senior artillery commander of Australia's first contingent. That fact alone was the stamp of his ability. While he would be the last to lay claim to special brilliance, or outstanding military genius, he nevertheless succeeded fully as the commander of a division, by his sound common sense, and his sane attitude towards every problem that confronted him. He possessed also the virtue of a large-hearted sympathy for all subordinate to him; and that gave him a loyal following, which carried him successfully through several great crises in the affairs of the Fifth Division.

This period was one of those crises. When, late on the afternoon of August 31st, he urged upon me with much earnestness the stress upon his troops, and repeated the anxious representations of his brigadiers—I was compelled to harden my heart and to insist that it was imperative to recognise a great opportunity and to seize it unflinchingly. His response was loyal and whole-hearted. His division followed the lead which he thus gave them, and he led them to imperishable fame.

Considerable re-dispositions followed upon the transfer of my battle front to the country east of the Somme. These, and the reasons which governed their nature, chief among which was the resumption of the enemy's rearward movement, I shall deal with in due course.

Battle problems on the grand scale were, for the moment, relegated to the background, and there now arose a multitude of other problems, almost equally burdensome, relating to the supply and maintenance of the corps.

Every corps must be based upon a thoroughly reliable and efficient line of supply, and for this a railway in first-class operating condition is a prime essential. Every kind of requisite must be carried by rail to some advanced distribution point called a "railhead". Thence supplies are distributed by motor lorry to the areas still further forward.

The appropriate distance of the railhead behind the battle front is conditioned by the available supply of motor lorries, and their range of action. If the distance be too great the stress upon the mechanical transport becomes so severe that it rapidly deteriorates, and an undue proportion of lorries daily falls out of service. As the facilities for repair in the mobile workshops are strictly limited, an excessive rate of wastage among these vehicles soon dislocates the whole supply arrangements.

The experience hitherto gained had demonstrated that a railhead could not conveniently be allowed to fall behind our advance more than ten or twelve miles. This limit had already been reached when the corps front arrived on the west bank of the Somme, and the strain upon the lorry service was already great.

For a further deep advance of the whole corps in pursuit of the enemy towards the Hindenburg Line, still distant another fifteen miles, it became imperative, therefore, that the railway service to Péronne and beyond should be speedily re-opened, or some equally efficient alternative provided. The great lattice girder railway bridge at Péronne had been irretrievably demolished. Engineers estimated that it would take two months to restore it, and at least a month to provide even a temporary deviation and crossing. Nevertheless, the work was put in hand without delay.

An alternative possibility was to construct a new line of railway to connect the existing military line at Bray to the Péronne railway station, a length of new construction amounting to some six miles. It was estimated that such a link could be built in a fortnight, and this work also was commenced forthwith.

There was a third possibility. This was speedily to repair that portion of the railway which lay west of the Somme, and to establish a railhead near Péronne, but on the opposite bank of the river. This proposal involved only a few days' work, for extensive sidings already existed on the west bank, and had been left more or less undamaged by the enemy. But it also involved the complete restoration of all road traffic bridges, both at Péronne and at Brie, for the service of the intense traffic which would ensue across the Somme from such a point of departure.

The rebuilding of the crossings was, in any case, a matter of urgent necessity. By this time all my heaviest guns had already been brought up to the vicinity of the west bank of the Somme, and had there perforce to wait; for a long detour, on the densely-crowded roads, to cross the Somme, say as far back as Corbie, where bridges were strong and grades were easy, was out of the question.

The problem, therefore, involved a stable and comprehensive reconstruction; half measures would not meet the case. But half measures were an inevitable necessity of the situation, to begin with, because troops had to be fed, and their supplies could be carried in no lighter way, in adequate quantities, than in the normal horse-transport wagons.

The order of procedure had, therefore, to be, firstly, hastily to reconstruct some sort of bridging, based generally upon the wreckage of the original bridge, and strong enough to carry loads up to those of horsed wagons; next to stay, strut and strengthen these temporary bridges to fit them for the passage of the lighter guns, and finally to reconstruct them in their entirety for the heaviest loads.

At a point such as the southern entrance to Péronne, where the approaches could not be conveniently deviated, the difficulties of such successive reconstructions, while the flow of traffic had to be maintained, can hardly be fully realised.

For many days, in the early part of September, Brie, Eterpigny and Péronne were scenes of feverish activity. Every available technical unit that could be spared from other urgent duty was concentrated upon this vital work. Most of the Engineer Field Companies, three of the five pioneer battalions, both Tunnelling Companies, and all the Army Troops Companies, laboured in relays, night and day.

Hundreds of tons of steel girders, of all lengths and sections, were hurried up, by special lorry service. Pile-driving gear was hastily improvised. The wreckage of the original bridges was overhauled for sound, useful timbers. The torn and twisted steelwork was dragged out of the way by horse or steam power, and tumbled in a confused mass into the river bed. Hammer, saw and axe were wielded with a zest and vigour rarely seen in peace-time construction. The whole work was supervised by my chief engineer, Brigadier-General Foott, and was later, when the advance of the corps was resumed, completed by the army authorities. The speed and punctuality with which the first temporary viaducts were completed and ready for use were exemplary, and reflect every credit upon Foott and his helpers. Within forty-eight hours bridges usable for ordinary supplies and for field guns became available, and thereafter were rapidly strengthened by successive stages.

The whole work of restoration, in which the Australian technical services played so prominent a part, won the highest praise from the field marshal, who expressed his appreciation in a special message of thanks to these services.

The congestion of traffic at the Péronne bottleneck was, however, serious. Blocks occurred, reminiscent of those which are familiar in the heart of London when the dense traffic is temporarily held up by a passing procession. Marching troops always had the right of way; and a division on the move up to or back from the line meant a severe super-load upon the already overtaxed road capacity.

Sometimes a block of traffic would occur for an hour at a time, and a motley collection of vehicles, stretching back for miles, would pile up on the roads. The capabilities of a very able road and traffic control service, numbering hundreds of officers and men, acting under the direction of my provost marshal, were often severely tested. More than once my own motorcar was unavoidably held up at this bottleneck for half an hour at a time, on occasions, too, when the situation required

The Hindenburg Line Wire—near Bony.

The 15-inch Naval Gun—captured at Chuignes, August 23rd, 1918.

my urgent presence at some important meeting.

All these minor embarrassments arising from the passage by the Australian Corps of a great military obstacle such as the Somme were, however, soon dissipated. The Somme had loomed large, for many days, in the minds of all of us—first as a problem of tactics, and next as a problem of engineering. Before the end of the first week of September the Somme had ceased to hold our further interest. It had become a thing that was behind us, both in thought and in actuality.

The enemy was once more on the move, and it became our business to press relentlessly on his heels.

CHAPTER 12
A Lull

During the closing days of August events had commenced to move rapidly; for the offensive activities initiated by the Fourth Army, three weeks earlier, began to spread in both directions along the Allied front.

The Third British Army had entered the fray on August 21st; the First British Army was ready with its offensive on August 26th, on which date the Canadian Corps, restored to its old familiar battleground, delivered a great attack opposite Arras.

The French, who, on my right flank, had along their front followed up the enemy retirement begun after the Battle of Chuignes, reached Roye on August 27th, and Noyon on August 28th. Their line, however, still bore back south-westerly from the vicinity of the river near Brie and St. Christ.

By August 29th the line of the First Army had reached and passed Bapaume, and that of the Third Army cut through Combles. The Third Corps, on my immediate left, had made good its advance as far as Maurepas. Thus, the thrust of the Australian Corps beyond the Canal du Nord, on August 31st to September, 3rd, formed the spearhead which pierced the Somme line, and the corps was still leading the advance both of the French and the British.

From the morning of September 4th, the evidences of the enemy's resolution to withdraw to the Hindenburg Line became hourly more unmistakable. His artillery fire died down considerably, particularly that from his long range and high velocity guns. These were probably already on the move to the rear, in order to clear the roads for his lighter traffic.

The high ground near Biaches (west of Péronne) provided a vantage point from which an extensive view of the whole country could be obtained. There lay before us, beyond the Somme, a belt about eight miles deep, which had scarcely suffered at all from the ravages of the previous years of war. It was gently undulating country, liberally watered, and heavily wooded, especially in the minor valleys, in which snuggled numerous villages still almost intact and habitable, although, of course, entirely deserted by the civilian population.

Beyond this agreeable region there began again an area of devastation, which grew in awful thoroughness as the great Hindenburg Line was approached some six miles further on. For, through the autumn and winter of 1917, and up to the moment of the German offensive in March, 1918, it was there that the British Fifth Army had faced the enemy in intensive trench fighting.

In all directions over this still habitable belt there were now signs of unusual life and activity. Columns of smoke began to rise in the direction of all the villages. Sounds of great explosions rent the air. These were sure indications that the enemy was burning the stores which he could not hope to salve, and was destroying his ammunition dumps lest they should fall into our hands.

A vigorous pursuit was now the policy most to be desired. But my troops in the line were very tired from the exertions of a great struggle, and many of the units, by reason of their battle losses, required time to reorganise and refit. It was also essential that no rapid advance should be attempted until the arrangements for supply, depending upon the completion of the Somme crossings, had been assured.

The general line of advance of the corps had, during August, been in a due easterly direction. The operations about Péronne had necessitated a drive north-easterly, and the advance of my Third Division up the Bouchavesnes Spur had carried them square across the line of advance of the Third Corps.

The first step was to restore our original corps boundaries, and to resume the original line of advance. By arrangement with General Godley, his 74th Division took over the ground captured by my Third Division, which was thereby released and enabled to concentrate, for a couple of days' rest, in the Cléry region. The Second Division employed its 7th Brigade on September 2nd and 3rd to advance our line beyond Haut Allaines, another two miles east of Mont St. Quentin, routing from the trenches of that spur the strong rear-guards which the enemy had posted for the purpose of delaying us.

On the night of September 4th, the 74th Division took over the Haut Allaines spur also, thereby releasing my Second Division, and the latter was withdrawn to the Cappy area for a thorough and well-deserved rest. Meanwhile, the 32nd Imperial Division, availing itself of the temporary crossings which had hastily been effected over the Somme, brought its front up, on the eastern bank of the river, level with the line which had by September 4th been reached by the Fifth Australian Division.

On September 5th, therefore, I had, east of the Somme, two divisions in the line, the 32nd on the right or south, the Fifth Australian on the left or north, each operating on a frontage of two brigades, with one brigade in reserve. This was, however, quite a temporary arrangement, devised merely to allow time for the Third Division to reorganise and resume its place in the front line of the general advance.

The general withdrawal of the enemy, over a very wide front, now began to effect a very substantial reduction of the length of frontage which he had to defend. The enemy *communiqués* and wireless propaganda of that time busied themselves with the explanation that the withdrawals in progress were being deliberately carried out for the very purpose of releasing forces from the line to form a great strategic reserve. These protestations did not deceive us, nor did we on our part fail also to take full advantage of the steady shortenings of the Allied front. Marshal Foch decided once again to readjust the international boundary, and my own front was thereby considerably shortened. The French took over from the 32nd Division all ground south of the main Amiens-St. Quentin road; and that road henceforth became my southern boundary.

This, coupled with the re-adjustment of the northern boundary with the Third Corps, as already narrated, reduced the total frontage for which I remained responsible to about ten thousand yards, an extent which was never again exceeded. It was still, however, in my judgment, too long a frontage for an effective pursuit by only two Divisions, and arrangements were initiated on the same day to bring back the Third Division into line.

During September 5th I advanced my front to the line Athies-Le Mesnil-Doingt-Bussy. Severe fighting took place near Doingt. Opposition came mainly from machine-guns; but isolated field-guns also gave us trouble. We captured that day about a hundred and fifty prisoners. Next day my Third Division came into the line on the north. I divided my frontage equally between the three divisions, placing each on a single Brigade front. This was, in fact, a repetition of the order of battle which had carried us so successfully and rapidly up to the Somme.

Each front line brigade took up the role of Advanced Guard to its division. The 11th Brigade led the Third Division; the 8th Brigade led the Fifth Division, while the 97th Brigade covered the 32nd Imperial Division. For the first time in the war I found an opportunity of employing my corps cavalry (13th Australian Light Horse) on other than their habitual duty of carrying despatches, or providing mounted escorts to convoys of prisoners of war. Here at last was a chance for bold mounted tactics, as the country was mainly open and free of wire and trenches. To each division I therefore allotted a squadron of light horse for vanguard duty, together with detachments of the Australian Cyclist Battalion. These troops more than justified their employment by bold, forward reconnaissance, and energetic pressure upon the enemy rear-guards.

So promising, indeed, was the prospect of the useful employment of cavalry, that I prevailed upon the army commander to endeavour to secure for my use a whole cavalry brigade. Brigadier-General Neil Haig (cousin of the field marshal) was actually sent for and placed under my orders. I duly arranged a plan of action with him, but before the 1st Cavalry Brigade, stationed many miles away, had completed its long march into my area, the situation had already changed, and the employment of cavalry on the Fourth Army front had to be postponed until a much later date.

A juncture had arrived when it became imperative for me to consider the possibility of affording some relief to the three line divisions; all of them had been fighting without respite since August 27th. The troops were so tired from want of sleep and physical strain that many of them could be seen by the roadside, fast asleep. These three divisions had almost reached the limits of their endurance.

It was essential, however, that they should be called upon to yield up the last particle of effort of which they were capable. Every mile by which they could approach nearer to the Hindenburg defences meant a saving of effort on the part of the fresh waiting divisions, whom I had earmarked for the first stage of our contemplated assault upon that formidable system; a system which I knew to be too deep to be overwhelmed in a single operation.

It was for this reason that I was compelled to disregard the evident signs of overstrain which were brought to my notice by the divisional generals and their brigadiers, and which were patent to my own observation of the condition of the troops. I arranged, however, two measures of immediate relief, the first being to set a definite limit of time for the further demands to be made upon the line divisions. This was fixed for September 10th. The second was to issue orders that the rate of our further advance was to be controlled by consideration for the well-being of our own troops, and not by the rate of the enemy's retreat. If, in consequence, any gap should eventuate, touch with the enemy was to be kept by the mounted troops and cyclists.

The preliminary steps for effecting the reliefs thus promised for September 10th were begun on September 5th. The corps was, as stated, on a three division front. I had only two fit divisions in Corps Reserve (*i.e.*, the First and Fourth), the Second Division being not yet rested. My representations to the army commander on this matter bore immediate fruit; for he placed under my orders the Sixth (Imperial) Division one of the first seven divisions of the original Expeditionary Force). Before, however, I could take advantage of this windfall, the constitution of the Fourth Army underwent a vital alteration, of which more will be told later.

The First and Fourth Divisions had been resting since August 26th. They had had time to reorganise their units, to reclothe and refit their troops, to receive and absorb reinforcements, and to fill vacancies among leaders. Staffs had been able to deal with a mass of arrears. The men had enjoyed a pleasant holiday in the now peaceful Somme Valley, far in rear, a holiday devoted to games and aquatic sports. Horse and man, alike, were refreshed, and had been inspired by the continued successes of the remainder of the corps.

They were however, by now, far in rear; and it was out of the question to tax their restored energies by calling upon them to march back to the battle zone. The Fourth Army, as always, extended its sympathetic help; two motor bus convoys, each capable of dealing with a brigade group a day, were speedily materialised from the resources of G.H.Q. The completion of the moves of these two divisions from the back area to within easy marching distance of the battle front therefore occupied three days. The use of mechanical transport for the execution of troop movements has now entirely passed the experimental stage, and in future wars, calculations of time and space will be vitally affected, whenever an ample supply of lorries or buses and suitable roads are available for the rapid concentration or dispersal of large bodies of troops.

The Australian soldier is individually philosophic and stoical, but in the mass, he is sensitive to a degree; and he is intelligent enough to realise how he is used or misused. It was the subject of complaint among the troops during the earlier years of the war, that while they were indulgently carried by lorries into the battle at a time when they were fresh and fit, they were invariably left to march long distances, out of the battle, when they were on the verge of exhaustion. I therefore tried, whenever possible, to provide tired troops with the means of transport to their rest areas, a facility which was always highly appreciated by them.

By the time the First and Fourth Divisions had thus been assembled in the forward areas, ready to relieve the Third and Fifth Divisions, these latter, together with the 32nd Division, had advanced our front approximately to the line Vermand-Vendelles-Hesbecourt, carrying it to within three miles of the front line of the Hindenburg defence system. There can be no doubt, however, that the rate of our advance, retarded as it had been for the reasons already explained, had proceeded much more rapidly than suited the enemy.

A steady stream of prisoners kept pouring in, captured in twos and threes, all along my front, by my energetic patrols. Numerous machine-guns were taken; and in the vicinity of Roisel, fully three hundred transport vehicles and much engineering material were captured, which the enemy had been compelled to abandon in haste.

At this juncture the British High Command arrived at the important decision to enlarge the Fourth Army, by adding another corps; doubtless contemplating the possibility of operations on a large scale against the Hindenburg defences in the near future.

A new Corps Headquarters, the Ninth, was to be reconstituted under Lieut.-General Braithwaite, and he was to become my neighbour on my southern flank, interposed between me and the French. Braithwaite had been chief of staff to Sir Ian Hamilton during the Dardanelles Expedition, and I had seen much of him there. I was to have the advantage, therefore, of having old Gallipoli comrades on either flank, Braithwaite on the south, and Godley on the north.

The immediate result of this decision, which came into effect early on September 12th, was that the 32nd Division, which had been under my orders for nearly four weeks, passed over to the Ninth Corps. Lambert, his staff and his division had served me well and efficiently, and I was sorry to lose them out of my corps.

With the impending further shortening of my front, I had no justification for pressing to be permitted to retain this division. On the contrary, my representations to General Rawlinson had always been in favour of shortening my frontage to the effective battle standard of

August 8th, so that the corps might at any time be in a position to embark on a major operation, with its whole resources in artillery and infantry concentrated, as on that occasion, upon a relatively narrow objective. My greatly extended front, and the direct control of the affairs of six separate divisions, had been a heavy burden, involving great and manifold responsibilities.

According to my promises to the remaining two line divisions, the Fifth and Third, these were duly relieved on September 10th by the First and Fourth Divisions, the former on the north, the latter on the south. Each division had a frontage of about four thousand yards, but this was to diminish rapidly, if the advance of the corps continued, by reason of the fact that my southern boundary now became the Omignon River, whose course ran obliquely from the north-east. While all these changes in dispositions were being effected, there was breathing time to give attention to a heavy mass of arrears of work; for there could be no question of undertaking an attack on the Hindenburg defences without most careful and exhaustive preparation.

For this the time was not yet ripe. It would still take some days to bring forward the remainder of my heaviest artillery, to advance the railheads, to replenish the ammunition depots and supply dumps, and to re-establish telegraph and telephone communications. Another good reason for a more leisurely policy on the front of the Fourth Army lay in the events on other portions of the Allied fronts. By September 4th the German withdrawal had become general on all fronts.

It had become clear that the enemy's retirement to his former position of March, 1918, was not to be confined to those fronts on which he had been receiving such punishment. All evidence pointed to the fact that his present strategy was to take up as speedily as possible a strong defensive attitude, behind the great system of field works, which had already served him so well during 1917, at a time when a considerable proportion of his military resources was still involved on the Russian and Roumanian fronts.

His retirement before the First and Third British Armies was proceeding methodically, and on September 5th the French were crossing the Vesle, between Rheims and Soissons. All was going well; and those in the confidence of our High Command knew that, on any day now, news might be expected of the first great attack to be made by the American Army, to be directed against the St. Mihiel Salient on the Alsace front. This latter attack actually opened on September 11th, and it was clearly sound military policy to wait for a few days, in order correctly to diagnose the effect of these operations upon the enemy's distribution of forces.

Information as to the locations and movements of all the enemy divisions was in these days voluminous, accurate and speedy. Prisoners and documents were daily falling into the hands of the Allies over the whole length of the Western Front. His divisions in the front line were identified daily by actual contact. As to those resting or refitting or in reserve, accurate deductions could be made from the mass of information at our disposal.

It was at this time that it began to be made clear to us that the enemy's mobile reserves had been almost completely absorbed into the front line. One division after another, particularly among those which had been engaged against the Australian Corps in August, was being disbanded. Among these were the 109th, 225th, 233rd, 54th Reserve, and 14th Bavarian Divisions.

The strength of the enemy's remaining divisions was also rapidly diminishing. From prisoners we learned that many battalions now had only three companies instead of four, many regiments only two battalions instead of three, and even the company strengths were at a low ebb. We could well afford to approach the immediate future with greater deliberation.

Since August 8th, the corps front had already advanced twenty-five miles, and it was not long before I had to abandon the luxurious *château* of the Marquis de Clermont-Tonnere, at Bertangles, whose spacious halls and spreading parks had formed so pleasant a habitation for the whole of my Corps Headquarters.

The scale of comfort possible for all senior commanders and staffs rapidly declined as the advance developed. Generals of corps, divisions and brigades had to be content with living and office quarters in a steadily descending gradation of convenience. From *château* to humbler dwelling house, and thence into bare wooden huts, and later still into mere holes hollowed out in the sides of quarries or railway cuttings, were the stages of progress in this downward scale.

My headquarters moved from Bertangles to a group of village houses at Glisy on August 13th; thence on August 31st to Méricourt, where the best had to be made of a derelict, much battered and almost roofless *château*, which the Germans had rifled of every stick of furniture, and even of all doors and windows, in order to equip a large collection of dug-outs in a neighbouring hill-side.

Again, on September 8th I moved into the very centre of the devastated area lying in the Somme bend, on to a small rise near Assevillers, where a number of tiny wooden huts served us as bedrooms by night and offices by day. Only one hut, more pretentiously brick-walled and evidently built for the use of some German officer of high rank, was available to fulfil the duties of hospitality.

In spite of such discomforts, the daily life at Corps Headquarters flowed on uninterruptedly in its several quite distinct activities. On the one hand, there was the grim business of fighting, the detailed conduct of the battle of today, the troop and artillery movements for that of to-morrow, the planning of the one to be undertaken still later; rounds of conferences and consultations; visits to divisions and brigades, and to artillery; reconnaissances to the forward zone; and an intent and ceaseless study of maps and Intelligence summaries.

Hourly contact with headquarters of Fourth Army and of flank corps had to be maintained. Then, following the day's strenuous activities out of doors, there was at nights a never-diminishing mass of administrative work, disciplinary questions, honours, awards, appointments, promotions, and a formidable correspondence which must not be allowed to fall into arrear.

Again, in the back areas there were the unemployed divisions of the corps, who must be regularly visited, both at training and at play. There were medals and ribbons to be distributed to the gallant winners; addresses to be delivered; and the work of reorganising and refitting the resting units to be supervised. Still further in rear, demonstrations of new experiments in tactics or in weapons, or in mechanical warfare, had frequently to be attended, for study and criticism.

And lastly there was the social life of the corps; for its performances were beginning to attract attention beyond the limited, if select, circles of the Fourth Army. A steady stream of visitors began to set in. It was a necessary burden that suitable arrangements for their reception and entertainment had to be maintained.

The duties of hospitality had been simple at a time when Corps Headquarters was still housed in palatial *châteaux*, situated in country hitherto untouched by the war, and within easy reach of all supplies. It was a very different matter to offer even reasonable comfort to a visitor at a time when government rations constituted the backbone of our fare, when there were only bare floors to sleep upon for those who were not fortunate enough to possess a camp bed or valise, and when even an extra blanket or pillow or towel was at a premium.

Yet we were always most glad to see visitors, and those of them who

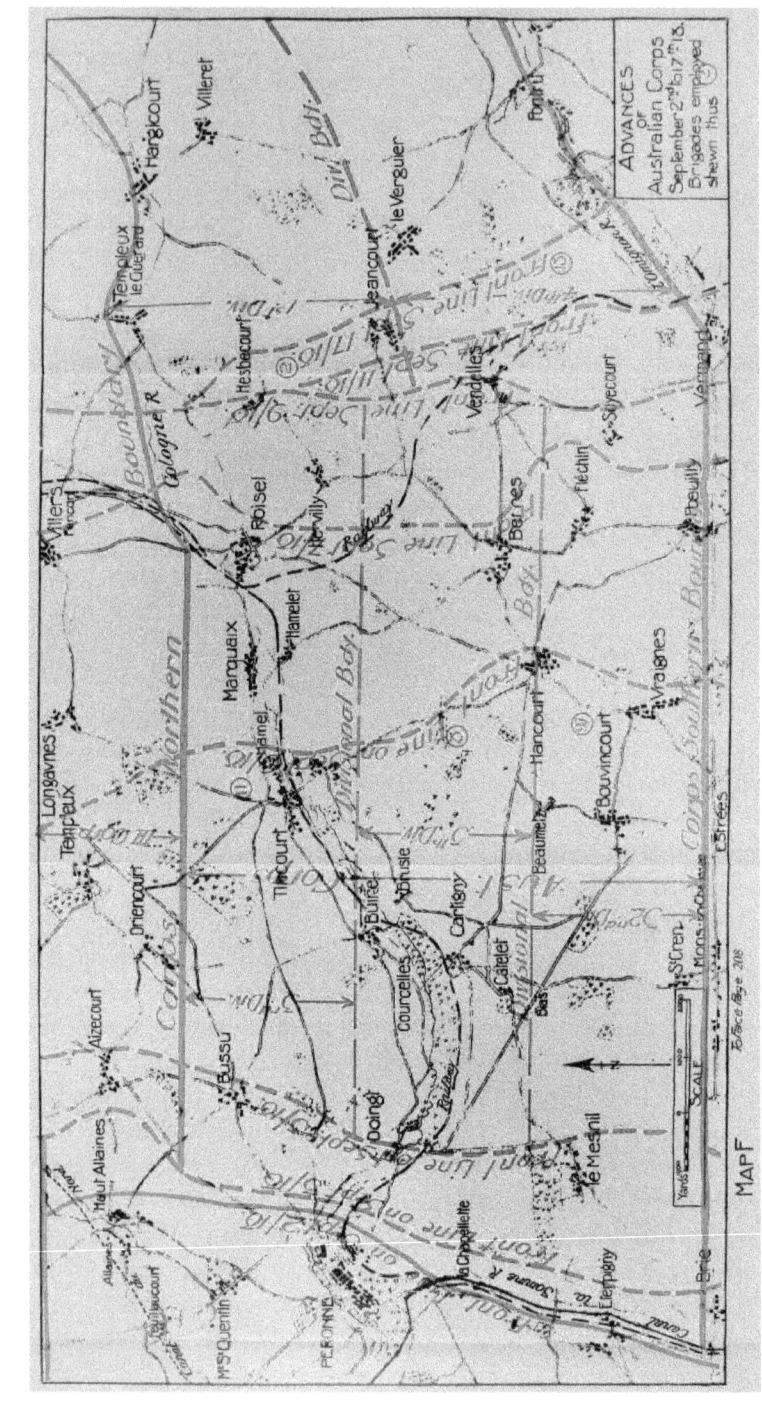

MAP F

were soldiers had, of course, a full understanding of our limitations. It was not always so with others who, in the earlier years of the war, when all corps had a fixed location and had achieved a high standard of domestic comfort, had been accustomed to an adequate reception.

Upon the whole, our guests were indulgent, and understood that the stress of current events placed a very strict limit upon the amount of time that the members of my staff or I could devote to them.

Among many other distinguished men whom I had the honour to receive were members of the War Cabinet, such as Lord Milner, then Secretary of State for War, and Mr. Winston Churchill, the Minister of Munitions; public men, such as Sir Horace Plunkett and Robert Blatchford; eminent authors, such as Sir Conan Doyle, Sir Gilbert Parker and Ian Hay; famous artists, such as Louis Raemakers, Streeton and Longstaff; celebrated journalists, like Viscount Burnham, Thomas Marlowe and Cope Cornford; together with many representatives of the Royal Navy, and of the armies of our Allies, and *attachés* from all the Allied Embassies.

The commander-in-chief, Field Marshal Haig, was a frequent caller, and never departed without leaving a stimulating impression of his placid, hopeful and undaunted personality, nor without a generous recognition of the work which the corps was doing.

General Birdwood, also, the former corps commander, who now commanded the Fifth Army, paid several visits to the corps, travelling long distances in order to speak a few encouraging words to the commanders and troops with whom he had formerly been so long and so closely associated. He, too, was always a most welcome visitor. Although since the previous May he had ceased to control the fighting activities of the corps, this did not lessen the intense pride which he took in its daily successes.

Many of our civilian visitors thirsted for the noise and tumult of battle, and were most keen to get under fire, even if only of long-range artillery fire. This was a constant source of anxiety to me, for it was an unwritten law that the responsibility of their safe sojourn in the corps area rested with me. More often than not they had to be dissuaded from visiting the forward zone, and induced to spend their available time in inspecting some of our show spots in the rearward areas, such as the Calibration ranges, or the corps central telegraph station, or the tank park, or even the prisoner of war cages, and the numerous depots of captured guns and war trophies.

The corps prisoners' cage was always, throughout the period of our active fighting, a scene both of great interest and much activity. Although all prisoners of war had to be evacuated to the rear usually within about twenty-four hours of their admission, and every day a batch marched out under escort, yet the corps cage between July and October was never empty.

When early in July the stream of prisoners began to flow in, and thereafter grew steadily stronger, my Intelligence Service, headed by Major S.A. Hunn, rose thoroughly to the occasion. Among our troops sufficient numbers of all ranks proficient in the German language were speedily found. After a little training they learned to deal expeditiously with the lengthy searchings and interrogations which followed the arrival of all newcomers.

Documents of every description found upon prisoners excepting their pay-books, were seized and examined. The German soldier is an inveterate sender and recipient of picture postcards. It was surprising how much information of an invaluable character could be gleaned from a postcard. A date, a place name, the number of a unit or regiment, the name of a commander, reference to a train journey or a fight, are often sufficient, when read by an expert in relation to the context, to furnish definite information of the whereabouts of a division, or of the fact that it has been or is about to be disbanded, or of its intended movement to some other part of the front, or of the losses which it has suffered.

All these scraps of information, when compared with similar items gathered on other fronts, soon enabled the whole story of all movement that was going on behind the enemy's lines to be deduced from day to day with wonderful completeness.

So, also, maps, sketches, copies of orders, or of battle instructions, and the contents of note-books and of personal diaries always repaid the closest scrutiny. Such study produced results which, even if not of immediate value to me, were nevertheless passed on to the army, and by them broadly promulgated, in daily summaries, for the benefit of all our other corps.

The oral interrogation of the prisoners, particularly of officers, often produced results of first-class importance. Information as to dispositions, intentions, new tactical methods or new weapons frequently emerged from these inquiries. It was rare that prisoners refused to talk, and rarer still for them to attempt to mislead with false information. If they did attempt it, the interrogating officer was usually sufficiently well-informed upon the subject of inquiry to be able to detect the inconsistency.

As the prisoners were invariably examined separately, it was never difficult to discriminate between the true, upon which the majority of them were in agreement, and the false, upon which the minority never agreed. Should the prisoner prove uncommunicative or deceitful, then if he were of sufficient education to make it worthwhile, the intelligence officer had yet another method, besides direct questioning, at his disposal.

For a certain number of our own men, who could speak German fluently, and who had been carefully tutored in their role, were provided with enemy uniforms, and allowed to grow a three-days' beard, so as to impersonate prisoners of war. These men, so equipped, were called "pigeons". A pigeon would be ostentatiously brought under escort into the prisoners' cage, and would sojourn for a day or more in a compartment of it among the specially selected genuine prisoners. He would indicate by a secret sign the time when he should himself be led to the Intelligence Office for interrogation. It was seldom that he came away empty-handed.

The demeanour of our captives, on reaching the cages, varied widely, according to the stress which they had undergone. Some wore an air of abject misery, and were thoroughly cowed and subservient. Others were defiant, sulky and even arrogant. Our treatment of them was firm, but humane. Physically, they had nothing to complain of; they were fed and quartered on the same standard as our own men. But they were given to understand from the very outset that we would stand no nonsense, and that they must do exactly what they were told. Few of them ever gave us any real trouble.

The subsequent employment of prisoners of war did not come under my jurisdiction, and it was seldom that any prisoner working parties were available to me. My corps area rarely extended sufficiently far back from the front line to carry it beyond the zone in which, by agreement between the belligerents, the employment of prisoners of war was forbidden.

Australian soldiers are nothing if not sportsmen, and no case ever came under my notice of brutality or inhumanity to prisoners. Upon the contrary, when once a man's surrender had been accepted, and he had been fully disarmed, he was treated with marked kindness. The front line troops were always ready to share their water and rations with their prisoners, and cigarettes were distributed with a liberal hand.

On the other hand, the souvenir-hunting instinct of the Australian led him to help himself freely to such mementos as our orders had not forbidden him to touch. Prisoners rarely got as far as the corps cage with a full outfit of regimental buttons, cockades, shoulder-straps, or other accoutrements. Personal trinkets, pay-books, money and other individual belongings were, however, invariably respected; unless, as often happened, the prisoners themselves were anxious to trade them away to their captors, or escorts, for tobacco, chocolates, or other luxuries.

Before I leave the subject of prisoners, I should mention my impression of the German officers, particularly of those who were more senior in rank. Whenever a regimental or battalion commander was captured, and time permitted, he was brought before me for a further interrogation. It was an experience which was almost universal that such officers were willing to give me little information which might injure their cause; on the other hand, they exhibited an altogether exaggerated air of wounded pride at their capture, and at the defeat of the troops whom they had commanded.

It was that feeling of professional pique which dominated their whole demeanour. They were always volubly full of excuses, the weather, the fog, the poor *morale* of their own men, the unexpectedness of our attack, the tanks, errors in their maps—anything at all but a frank admission of their own military inferiority.

There were two amusing exceptions to this experience. The day after the fighting for Péronne, when a large batch of the prisoners then taken was being got ready to march out of the corps cage, officers in one enclosure, other ranks in another, the senior German officer, a regimental commander, formally requested permission to address some eighty other officers present in the cage. This request was granted.

He told them that they had fought a good fight, that their capture was not to their discredit, and that he would report favourably upon them to his superiors at the first opportunity. He then went on to say that on his own and on their behalf he desired to tender to the Australians an expression of his admiration for their prowess, and to make a frank acknowledgment to them that he fully recognised that on this occasion his garrison had been outclassed, outmanoeuvred, and outfought. The whole assembly expressed their acquiescence in these observations by collectively bowing gravely to the small group of my intelligence officers who were amused spectators of the scene.

On another occasion—it was just after the battle of September 18th—I was asking a German battalion commander whether he could explain why it was that his men had that day surrendered in such large numbers without much show of resistance.

"Well, you see", said he, with a twinkle in his eye, "they are dreadfully afraid of the Australians. So, they are of the tanks. But when they saw both of them coming at them *together*, they thought it was high time to throw up their hands."

But this story is slightly anticipatory. The short breathing-space which had been afforded by our more leisurely advance towards the Hindenburg system was over. By September 12th I was once again immersed in all the perplexities of shaping means to ends. I had to decide, in collaboration with the army staff and the corps on my flanks, first, the extent of the resources which would be required, and second, the successive stages which would offer promise of success in overthrowing the last great defensive system of all those which the enemy had created upon the tortured soil of France.

Chapter 12

Hargicourt

The great Hindenburg system, by which name it has come to be known to English readers, or the "Siegfried Line", as it is called by the Germans, was brought into existence during the winter of 1916 and early spring of 1917 in order to fulfil a very definite strategic purpose. This was to put into effect, on a stupendous scale, a very elementary principle of minor tactics, namely, that field works are constructed for the purpose of reducing the number of men required to defend a given front or locality.

In themselves, field fortifications have, of course, no offensive value whatever, but their use permits a reduced number of men to defend one place, in order that a greater number of men may be available to attack another place.

The German High Command proceeded to make use of this principle on a scale previously unknown in history. The whole of the Western front, in Belgium and France, was to be held defensively throughout 1917. The military resources required to defend that front were to be reduced to a minimum, by the provision of a line of defences protected by powerful field works, believed to be impregnable. This would liberate the greatest possible resources for the Eastern front, where an end could be made of the Russians and Roumanians there. As soon as these were disposed of, those troops, guns and aeroplanes could again be transferred to the West, in order similarly to dispose of the remainder of our Alliance.

This great strategic plan was carried out in its entirety until the middle of 1918. It was the great Hindenburg Line which had been the kernel of the whole conception, and, until the days which we are now approaching, it had remained, practically over its whole length, an impregnable barrier against the assaults of the French and British.

It is to be remembered that the very basis which justified the expenditure of such enormous labour on the creation of these defences was the saving in manpower. It is an accepted principle of tactics that in any given battle the advantage always rests heavily on the side of the defence. Where numbers, resources and *morale* are equal, no attack can hope to succeed.

If, in the teachings before the war, it was correct to say that a commander should hesitate to attack unless he had a preponderance of men and guns of at least two to one, such a *dictum* assuredly did not take into account field defences of the permanent and elaborate character of the Hindenburg Line. I should hardly venture to fix a ratio of relative strength appropriate in such circumstances.

But this much is clear. The Germans had once already relied successfully upon the impregnability of this great work. They had every justification for believing that it would once again serve them to keep us at bay for just a few weeks longer. Winter was very near, and the *Entente* peoples might not have been able to hold together to face another year of war.

We, on our part also, had as much justification for the resolve that every sacrifice must be made to overthrow these defences before the end of 1918, and for believing that it would require a great, concerted and intense effort to succeed in this.

It is quite necessary, for a due appreciation of the magnitude of the effort which was actually made, and of the wonderful success with which it was rewarded, that the nature of the defences of the Hindenburg Line should be clearly understood. This can best be done, I think, by making an endeavour to realise the sense of security which the possession of such a line of defence must have afforded to the enemy. We are here interested only in that portion of the line which extends from St. Quentin northwards towards Cambrai.

Between these two cities the country is higher than that adjoining it on the north and the south. It forms, therefore, a watershed, dividing the basin of, the Somme from that of the Scheldt. Early in the nineteenth century, Napoleon realised the ambitious project of connecting these two river systems by a great Canal scheme, cutting right through this high country from south to north.

The canal is called, in its southern reaches, Canal de St. Quentin. Before Cambrai is reached it merges into the Canal de l'Escaut. Throughout the whole of that portion which concerns us, it runs in a deep cutting, reaching, for great stretches, a depth of 50 to 60 feet. In certain places where the ground rises still higher, the canal passes through in great tunnels. The southernmost, or Le Tronquoy Tunnel, near St. Quentin, is but short; the northern boasts of the imposing length of 6,000 yards, and extends from Bellicourt, (see Map H), at its southern portal, to Le Catelet at its northern one. From that point northwards the canal flows in "open cut" which gradually becomes shallower as Cambrai is approached.

The canal excavation—except where the tunnels occur—itself affords an excellent military obstacle, the passage of which could be stoutly contested by resolute troops well dug in on its eastern banks, for the descent and ascent of the slopes could be obstructed by wire entanglements, and swept with fire. The water alone, which is too deep to be waded, would seriously impede infantry, while the passage of tanks, guns and vehicles would be impossible once the few high level bridges over the canal had been destroyed.

Such an obstacle would not, however, of itself fulfil the requirements of modern war, with its searching and destructive artillery fire. It was to be regarded more as the foundation upon which a complete system of defences could be built, and as a last line of resistance *à outrance*.

The canal had been, naturally, located by its engineers, in the lowest ground available, so that its course closely follows the lines of the minor valleys and depressions of the ground. On both sides, therefore, the canal is flanked by somewhat higher ground, from which its immediate banks can be overlooked. On the western side particularly, there is a regular line of such higher plateaux on which the villages of Villeret, Hargicourt and Ronssoy once stood.

It was clearly desirable both to deprive a besieger of such vantage ground, and also to provide the canal defences with a stout outpost defence. For these reasons, the Germans had constructed an elaborate system of trenches on a line generally parallel to and on the average a full mile west of the canal. These trenches had been perfected with dug-outs, concrete machine-gun and mortar emplacements, and underground shelters. They were protected by belt after belt of barbed wire entanglements, in a fashion which no one understood better, or achieved more thoroughly, than the Germans.

But much more remained. Deep communication trenches led back to the canal banks, in the sides of which tier upon tier of comfortable living quarters for the troops had been tunnelled out. Here support and reserve troops could live in safety and defy our heaviest bombardments. They could be secretly hurried to the front trenches whenever danger threatened.

There was, indeed, a perfect tangle of underground shelters and passages. Roomy dug-outs were provided with tunnelled ways which led to cunningly hidden machine-gun posts, and the best of care was taken to provide numerous exits, so that the occupants should not be imprisoned by the blocking of one or other of them by our bombardment. But it was the barbed wire which formed the groundwork of the defence. It was everywhere, and ran in all directions, cleverly disposed so as to herd the attackers into the very jaws of the machine-guns.

The stretch of 6,000 yards of the canal which had been tunnelled was, however, both a hindrance and a benefit to the perfection of the scheme. On the one hand, the advantage of the open cut, as a last obstacle, was lost. Its place had to be taken by a second complete system of trench and wire defences, roughly following the line of the tunnel, but of course far above the latter. On the other hand, the tunnel itself afforded secure living accommodation for a substantial garrison.

The Germans had collected large numbers of canal barges, and had towed them into the interior of the tunnel, mooring them end to end. They served as living quarters and as depots for stores and munitions. It was no great business to provide electric lighting for the tunnel. Indeed, the leads for this purpose had been in existence before the war. Here, again, underground shafts and ways were cut to enable the troops rapidly to man the trenches and machine-guns, and as rapidly to seek a safe asylum from the heaviest shell fire.

The whole scheme produced, in fact, a veritable fortress—not one, in the popular acceptation of the term, consisting of massive walls and battlements, which, as was proved in the early days of the war at Liége and Namur, can speedily be blown to pieces by modern heavy artillery—but one defying destruction by any powers of gunnery, and presenting the most formidable difficulties to the bravest of infantry.

Even this was not all. On the east side of the St. Quentin Canal and parallel to it were built still two further trench lines, both fully protected by wire entanglements, and capable of determined defence.

Australian Artillery—going into action at Cressaire Wood.

Battle of August 8th, 1918—German prisoners being brought out of the battle under the fire of their own artillery.

The first of these is the Le Catelet line, about one mile distant from the canal. It skirts and embraces the villages of Nauroy and Le Catelet, while two miles still further east is the Beaurevoir Line, the last or most easterly of all the prepared defences which the Germans had in France.

Neither of these latter trench systems was nearly so formidably prepared as the main systems previously described, but together with them they go to make up the whole Hindenburg defensive system. In this region that system runs generally due north and south, with many minor convolutions in its line. It is altogether some 4½ miles across from west to east.

As its overthrow could not be attempted in a single operation, it is necessary for clearness of description to give definite names to each of the successive lines of trenches which go to form the whole defence system. Taking them in the order in which we attacked them, from west to east, they will be referred to as:

The Hindenburg Outpost Line (known also in this part of the field as the Hargicourt Line).
The Hindenburg Main Line (*i.e.*, the Canal and Tunnel Line).
The Le Catelet Line.
The Beaurevoir Line.

During the winter of 1917-1918 the British Fifth Army and the Germans had faced each other in this region for many months. On our side, also, a system of field defences had been developed. They fell far short, indeed, of the completeness and ingenuity of the German works, because the latter had been constructed at leisure, long before, while ours had been built under the very fire of the German guns.

For months the opposing artilleries had pounded the country to pieces, effaced every sign of civilization, and churned up the ground in all directions over a belt some three miles wide. Heaps of broken bricks marked the sites of once prosperous villages. Broken telegraph poles, charred tree trunks, twisted rails, a chaos of mangled machinery, were the only remains of what had once been gardens, orchards, railways and factories. The whole territory presented the aspect of a rolling, tumbled desert from which life itself had been banished.

This was the region whose western verge the vanguard of the Australian advance approached on September 11th, on a frontage of about 8,000 yards, the northern extremity directed on Bellicourt, the southern on Bellenglise. That is to say, if our further advance had but continued unimpeded in the same due easterly direction, it would have brought us square upon the open excavation of the canal, and just clear and to the south of the Bellicourt–Le Catelet tunnel. Some significance attached to this circumstance, as will later appear.

Now, some little time before, an event of peculiar interest had occurred. This was the capture, on another front, of a very ordinary-looking transport vehicle loaded high with miscellaneous baggage. Little escaped the inquisitive eyes of the British Intelligence Service, which speedily discovered that among this baggage there safely reposed a large collection of maps and documents. On examination these proved to be nothing less than the complete Defence Scheme of the whole "Siegfried" system, in that very sector which now lay before the Australian Corps.

These papers were carefully overhauled and arranged. There were dozens of accurately drawn detailed maps, and minute descriptions of every tactical feature of the defences. The position of every gun emplacement was given; every searchlight, machine-gun pit, observation post, telephone exchange, command station and mortar emplacement was clearly marked; the topographical and tactical features of the ground were discussed in minute detail, and plans for the action of every individual unit of the garrisons were fully displayed.

Naturally, an army of translators and copying clerks was set to work upon this precious find, and my Intelligence Service was kept busy for many days in making for me digests of those items likely to prove of special interest. It had, of course, to be remembered that the Defence Scheme had been brought into operation for the campaign of 1917, and it remained to be seen to what extent it might by now have become obsolete.

It was hardly to be expected that the enemy would adhere to it in its entirety, especially if he were aware, as I was bound to assume that he was, that all this information had fallen into our hands. But the scheme contained a full exposition of many important topographical facts which it was in any case beyond his power to alter, and which it was of priceless value for me to know.

Although I had to devote hour upon hour to a concentrated study of these papers, it proved to be in greater part labour in vain so far as the Australian Corps was concerned, because it ultimately came about that although I did carry out the attack upon the Hindenburg outpost line in my present sector, the attack upon the Hindenburg main line, which I was, later, called upon to make, took place in the next adjoining sector to the north, *i.e.*, the Bellicourt tunnel sector, to which these captured documents only incidentally referred. Nevertheless, the Ninth Corps, under Braithwaite, ultimately got the full benefit of these discoveries.

The production of these documents on September 10th formed the starting point of the discussions which were now initiated in the Fourth Army upon the question of the series of operations necessary to overthrow the Hindenburg defences. General Rawlinson, on September 13th, asked his three corps commanders (Butler, now restored to health and back at duty, Braithwaite and myself) to meet him at my newly-installed hutted camp at Assevillers. There, quite informally, over a cup of afternoon tea, the great series of operations took birth which so directly helped to finish the war.

It was decided that the operation must necessarily be divided into two main phases—separated in point of time by an interval of several days for further preparation. All of us recognised the impossibility of overrunning, in a single day, so deep and formidable a system of defences, in such tortured country, and in weather which was already becoming unsettled.

The first phase was to be an attempt to capture the Hindenburg outpost line, along the whole army front. The French and the Third British Armies were to be asked to make a synchronised attack on the same objective. The three corps of the Fourth Army were to attack upon the frontages and in the sectors on which they then stood. The date was left undecided, but all were to be ready at three days' notice.

One important consideration was the meagre supply of tanks available. The operations of August had been costly, not to say extravagant, in tanks, and General Elles' repair workshops, manned largely by very competent Chinese *coolie* mechanics, had been working night and day ever since to repair the minor damages, and new tanks were steadily arriving from England to replace those damaged beyond repair. But no large contingent of tanks was to be expected until towards the end of the month. The upshot was that I was to be content with only eight tanks for use in the contemplated operation.

Late the same afternoon I communicated to Generals Maclagan and Glasgow an outline of the probable role of their respective divisions in the very near future.

In the meantime, the front-line troops had not been idle. My orders were that the First and Fourth Divisions were to carry the line forward as far as possible towards the Hindenburg outpost line, without committing the corps to an organised attack. They were to operate by vigorous patrol action against enemy points of resistance, for the enemy had evidently no intention of quietly giving up the ground which lay between us and the Hindenburg outpost line. On the contrary, he had posted strong rear-guards on every point of tactical value, and did his best to keep us as long as possible at arm's length, and beyond striking distance of his first great line of defence.

These orders were entirely to the taste of the two divisions now in the line. The First Division had served its apprenticeship to that very kind of fighting in the Merris area in the previous spring, and the Fourth Division did not mean to be a second best. Each division stood on a one-brigade front, being ordered to keep its other two brigades well out of harm's way and resting, for any great effort that might be required.

The next few days witnessed some daring exploits on the part of the 13th Brigade of the Fourth Division and the 2nd Brigade of the First Division in the capture of tactical points, and in the bloody repulse of all attempts by the enemy to recapture them. In this way our line was carried up to and a little beyond what had been the old British reserve line of trenches of March, 1918, which lay within 5,000 yards of the final objective of the first phase of the contemplated operations.

On September 16th I called together the whole of the commanders who were to participate in the next great battle, Maclagan (Fourth Division), Glasgow (First Division), Courage (Tanks), Chamier (Air Force), Fraser (Heavy Artillery), and the four generals of my own staff. The conference took place in a Y.M.C.A. marquee erected near Maclagan's Headquarters, and I was able to announce that the date had been fixed for September 18th.

The contemplated battle presented only a few novel features. The methods of the corps were becoming stereotyped, and by this time we all began to understand each other so well that most of what I had to say could almost be taken for granted. Each commander was ready to anticipate the action that would be required of him, almost as soon as I had unfolded the general plan.

The shortage of tanks was a source of much anxiety to me. I felt that it would mean a heavier risk to the infantry, and the contemplation of losses among our splendid men, which might be lessened by the more liberal use of mechanical aids, always sorely troubled me. I endeavoured to meet the situation by adopting two unusual expedients.

The first was to *double* the machine-gun resources of the two battle divisions. This was effected by bringing up the complete machine-gun battalions of the Third and Fifth Divisions, and adding them to those of the line divisions. This gave me a total of 256 Vickers Machine-guns on a frontage now reduced to 7,000 yards. It enabled me to deliver so dense a machine-gun barrage, advancing 300 yards ahead of the infantry, that to quote the words of a German battalion commander who was captured on September 18th:

> The small-arms fire was absolutely too terrible for words. There was nothing to be done but to crouch down in our trenches and wait for you to come and take us.

The other expedient was amusing, although no less effective. This was to make up for the shortage of real tanks by fabricating a number of dummy ones. As soon as the word went round engineers and pioneers vied with each other in rapid "Tank" manufacture. Dumps and stores were clandestinely robbed of hessian, paint, wire nails, and battens, and some weird monstrosities were produced. The best and most plausible of them were selected, and actually used on the day of the battle. Four men dragged out each dummy, before dawn, into a position from which it was bound to be seen by the enemy and there abandoned it. There is little doubt that this trick contributed its share to the day's astonishing success.

Once again, also, I put into practice the principle of an artillery barrage plan reduced to the utmost simplicity. This, as already described, consisted in having the line, on which were to fall the shells from the whole of the barrage guns employed, perfectly straight across the whole front, so as to avoid all complexities in fire direction.

The first line on which the barrage fell was called the artillery "Start Line", and from such a line the barrage advanced, by regular leaps or "lifts" of 100 yards at a time, in perfectly parallel lines, until the final objective was reached. Now, experience had shown that such a start line for the artillery should be at least 200 yards in advance of the line on which the infantry were to form up ready for the assault. A liberal margin of space had to be allowed, in order to minimise the risks to our own infantry.

The artillery "Start Line" was defined on our fighting maps. The guns were laid upon it by methods which depended upon accurate surveys, on the ground, of the exact position of every gun. When that had been determined, the map and compass helped to decide the range and alignment upon which the gun should open fire. On the map, also, was drawn another line 200 yards short of, or on our side of the artillery "Start Line", and this was called the infantry "Start Line".

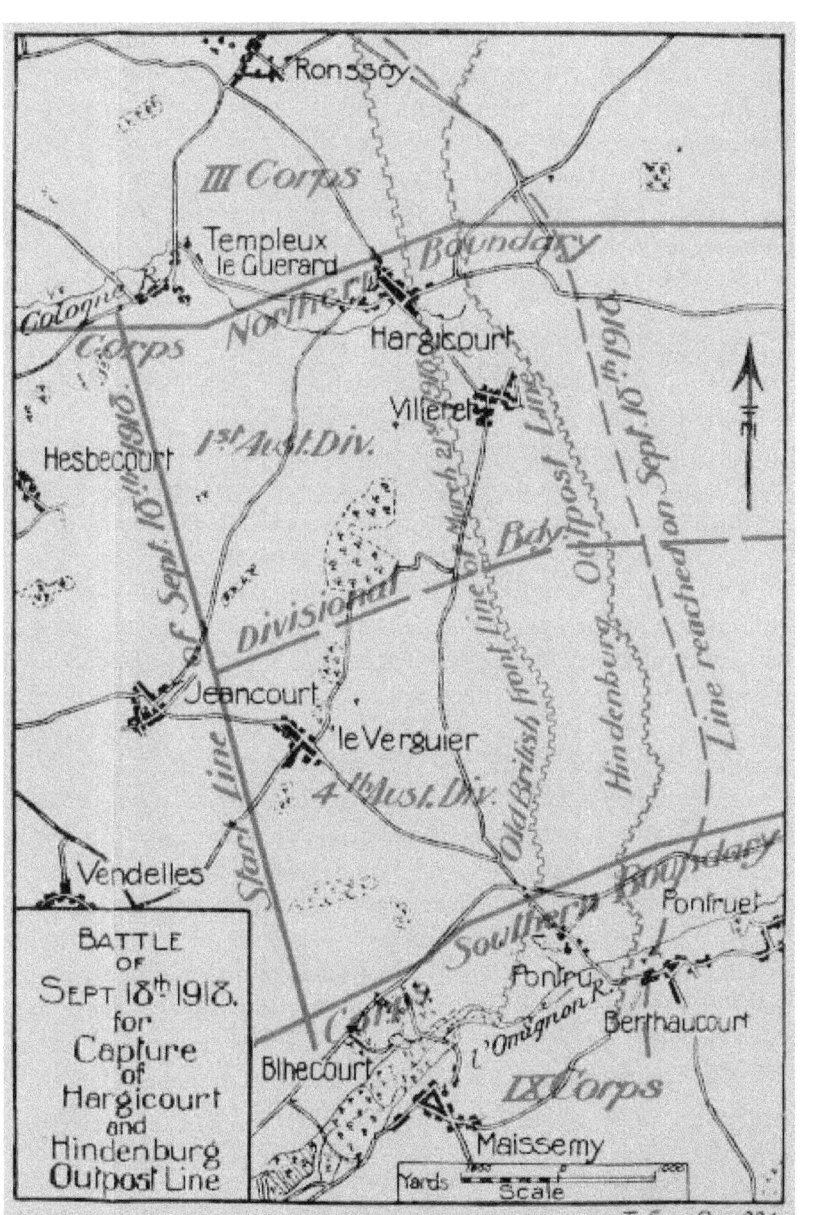

It then became necessary to determine, upon the actual ground, the position of this infantry Start Line, and to mark it in such a way that the infantry would be enabled to take up their correct positions. This would ensure that the infantry would know that the fall of our opening barrage would be 200 yards in advance of the line so marked.

This delicate work of marking out of the infantry Start Line on the ground was invariably entrusted to the engineers attached to the brigades co-operating in the attack. The marking was done by laying out and pegging down broad tapes of white linen, which could be recognised in the dim light of early dawn. The whole work, had, of course, to be done unobserved by the enemy, and it was always a dangerous task.

Only the fact that we were in possession of reliable large scale maps, recording every feature of the ground, made it possible for the engineers, resourceful as they were, to do this delicate work with reasonable accuracy. The battered condition of the country was always a difficulty; for it was never easy to recognise, on the ground, reference points, such as a road intersection, or the corner of a field, or a crucifix or similar land mark, which might aid the surveyors in getting their bearings.

The infantry Start Line had, naturally, to be located so that the ground upon which the tapes were to be pegged down was ground which was already within our possession, or accessible to us without coming dangerously near the enemy. It was a necessary consequence that portions of our always irregular front line of posts or trenches would lie beyond or on the enemy's side of the tape line.

It was always a rule of our practice, therefore, that any infantry posted in advance of the taped line should be withdrawn, behind the tapes, an hour before the time of Zero. It was also customary to order that all assaulting troops should be spread, in their appropriate dispositions, along the tape line, also one hour before Zero.

The result of these arrangements was that for the last hour before the actual opening of the battle, all infantry intended to take part in the assault was deployed along the tapes in a perfectly straight line, all along the battle front, while no troops previously in occupation of posts or trenches in advance of the tapes were left out in front, exposed to the risk of either being hit by our own artillery, or mistaken, in the half light of dawn, for enemies by our own infantry.

Complex and difficult as these arrangements may appear from this description, they worked out in actual practice with the utmost smoothness. The resulting simplification of the artillery plans, in this as in similar previous battles, more than justified their adoption.

A liberal use was also made of direction boards, which marked the routes by which each separate body of assaulting infantry should, during the last night, march from its place of assembly to the taped line or "jumping off" line, and also to mark the position which it was to take up upon that line. Each board had painted upon it the name of the unit to which it referred. Such preparatory measures, troublesome as they were, greatly reduced the risk of any confusion or mistake, and lessened the fatigue of the assaulting troops.

The moon would set, on the morning of the battle, at 3.37 a.m., and the sun would rise at 6.27 a.m. Zero hour, for the opening of the attack, was therefore fixed for twenty minutes past five.

Operations began inauspiciously. A soaking rain set in some two hours before, and made movement over the broken, clayey surface anything but pleasant. Although the troops were soon drenched to the skin, this did not in any way damp their spirits. It probably added much to the misery of the enemy, who could hardly fail to realise that, on any morning, a fresh attack might break upon him.

Modern war is in many ways unlike the wars of previous days, but in nothing so much as in the employment of what I have more than once referred to as "set-piece" operations. The term is one which should convey its own meaning. It is the direct result of the great extension, which this war has introduced, of mechanical warfare. It is a "set-piece" because the stage is elaborately set, parts are written for all the performers, and carefully rehearsed by many of them. The whole performance is controlled by a time-table, and, so long as all goes according to plan, there is no likelihood of unexpected happenings, or of interesting developments.

The artillery barrage advances from line to line, in regular leaps, at regulated intervals of time, determined beforehand, and incapable of alteration once the battle has begun. Should the rate prove too slow and the infantry could have advanced more quickly, it cannot be helped, and no great harm is done. On the other hand, if there be any risk of the barrage rate being too fast, one or two halts of ten or fifteen minutes are often introduced into the time-table to allow the infantry line, or any part of it which may be hung up for any reason, to catch up.

Following the barrage, comes line upon line of infantry in skirmishing order, together with the line of tanks when such are used. The foremost lines advance to capture and hold the ground, the lines in rear to "mop up" and deal with the enemy either showing fight or hiding underground, the rearmost lines collect prisoners or our own wounded, or carry supplies, tools and ammunition.

In a well-planned battle of this nature, fully organised, powerfully covered by artillery and machine-gun barrages, given a resolute infantry and that the enemy's guns are kept successfully silenced by our own counter-battery artillery, nothing happens, nothing can happen, except the regular progress of the advance according to the plan arranged. The whole battle sweeps relentlessly and methodically across the ground until it reaches the line laid down as the final objective.

Such a set-piece battle lasts usually, from first to last, for 80 to 100 minutes; seldom for more. When the artillery programme is ended the battle is either completely won, or to all intents and purposes completely lost. If the barrage for any reason gets away from our infantry, and they are relegated to hand to hand fighting in order to complete their advance, the battle immediately assumes a totally different character, and is no longer a set-piece affair.

It will be obvious, therefore, that the more nearly such a battle proceeds according to plan, the more free it is from any incidents awakening any human interest. Only the externals and only the large aspects of such battles can be successfully recorded. It is for this reason that no stirring accounts exist of the more intimate details of such great set-pieces as Messines, Vimy, Hamel and many others. They will never be written, for there is no material upon which to base them. The story of what did take place on the day of battle would be a mere paraphrase of the battle orders prescribing all that was to take place.

On the other hand, battles such as the second phase of August 8th, the battle for Mont St. Quentin, and the later Battles of Bony and Beaurevoir were not set-piece operations. Therefore, the developments from hour to hour, and even from moment to moment, are full of intense human interest, and replete with tales of individual courage and initiative. Someday, when all the material has been gathered, an abler pen than mine will write their story.

If the reader will bear in mind all these considerations, with special reference to the Battle of Hargicourt on September 18th he will realise that, in describing the dispositions, the objectives, the timetable and the preparations for the battle, I have told practically all that there is to tell of the course it took, except only as regards the results actually achieved, in ground won and prisoners taken.

It has been difficult, nevertheless, to refrain from dwelling in detail upon the performances and experiences in battle of the individual fighting men. Any attempt to do so would, however, prove hopelessly inadequate. The numbers engaged were always so large, their activities so varied, the conditions of each battle so different in detail, that to do adequate justice and avoid unfair discrimination would make impossible demands upon the space available to me.

Popular interest naturally centres upon the infantry, not only because they are the most numerous, but also because they are invariably in the forefront of the battle and often in immediate contact with the enemy. Without the slightest disparagement to the important role of the infantryman and to the valour which its performance demands, it must never be forgotten that the work of the Artillery, Engineers, Pioneers, Machine-gunners, Trench Mortars, Air Service and Tanks is in every way equally important and essential to the success of any battle operation. Yet it is equally true that no battle can be won without the infantry.

In a deliberately prepared battle it is not too much to say that the role of the infantry is not, as a rule, the paramount one, provided that all goes well and that there is no breakdown in any part of the battle plan. That does not, however, imply that the infantry task makes no high demand upon courage and resolution. On the contrary, these are the essentials upon which the success of the infantry role and therefore of the whole battle depends.

The primary duty of the infantry, in an assault covered by an artillery barrage, is to follow up the barrage closely. The barrage is nothing more nor less than a steady shower of shells, bursting over the very heads of the leading lines of infantry, and striking the ground some 80 to 120 yards in front of them. This shower is usually so dense that three to four shells per minute fall on every twenty yards of frontage. It is so intense a fire that no enemy, however courageous, could remain exposed to it. It falls on one line for three or four minutes, while the infantry lie down flat. Suddenly, the barrage "lifts" or advances 100 yards. At a signal from the platoon or company commander the whole line rises and rushes at top speed to catch up to the barrage, again to throw itself flat upon the ground.

So long as no enemy are encountered, these successive rushes may go on without check for hundreds of yards. If during the course of any rush, trenches or strong points are met with and they contain enemy who do not immediately surrender, prompt use must be made of rifle and bayonet. But it is the primary business of the leading line of infantry to push on and not to delay by engaging in close combat. The second and third lines of infantry are there to "mop up", that is, to dispose, by destruction or capture, of any enemy overrun or ignored by the leading line. Where tanks co-operate that is also their special business, and when it has been attended to, they go forward at top speed to rejoin the leading line.

In such a methodical way the advance continues until the final objective is reached. This event can be recognised by the infantry in any of three ways, firstly by reference to the clock time; for the arrival of the barrage at any line on the map or ground occurs in pursuance of a definite time-table; secondly by the topographical features, and thirdly by the expedient of maintaining the barrage stationary at the final objective for fifteen to thirty minutes. In some battles, I also adopted the device of firing from every gun in the barrage, three rounds of smoke shell in rapid succession, as a signal to the commanders of the leading line of infantry to call the final halt, to select a good line for trenches, and to dig-in rapidly, a process technically called "consolidation".

It would be too much to hope that in an attack covering a front of four or five miles, every part of the line should be able to advance without any check whatever up to the final halting place. But the expectation always is that by far the greater part of the whole line will be able to do so. If, here and there along the front, platoons or even whole companies were to be held up or delayed by special difficulties or obstacles such as thickets, or copses strongly manned by the enemy, or by belts of wire, or village ruins, such breaks in the general line of advance would matter but little to the success of the operations as a whole. The gaps discovered in the leading line of infantry, when it had come to a halt at the final objective, would be speedily filled by supporting troops from both flanks of the gap, and thereby the enemy holding out further back, would be completely enveloped. His surrender would follow as soon as he realised his position, and that he had been cut off from any contact with his friends in his rear.

Such is the normal course of the infantry action in a pitched battle. It makes great demands upon the iron resolution of the infantryman to push on vigorously against all obstacles, and to put forth his utmost physical powers to keep up with the barrage, especially when the ground is wet and sticky, or when uncut wire has to be crawled through. All this he must do, utterly regardless of the enemy fire which may be directed against him, whether from artillery or machine-guns. His best hope of immunity is always to make his rush rapidly and determinedly, and to get to ground immediately that he reaches the halting place, close up to the barrage, when signalled by his officer.

Very different from such a stereotyped procedure is the action of the infantry in any operation or any part of an operation which partakes of the character of open warfare. The main tactical purpose is still, as before, to advance to the seizure of an appointed objective, but there is no barrage, no time-table, no fixity of route, no prescribed formation or procedure. Everything must be left to the judgment, initiative and enterprise of the leader on the spot.

The tactical unit of infantry is the platoon. The action of a whole battalion is compounded merely of the separate actions of its sixteen platoons, each performing the separate role, in a general plan, that may be laid down by the battalion commanders, some to advance and fight, some to act in support, some to lie in reserve, some to engage in a flank attack, others to fetch and carry food, water and munitions.

The platoon is commanded by a lieutenant and comprises four sections, each under a sergeant or corporal. There are two sections of riflemen, a Lewis gun section and a section of rifle grenadiers. Each section may consist of from five to eight men. Let it be supposed that it is the business of the platoon to capture a small farmhouse which the enemy has fortified and in which he is holding out. Always supposing that the enemy garrison is not of a strength requiring more than one platoon for its capture the normal action of the attacking platoon would be somewhat as follows. The Lewis gun section would, from a concealed position, on one flank, keep the place under steady fire. The rifle grenadiers from the same or another flank would fire smoke grenades to make a smoke screen. One section of riflemen would endeavour to sneak up depressions and ditches or along hedges, so as to get well behind the farm and threaten it by fire from the rear. The other section of riflemen would choose some direct line of attack, over ground which offered concealment to them until they were close enough to take the objective with a rush.

Such in very bare outline is merely an imaginary example, but it is sufficient to show the amount of skill, resource and energy required on the part not only of the leader, but also of every man in the platoon. The secret of success of the Australian open fighting lay in the extraordinary vigour, judgment and team-work which characterised the many hundreds of little platoon battles which were fought on just such lines as I have tried to suggest in this example.

It will be readily seen that no comprehensive description is possible which would present an adequate picture of the widely varying activities of the Australian infantryman in this campaign. There is only one source from which reliable narratives of individual fighting can be gathered, and that source is so voluminous that space forbids any but a meagre attempt to supply extracts from it. I refer to the recommendations made by commanders for honours and rewards for individual acts of gallantry. A very small selection of these has been made and is presented in an appendix to this book. (See Appendix B.)

But to return to my narrative of September 18th. On that day each division attacked on a frontage of two Brigades. No serious opposition was encountered except at La Verguier, which was not far from our start line. Nevertheless, the whole of the "red" line, which was the objective of the "set-piece" phase of the day's battle, was in our possession, throughout the whole length of the corps front, well before 10 o'clock.

This gave us complete possession of the old British front line of March, 1918; but the Hindenburg outpost line yet lay before us, still distant another 1,500 to 2,000 yards. This latter line was to be the ultimate or exploitation objective of the day's operations, and I could hardly have dared to hope that a trench system of such considerable strength, which had defied the Fifth Army for so long, would fall into our hands so easily as it did.

Glasgow's division pushed on without pause, and before nightfall had overwhelmed the garrison of the Hindenburg outpost line along its front. Maclagan's division also fought its way forward to within 500 yards of that line. But the troops were by then very exhausted; all movement was in full view of the enemy; and the ground was very difficult. After a consultation with Maclagan I decided to rest the troops, and to make an attempt to reach the final objective (blue line) that same night.

Advantage was taken of this pause to advance the artillery, so that the enemy's defences could be thoroughly bombarded before the final assault. At 11 o'clock the same night, the Fourth Division again attacked, and after severe fighting also captured the whole of the objective trench system. It was a great victory. The Hindenburg outpost line had been vanquished. From it we could now look down upon the St. Quentin Canal, and sweep with fire the whole of the sloping ground which lay between us and the canal, denying the use of that ground to the enemy, and making it impossible for him to withdraw the guns and stores which littered the area.

The overwhelming nature of the success can best be realised by the following almost incredible analysis of the material results of the day's fighting. The First Division attacked with a total strength of 2,854 infantry. They suffered only 490 casualties (killed and wounded). They captured 1,700 prisoners, apart from the large numbers who were killed, and the wounded enemy who made good their escape.

The Fourth Division had a total assaulting strength of 3,048 of all ranks, of whom 532 became casualties. Their captures of live prisoners amounted to 2,543. In addition, the corps gathered in upwards of 80 guns, which had been overrun, and had to be abandoned by the enemy. There is no record in this war of any previous success on such a scale, won with so little loss.

The corps on either flank of me had successes of varying quality. The Ninth Corps on the south had reached the red line, but the exploitation phase of the operation was not pressed until a later day. The Third Corps, on my left, however, made indifferent progress. Their line still bent back sharply from my left flank, and none of the enemy's outpost system had been gained. This portion of the army front was that which lay square opposite the Bellicourt tunnel, and the fact that in this part of the field the Fourth Army had not yet mastered the Hindenburg outpost system was to be fraught with very serious difficulties for me, not many days later.

The general plan propounded by General Rawlinson on September 13th had been realised in part, although not in its entirety. The successes gained on September 18th were nevertheless sufficiently important and decisive to justify immediate preparations for working out the plan for a great, combined and final effort to sweep the enemy out of the remainder of the last lines of defence which he had established in France.

The First and Fourth Australian Divisions had, however, as it turned out, fought their last fight in the war. Their long and brilliant fighting career, which had been opened three and a half years before, the one on the cliffs of Gallipoli, and the other in the desert of Egypt, thus ended in a blaze of glory. Although a number of the officers and non-commissioned officers of both these divisions were called upon, very shortly after, to render one more valuable service to the Australian Corps, the divisions themselves were destined, because of the termination of hostilities, not again to make their appearance on any battle front. Their labours ended, the troops were taken by motor bus and railway to a coastal district lying to the south-west of Amiens, there to rest and recuperate in the contemplation of a noble past devoted to the service of the Empire.

Chapter 14
America Joins In

I had foreseen that the battle to be fought on September 18th was the last in which the First and Fourth Divisions could be called upon to participate during the remainder of the 1918 campaigning season. The wastage of their battalions had gone on faster than the inflow of fresh drafts, or the return of convalescent sick and wounded. These two divisions contained the original sixteen battalions who had immortalised themselves, in 1915, in the landing on Gallipoli. I was strongly averse from disbanding any one of them to furnish drafts for the remainder. My hope then was that, if these divisions could be allowed to rest over the winter, they could be sufficiently replenished by the spring of 1919 to be able to maintain all sixteen battalions at a satisfactory fighting strength.

Of the remaining three divisions, the Third and Fifth required at least another week's rest; and I had promised the Second Division that after their heroic efforts at Mont St. Quentin, they would not be again called upon until towards the end of September. I would thus be left with insufficient resources to maintain an immediate continuance of the pressure upon the enemy.

On explaining the situation to General Rawlinson, he suggested the interesting possibility of being able to obtain, very shortly, the services of the Second American Corps of two divisions, and asked me whether I would be prepared to accept the responsibility of taking this large force under my command for the continuance of the operations.

I had no reason to hesitate. My experience of the quality of the American troops, both at the Battle of Hamel and on the Chipilly Spur, had been eminently satisfactory. It was true that this new American Corps had no previous battle service, but measures were possible to supply them with any technical guidance which they might lack.

I therefore accepted the suggestion, and Rawlinson then asked me to submit a proposal for a joint operation to take place towards the end of the month by these two American and the remaining three Australian Divisions, with the object of completing the task, so well begun, of breaking through the Hindenburg defences. I was to propose my objectives, to show how I intended to employ each of the five divisions, and also to set out my requirements in artillery, tanks and other services.

It was anything but an easy task, and it had to be undertaken at a time when the preparations for the Battle of Hargicourt were uppermost in my mind. Much time also had to be devoted to numerous distinguished visitors.

The outcome was a letter to the Fourth Army which foreshadowed, almost in its entirety, the battle plan which subsequently was actually employed. The substance of this letter is here reproduced. The text has been modified only by the omission of the reference letters to a large coloured map which accompanied it:

Corps Headquarters,
18th September, 1918.

Fourth Army.

1. I beg to submit the outlines of a plan for a series of operations for the capture of the Hindenburg Line in the Sector Bellicourt-Vendhuille, based upon the expectation that two American Divisions will be available immediately to supplement this corps.

2. The resources of the corps in infantry, which will be available, are exclusive of the First and Fourth Australian Divisions, although the artillery, technical troops and machine-gun battalions of those divisions will continue to be available.

3. The plan is based upon the assumption that the objective Blue Line of the operations of September 18th is in our possession all along the army front, or can be seized in the very near future.

4. The accompanying map shows the coloured lines referred to in the following description, as also the reference letters.

5. This plan is in outline only, and the various objective lines and boundaries suggested are merely tentative, to form the basis for a general plan.

6. The Blue Line is the line of eventual exploitation for the operations of September 18th.

7. The present corps front on the Blue Line extends a distance of 6,000 yards. It is suggested, either that the corps front should be extended to a total frontage of 10,000 yards, or that it should be side-slipped northwards to a frontage of 6,000 yards. The latter would obviously be preferable, so far as the corps is concerned, as enabling all its resources to be concentrated upon a smaller frontage.

8. The major outlines of the plan are as follows:

(*a*) An attack by two American divisions for the capture of the Green Line.

(*b*) A subsequent attack by two Australian divisions for the capture of the Red Line.

(*c*) Exploitation by the cavalry from the Red Line, in an Easterly and north-easterly direction.

(*d*) A turning movement by the Ninth Corps, through Bellicourt and Nauroy to turn the canal defences, operating from north to south—or alternatively.

(*e*) A turning movement by the Third Corps, operating through Le Catelet northwards.

9. The details of the above plan will run on the following lines:

(*a*) The new corps front to be taken over at the earliest possible moment by two American divisions, each division deploying for this purpose only one regiment of one brigade. This will place in Line six battalions on the corps front, giving each battalion about 1,000 yards. These troops will hold the line defensively, and will, with the assistance of technical troops, prepare the battle front.

(*b*) The battle troops of the two American divisions will thus comprise three regiments or nine battalions for each division. The allocation of objectives to these troops will be as follows:

(1) One brigade (two regiments) of the right division to advance 4,500 yards on a frontage of 3,000 yards. This brigade (six battalions) would attack with four battalions in line (750 yards frontage each) and two battalions in support for "mopping up" duties. Its principal objective, apart from the main trench systems, is Bellicourt.

(2) Similarly, one brigade (two regiments) of the left division, with similar dispositions. Its principal objective, apart from the main trench systems, is Catelet.

(3) The odd regiment of the right division to be responsible for forming the south defensive flank.

(4) The odd regiment of the left division to be responsible for forming the north defensive flank.

(*c*) It will be noted that the Green Line has been drawn so as to include all ground giving good observation northward, eastward and southwards, and to deny observation to the enemy. It is probable that the field artillery barrage will not be able to penetrate to the extreme limits of this proposed objective along the whole battle front without moving forward some of the batteries, particularly in the Northern Divisional Sector. This will probably necessitate a halt of an hour or an hour and a half, to enable artillery to be advanced.

(*d*) Assuming that the battle opens about 6 a.m., the Green Line should be reached by 10 a.m. or earlier. By mobilising ample resources in technical troops, both American and Australian, and ample tools and engineering material, it should be easily possible to construct not less than four roads, sufficiently developed for horse transport, from the Blue Line to the Green Line, by 2 p.m. These roads would be located so as to make use of existing roads, and trench crossings would be made by filling in with earth and not by bridging. It is estimated, therefore, that mobile artillery could move forward not later than 2 p.m. on Zero day.

(*e*) The Australian infantry of two divisions would move at such an hour as would enable them to reach and be deployed upon the Green Line by 2 p.m., shortly after which hour they would be joined by the necessary mobile artillery. This phase of the operation would also involve the capture of the Beaurevoir Line. It is assumed that tanks would be available to deal with the crossing of the wire entanglements covering this line.

(*f*) The completion of the defensive flanks would be allocated to American troops.

(*g*) As soon as the Australian infantry had passed the Green Line, the four American regiments who had participated in the capture of the Green Line, would be concentrated, refitted and rested for operations eastwards.

10. The following considerations should be kept in view, in connection with this plan.

(*a*) There should be sufficient field artillery, not merely to provide an effective barrage for the time-table advance to the Green Line and its flanks, but also, in addition, sufficient mobile field artillery, not employed in the barrage, to enable the Australian infantry to be provided with at least six artillery brigades for the exploitation phase of the operation.

(*b*) There should be at least 60 tanks available for the first phase, in order absolutely to guarantee the breaching of the main Hindenburg trench systems. There should, in addition, be available not less than 30 tanks to assist the Australian infantry through the Beaurevoir Line.

11. There should be a systematic destructive bombardment of the whole of the Hindenburg trench system on the battle front, lasting at least four days, in order not merely to destroy the defensive organisation, but also to demoralize and starve the trench garrisons. This destructive bombardment should extend a considerable distance to the north and south of the battle front.

12. The rapid construction of usable roads, both for horse transport

Mont St. Quentin—Collecting Australian wounded under the protection of the Red Cross flag, September 1st, 1918.

An Ammunition Dump—established in Warfusee village on August 8th, 1918, after its capture the same morning.

and mechanical transport, across the canal tunnel, would have to be a special feature of the organisation, so that the whole of our battle organisation could be rapidly carried forward to maintain the battle eastward of the Red Line. This would involve the mobilization of a large amount of mechanical transport, ready loaded with road-stone, so that road-making can commence after Zero hour without any delay. For these works, there would be available the greater part of the Australian and American technical troops of seven divisions, as well as army troops companies.

John Monash,
Lieut.-General.
Commanding Australian Corps.

Some comment is necessary upon this proposal. The composition of the American divisions, following the French and not the British precedent, differed materially from my own divisions. The American division consisted of two brigades, each of two regiments, each of three battalions. Its total strength was nearly double that of an English division.

It will be noted that my proposal involved a concentrated attack, not upon the canal, but upon that sector of 6,000 yards which lay over the Bellicourt-Catelet tunnel. This zone at that time lay clear of and to the north of my corps area, and that is what involved the necessity of "side-slipping" the corps front to the north.

Moreover, I put forward no suggestion that the canal sector, then in front of me, should be the subject of a frontal attack at all. My proposal was that it should be taken by envelopment, through the breach to be made over the tunnel. At the time I regarded it as unlikely that the deep canal itself could be stormed except at great cost. I was not prepared to commit any Australian troops under my command to such an enterprise, and therefore naturally hesitated to propose that any other corps should attempt it. For this reason, I submitted an alternative plan of envelopment.

This was, however, a matter for the army commander to decide. My business was merely to show that the proposed action of my own corps permitted of the co-operation of the other corps of the army in a specified way.

General Rawlinson's decisions were given on September 19th, at a conference which he assembled at my headquarters. My plan for the action of the Australian and American Corps was to be adopted in its entirety, with the sole exception that the capture of the Beaurevoir Line, on the first day of battle, was not to be included in the plan. It was to be left to await the results of the prior stages. In this modification I could readily concur.

As regards the action of the flank corps, General Rawlinson held the view that a direct assault on the canal itself ought to be attempted, and that this should be entrusted to the Ninth Corps. He was doubtless influenced, in this view, by the knowledge, disclosed to us for the first time on that day, that he intended to propose that the attack on the Hindenburg Line would, if undertaken, extend over the front of at least three armies, the French on the south, and the Fourth and Third British Armies. Such a simultaneous attack, over a very wide front, would naturally increase the prospects of success for every Corps participating.

As to the Third Corps, it was to take part only in the preliminaries of the battle, and not in the battle itself. Another corps, the Thirteenth (Lieut.-General Sir T.L.N. Morland) was to join the Fourth Army. If the Australian Corps succeeded in effecting the breach of the Hindenburg Line as I had proposed to do, it was to be the Thirteenth Corps, and not the Third Corps, which, pouring through the breach, was to envelop the flank of the Hindenburg Line towards the north.

The main consideration that affected me was the approval of my plan for the action of the two American and three Australian divisions. I was able to begin immediately the development in detail of that plan, a task which proved at once the most arduous, the most responsible, and the most difficult of any that I have had to undertake throughout the whole of the war.

The first step was to get the American divisions into the line opposite their prospective battle fronts, and the next was to hand over what had hitherto been the Australian Corps front to the Ninth Corps.

The Ninth Corps battle front was to extend from Bellenglise to Bellicourt, mine from opposite Bellicourt to opposite Le Catelet.

The necessary troop movements and inter-divisional reliefs required nearly a week for their completion. By the evening of September 23rd, the last of the two Australian divisions had been relieved by the Americans and the Ninth Corps, and on that night, these stood on their respective battle frontages. I took over command of this new front, thus manned by Americans, in the forenoon of September 25th.

It is a somewhat noteworthy circumstance, but one which attracted no attention at the time, that between September 25th and September 29th, there was a period of five days during which *no* Australian troops were in the front line in any part of the French theatre of war. This was a situation which had never arisen since the first contingent of Australians arrived from Egypt in April, 1916. For nearly two and a half years, there had never previously been a moment when some Australians had not been confronting the enemy, somewhere or other in the long battle front in France.

I have said that I had been called upon to undertake the responsibility of directing in a great battle two divisions (the 27th and 30th) of United States troops, numbering altogether some 50,000 men. These had been organised into a corps, called the Second American Corps, and commanded by Major-General G. W. Read. It was certainly anomalous that a whole organised corps should pass under the orders of a Corps Headquarters of another nationality, but in authorising such an arrangement, General Rawlinson relied upon the good sense and mutual forbearance of the corps commanders concerned.

I am bound to say that the arrangement caused me no anxiety or difficulty. General Read and his staff most readily adapted themselves to the situation. He established his headquarters quite close to my own, and gave me perfect freedom of action in dealing direct with his two divisional commanders, so far as I found it necessary to do so. Read was a man of sound common sense and clear judgment, a reserved but agreeable and courteous personality. His only desire was the success of his divisions, and he very generously took upon himself the role of an interested spectator, so that I might not be hampered in issuing orders or instructions to his troops. At the same time, I am sure that in his quiet, forceful way he did much to ensure on the part of his divisional commanders and brigadiers a sympathetic attitude towards me and the demands I had to make upon them.

The Australian Corps had specialised in comprehensive and careful preparations for battle. Its methods had been reduced to a quite definite code of practice, with which every staff officer and battalion adjutant had, by experience, become intimately familiar. All this procedure was a closed book to the American troops, and they were severely handicapped accordingly.

I therefore proposed to General Read, and he gratefully accepted, the creation of an "Australian Mission" to his corps, whose role would be to act as a body of expert advisers on all questions of tactical technique, and of supply and maintenance. This idea once accepted was worked out on a fully elaborated scale.

To the head of this mission I appointed Major-General Maclagan, not only to command the personnel of the mission itself, but also to live with and act as adviser to General Read's own staff. The mission comprised a total of 217 men, chosen from the First and Fourth Australian Divisions, and consisted of specially selected and very experienced officers and N.C.O.'s. The American Corps Headquarters was provided with a major-general, assisted by one general staff, one administrative, one signal, one intelligence, and one machine-gun staff officer. Each American division had assigned to it an Australian brigadier-general, assisted by several staff officers; each American brigade had an Australian battalion commander and signal officer; and so on down the chain. Each American battalion, even, had four highly expert warrant or non-commissioned officers to advise on every detail of supply, equipment and tactical employment of the troops.

By such an arrangement it became possible to talk to the whole American Corps in our own technical language. This saved me and my staff a vast amount of time and energy, because the members of this mission acted as interpreters of the technical terms and usages customary in the orders and maps of the Australian Corps, which were necessarily quite unfamiliar to the American troops.

Maclagan was a man eminently fitted for this task. In appearance and in temperament he is every inch a soldier. Of all my divisional commanders he was the only one who, immediately before the war, was a professional soldier of the Imperial Army. Although not Australian born, he was whole-heartedly Australian, for he had spent some years as Director of Military Training at the Royal Military College at Duntroon. On the outbreak of war, he received the command of the 3rd Australian Brigade, and with it carried out the most difficult preliminary phase of the landing on the Gallipoli peninsula. He commanded the Fourth Australian Division from the autumn of 1917 until the conclusion of hostilities. His characteristic attitude of mind, so strongly in contrast to that of Rosenthal, was pessimistic. But that was not because he looked for difficulties, but because he preferred squarely to recognise and face all the difficulties there were. Yet he never failed in performance, and invariably contrived to do what he had urged could not be done. One could not afford to take him at his own modest estimate of himself. Both he and his division always bettered any promise they gave.

I entertain no kind of doubt that it was only because of the creation of this Australian Mission to the Americans, and of Maclagan's tact, industry and judgment in controlling it, that the combined action of the two corps in the great battle of the closing days of September proved as successful as it did. Under no other conditions would it have been possible to bring about any reasonable degree of co-operation between two forces whose war experiences, outlook, attitude towards their problems, training and temperament were so fundamentally different.

It is not necessary to indulge in either a panegyric or a condemnation of these American divisions. Neither would be deserved or appropriate. They showed a fine spirit, a keen desire to learn, magnificent individual bravery, and splendid comradeship. But they were lacking in war experience, in training, and in knowledge of technique. They had not yet learned the virtues of unquestioning obedience, of punctuality, of quick initiative, of anticipating the next action. They were, many of them, unfamiliar with the weapons and instruments of fighting, with the numerous kinds of explosive materials, or with the routine of preparing and promulgating clear orders. They seriously underrated the necessity for a well-organised system of supply, particularly of food and water, to the battle troops. They hardly, as yet, appreciated the tactical expedients available for reducing losses in battle.

Yet all these shortcomings were the results only of inexperience, and it is perhaps unfair to contrast them with the Australian troops who had seen front-line service in France for two and a half years continuously, and whose leaders, high and low, had served a long and graduated apprenticeship in every branch of their duties.

The Australian Mission assisted greatly to minimize these difficulties. Although its members were vested with no executive powers, their advice and help were eagerly sought, and zealously adopted. In many ways, large and small, their assistance must have proved invaluable. How to interpret orders from above and how to issue them to those below, how to draw stores and how to distribute them, how to organise the signal service and how to ensure a flow of information—these ranked among the greater matters. In quite small things also, help was needed, such as the way to detonate mortar bombs, to equip the infantryman for battle, to organise and use the messenger (*i.e.*, runner) service, and to keep battle stations clear of people who had no urgent business there.

It is not, of course, intended to convey that all these defects were present in every regiment. Some, however, were met with, by the officers of the Australian Mission, in all of them.

It greatly added to the burden cast upon the American divisions that they were called upon to fight almost as soon as they had taken up duty in the line. The necessity for this was really a legacy from the Third Corps, whom they had relieved, and it is essential for an understanding of the course of events during these days to narrate them in proper chronological order.

I have explained that as the result of the Battle of Hargicourt, the Australian Corps had succeeded in mastering the whole of the Hindenburg outpost line opposite its front, as far as a point a little north of and opposite to Bellicourt. The advance of the Third Corps, however, had failed to reach the same line, and had stopped short of it by an average distance of nearly a thousand yards. On my pointing out that the front I had taken over did not comply with the stipulations which I had made in my battle plan, (shown earlier), the army commander decided that prior to the main attack, the northern of the two American divisions should make good this shortage, by an attack aiming at the capture of the remainder of the Hindenburg outpost line opposite the tunnel sector.

I must now anticipate an explanation of the main outlines of the plan which I had prepared for the great battle, by a brief reference to the situation and disposition of troops on September 25th. The two American divisions were respectively the 30th, commanded by Major-General Lewis, on the right or south, and the 27th, commanded by Major-General O'Ryan, on the left or north, each lying on a frontage of three thousand yards. These two divisions comprised, in all, eight regiments, each of three battalions. I had instructed each of them to place one regiment in the line, and to keep the remaining three, *i.e.*, six in all, in reserve, for the main operation.

My first corps conference dealing with the forthcoming operations was held at my headquarters at Assevillers, on September 23rd. The American Generals Read, Lewis and O'Ryan, with their respective staffs, attended, as also did the Australian Generals Maclagan, Brand and Mackay, who were members of the Australian Mission to the American Corps. None of the Australian commanders destined to take part in the operations attended on this day, for two reasons, firstly, because I intended to confine myself entirely to that portion of the operation which concerned the American troops only, and secondly, because the date of the battle had not then been decided, and I wished to run no risk of confusing executive action by any premature announcements to the Australians, which subsequent events might modify.

The American role, had, however, sufficiently crystallised to enable me to explain it to the assembled generals in great detail. As will subsequently appear, it was a plan which had, intentionally, been reduced to the simplest possible elements. It was to be a straightforward trench to trench attack, from a perfectly straight "jumping off" line to a perfectly straight objective line, under a dense artillery and machine-gun barrage, and with the assistance of a large contingent of tanks. The advance was to be at a deliberate pace, and if due regard were had to a few elementary precautions, should prove a simple task for the American infantry. It was, indeed, on quite stereotyped lines, such as had so often carried the Australian infantry to victory in set-piece battles such as Messines, Broodseinde, Hamel and the first phase of August 8th.

It was, however, borne in upon me, very soon after this conference opened, that I was now confronted with quite a different proposition from that to which I had been accustomed in the conferences attended by my own divisional generals. The exposition of the plan itself was brief and simple, but it elicited such a rain of questions, that in the end I found myself compelled to embark upon a very detailed exposition of the fundamental principles of my battle practice.

With blackboard and chalk, maps and diagrams, I had to speak for more than three hours in an endeavour to explain methods and reasons, mistakes and remedies, dangers and precautions, procedures and expedients. The proceedings left me with no doubt that the American generals became fully informed as to the tasks and duties allotted to them, and fully understood them.

In the light of after events, I am not so sure that they succeeded in passing on the information to their subordinates—not by reason of any shortcomings on their own part, for they impressed me as able, strong men—but because their divisions had not yet learned the methods and machinery of effectively and rapidly conveying instructions to large bodies of troops.

In one particular, subordinate though vital, there certainly was a serious failure to reach the troops. The enemy had, during 1916, met our assault tactics with an answer which proved disastrously effective against us until we had learned how to meet it. He provided his trench systems with many and roomy shell-proof dug-outs. Whenever our barrage fell upon his trenches, his garrisons promptly took cover in these dug-outs. When our assaulting infantry reached the enemy trenches, they found but few of the enemy there, and they rushed headlong forward to the next objective trenches. From out of their dug-outs streamed the enemy, faced about, attacked our assaulting lines in rear and withered them with fire. Many an attack by the British on the Somme failed for just such reasons.

In 1917 we evolved, and applied for the first time at the Battle of Messines, an effective answer to such tactics. Close on the heels of our first line of assaulting troops came a second line, whose role was to occupy the captured trench immediately, and to "mop it up". This meant the killing or disarming of all enemy found in hiding, the picketing of the entrances and exits of all dug-outs, and laying siege to them until their occupants surrendered, a course to which they were encouraged by a liberal use of phosphorus bombs or Mills's grenades.

This process of "mopping up" became an integral part of our attack procedure. Australian infantry soon learned its importance, and practised the method with a thoroughness and efficiency to which I remember no exception. Even a junior sergeant commanding a dozen men could be relied on to take all measures necessary to ensure that no enemy was ever left in hiding and unguarded behind his little party as they advanced.

In the forthcoming attack upon the Hindenburg defences, the process of "mopping up" became of supreme importance, because of the very fact, of which we had become well aware, that the whole defensive system had been provided, on quite an exceptional scale, with underground shelters, galleries, passages and dug-outs. I made the most of this knowledge in my talks to the Americans, emphasized the dangers as strongly as I was able, insisted that the "mopping up" organisation of their infantry must be absolutely perfected, and ordered that of the total infantry participating in the assault, not less than one-half should have the special role of safeguarding all underground exits and entrances.

The great fear was, of course, that these new troops, eager to show their mettle, would be carried away in the excitement of the moment, and would rush headlong forward, regardless of the dangers that lurked behind them. It is, after all, no small demand to make upon the discipline of an infantry soldier, to expect him patiently and obediently to stand guard over some dug-out entrance, allowing the battle to sweep on, and his comrades to go forward to the excitement and glory of achieving the final objectives.

So indeed, it happened. The American infantry had either not been sufficiently tutored in this important matter, or the need of it had not penetrated their understanding. In the attacks carried out by these troops, while under my command, the "mopping up" was always badly done, even in the few cases where it was attempted. The result was failure to achieve a clean success, and a great addition to their own casualty list. This criticism will be fully borne out by the narrative of the great battle itself.

A second and much larger conference was held at my headquarters on September 26th, for the really complete and final co-ordination of the whole of the procedure for the forthcoming battle. It was attended not only by the American divisional generals and brigadiers, but also by the commanders of the Second, Third and Fifth Australian divisions, their staffs, the tanks, air force and cavalry.

It was much the largest and was also destined to be the last of any assemblage of commanders that it had been my privilege to call together in the course of this memorable campaign.

No one present will soon forget the tense interest and confident expectancy which characterised that meeting. America, a great English-speaking democracy on one shore of the Pacific, was to co-operate with Australia, its younger sister democracy on the opposite shore, in what was the greatest and what might be the most decisive battle of the great European War. Few present doubted that, if we were successful, the war could not last much longer—because the loss of the Hindenburg system would inevitably mean for the enemy his final enforced withdrawal from France.

While the conference was in full swing, the field marshal himself paid me a call. He had come to wish me success in the task before me. He was interested to find so many divisional commanders assembled, and was persuaded to address a few words to the gathering.

The conduct of the proceedings of this conference was a heavy strain. The main battle was to take place on September 29th, or within seventy-two hours, and part of my front line still stood a thousand yards west of the Hindenburg outpost lines. General Rawlinson had decided that this defect was to be made good prior to the main operation, and the attempt to do so had been timed to take place on September 27th, the day after the conference.

I had, therefore, to complete my organisation upon the basis of a set of precedent conditions which had not yet been entirely realised. It was a new and a difficult situation. The whole of the powerful artillery at my disposal for the battle, amounting now to over a thousand guns, was naturally clamouring for final decisions, so that final barrage maps could be submitted for my approval, printed by my very diligent and competent body of lithographic draughtsmen, and circulated to all the batteries and infantry.

To await the result of the operation of the next day would have allowed insufficient time to complete the necessary maps and to distribute them before nightfall on September 28th. There was no option but to assume that General O'Ryan (27th American Division) would succeed in capturing the northern section of the outpost line still in enemy hands, and upon that assumption to fix the artillery "start line" as falling to the east of that objective. For the first time I had to gamble on a chance. It was contrary to the policy which had governed all my previous battle plans, in which nothing had been left to chance.

At 5.30 a.m. next morning the 27th American Division carried out the attack, under a barrage, and assisted by tanks. The principal objective points in the trench system under attack were Quennemont Farm and Gillemont Farm. Every trace of these once prosperous homesteads and plantations had, of course, long since disappeared. The names alone remained as memories of the fighting there of 1917.

What happened on that day will never be accurately known. For once, the information from the air did not harmonize with the claims made on behalf of the assaulting troops, perhaps because the troops, being untrained in the use of flares, or having been left unsupplied with them, failed to assist the aeroplanes in identifying their correct positions. However, that may be, it became sufficiently clear, as the day proceeded, that no proper success for the operation could be claimed.

There remained no doubt that some enemy were still left in occupation of trenches on our side of the objective for that day, and such American troops as may have gained their objective could not therefore be reached. It appeared afterwards that small parties of Americans had reached the vicinity of their objectives and had very gallantly maintained themselves there, although surrounded on all sides, until relieved by the Australians on September 29th.

The non-success of this operation of September 27th appeared undoubtedly to be due to a failure to carry out "mopping up" duties satisfactorily. It considerably embarrassed the preparations for the main attack on the 29th. The knowledge that a number of American wounded were still lying out in front, and the suspicion that some of the American troops had succeeded in reaching Gillemont Farm, precluded any alteration of the artillery plans for September 29th, even if there had still been time to do so without creating untold confusion. To have brought the artillery start line, proposed for September 29th, back to the start line of September 27th would have brought our own barrage down upon these forward troops of ours.

I hastened to the army commander to put the position before him, stating that I felt grave concern for the success of the main operation, in view of the fact that my artillery barrage would have to come down fully a thousand yards in front of what was still the front of the 27th Division. I suggested a postponement for a day to give this division, which had ample resources in troops, another opportunity of retrieving the position. He explained, however, that it was now too late to alter the programme, because three whole armies were committed to the date first appointed. He said that he was, under the circumstances, quite prepared for a partial failure at this point, and requested me to do my best to pursue the original plan, in spite of this difficult situation.

He agreed, however, to my further request, that additional tanks, out of army reserves, should be placed at my disposal, so that I might allot them to the 27th Division, to assist them in passing over the thousand yards which would bring them up level with the artillery barrage. I hoped that this would enable the division to catch up with the southern half of the battle line.

It was an unsatisfactory expedient, and gave no promise of certain success. It proved futile, and gravely affected the actual course, although not the ultimate success, of the battle still to come. It was the only occasion in the campaign on which I was compelled to accept preliminary arrangements which were not such as would absolutely guarantee success.

The genesis of the difficulty thus created had, however, been the failure of the Third Corps to complete their programme of September 18th. It had been confirmed by the subsequent failure of the 27th American Division to make up the deficiency on September 27th. I still think, as I then urged, that I should have been allowed to accept the situation as I found it on taking over this front on September 25th, and that the 27th Division should not have been called upon, at the eleventh hour, to endeavour to establish that new situation which had been originally assumed as the basis for the battle plan of September 29th. My original proposal of September 18th, in my letter of that date, paragraph 3 (see above), had, of course, been made before I could foresee that the Third Corps would fail to capture the start line contemplated in my first plan.

Of course, all is well that ends well. But, for an anxious and turbulent period of twenty-four hours on September 29th and 30th, the issue of the battle hung in grave doubt. The operation, although successful, did *not* proceed "according to plan" in its entirety, and it was due to the wonderful gallantry and skilful leading of the Third Australian Division that a very ugly situation was retrieved, a result to which the Fifth Australian Division also contributed in no small degree.

Chapter 15
Bellicourt and Bony

A full account of the battle plan for the forcing of the main Hindenburg Line, on the front of the Australian Corps, would alone fill a volume. Nothing but brief references to the main outlines of the plan can be attempted here.

The forces now at my disposal, for immediate use, were greater than I had ever before committed to a single operation. They comprised, in all, five divisions, of which two were American and three Australian, besides the whole of the corps troops. The total personnel employed on that occasion, under my orders in one capacity or another, almost reached 200,000 men.

Besides 58 battalions of infantry, there were over 20,000 technical troops, including engineers, pioneers and signallers, upwards of 1,000 guns of all calibres, more than 500 machine-guns, over 200 tanks, a brigade of cavalry, a battalion of armoured cars, and numerous air squadrons. The subsidiary services made an imposing array, comprising observation balloons, supply trains, ammunition columns, auxiliary horse transport, ambulances, motor convoys and mechanical transport, together with railway, veterinary, sanitary and labour units.

It was no small task correctly to apportion to each fighting unit and to each service its appropriate place in the general scheme, so that these great resources should be employed to the best advantage, without overtaxing the capacity of any one of them. I had also to secure the greatest measure of co-operation between them all, and the punctual performance by each of the work prescribed.

In contrast with the great battle of August 8th, there was on this occasion no possibility of securing any advantage from surprise. The enemy command was bound to know quite as well as we did that, we intended to deliver an attack on a gigantic scale, and there is no doubt that they put forth their utmost efforts, and marshalled their fullest resources in men and guns, to meet it. There was, therefore, no object to be served by any measures of concealment, and our task could not be made any the harder through heralding the approach of the actual attack by adequate artillery preparation.

The programme, therefore, began on the night of September 26th. There was an intense artillery action, extending over some sixty hours, with every gun that could be brought to bear. This does not, of course, imply that every individual gun or battery remained in action during the whole of this period; ammunition supplies were not inexhaustible, and gun detachments required periods of rest. But the programme of times and targets was so arranged, and the tasks were so distributed over the available batteries, that throughout this period there was no respite for the enemy in any part of the field.

For some days prior to the opening of this bombardment, railway trains and motor lorries had been working at the highest possible pressure, to enable gunners to accumulate at their gun pits and in all their dumps a sufficient supply of artillery ammunition for this purpose. In the short period which had elapsed since the forcing of the Somme, in the early days of September, the railway diversion from Bray to Péronne had been completed. The railway from Péronne to Roisel, although seriously damaged by the enemy in many places, had been restored, and Roisel had become the railhead for the delivery of ammunition. It was a noteworthy performance, for all the corps services concerned, to carry out the whole supply of this battle in so smooth and expeditious a manner.

The first phase of this bombardment was of a novel character. For over two years the enemy had been using a shell containing an irritant and poisonous gas known to us as "mustard" gas. It was so called only because of the smell. For a long time, we had been promised that the British artillery service would shortly be supplied with a gas shell, of similar character, but even more potent. It was, moreover, anticipated that the German gas mask would prove no adequate protection against this kind of gas.

At last the new shell was forthcoming, and the first shipment from England, amounting to some fifty thousand rounds, was placed at the disposal of the Australian Corps. My artillery action, therefore, opened with a concentrated gas bombardment for twelve hours, attacking probable living quarters, occupied defences, and all known or suspected approaches to them. Apart from being the first occasion, I believe that it was also the only occasion during the war when our "mustard" gas shell was used. No suitable opportunity for further use occurred before the close of hostilities.

The gas bombardment was followed by forty-eight hours' destructive bombardment with high explosive shell. This was directed partly

Australian Light Horse—the 13th A.L.H. Regiment riding into action on August 17th, 1918.

"The Sniper sniped"—an enemy sniper disposed of by an Australian Sharp-shooter, August 22nd, 1918.

against the enemy's artillery, as far as the short time available had permitted us to locate his batteries.

Another part of the bombardment was devoted to the approaches from the enemy's rear to his forward defences. The object was to render his roads and tracks unusable, and thereby to prevent the delivery of rations, or, at any rate, of hot food to his garrisons, or of ammunition to his guns. By these means we expected, by partially starving him out, to impair the enemy's morale.

The main weight of the bombardment was, however, devoted to the destruction of the enemy's defences, of which his barbed-wire entanglements-were for us the most formidable feature. Much of this wire was disposed in concealed positions, either in depressions of the ground, or in sunken moats, artificially prepared. It was, therefore, difficult to locate, and still more difficult for my gunners to direct their fire upon it. Nevertheless, there was a considerable quantity of wire which was plainly visible, and every band of entanglements through which breaches could be blown was so much to the good, in clearing the path for the infantry assault.

In earlier years it had been the custom to attack barbed wire with our lighter guns, using shrapnel shell. This shell is, however, essentially a "man-killing" projectile, and has no great destructive power against field works. On the other hand, our heavier guns were scarcely more useful for wire cutting, because the great craters which were made by the explosion of their shells destroyed the wire only very locally, and, by upheaving the ground, increased rather than reduced the difficulties of the infantry.

This was due to the employment of fuses, which permitted the projectile, after striking, to bury itself in the ground for a small fraction of time before igniting the explosive charge which it contained. Hence the great shell craters. It was a very proper fuse to use for destroying trenches, dug-outs, gun-pits and emplacements, but of little use for cutting wire.

In due course the British service evolved an "instantaneous" fuse, which became known to the gunners as the "106 Fuse". This had the merit of being perfectly safe to handle, up to the moment of firing the gun, but by means of a most ingenious mechanism it became highly sensitive while the projectile was in flight between the gun and the target. The result was that the very slightest obstacle met with, even a strand of wire, was sufficient to set off the fuse and explode the shell. Even if the shell met no obstacle before striking the earth, the explosion would take place above instead of below the surface of the ground, and would exert so great a horizontal force in all directions that great bands of wire entanglements would be bodily uprooted, over considerable areas, and literally blown to one side in a jumbled mass.

Our heavy guns, therefore, using 106 fuses, became ideal wire cutters, and it was in this way that much of the artillery action during the forty-eight hours prior to the battle was applied.

The infantry and field artillery plan, which I prepared, was very similar in its general character to the battle plan of August 8th. It differed only in subordinate details due to local topographical variations from the former conditions.

Of the five divisions available, one—the Second Australian—was to remain in corps reserve, but handy. For that purpose, it was brought up from its rest near Cappy, by motorbus, to the vicinity of Péronne, the move being completed by nightfall on September 27th.

The battle divisions and their prior dispositions were as follows:

Line Divisions:
On the right, the 30th American Division, to attack with the 60th Brigade, and to employ the 59th Brigade to form a southern defensive flank in the event of the failure of the Ninth Corps to cross the Canal.

On the left, the 27th American Division, to attack with the 54th Brigade, and to employ the 53rd Brigade to form a northern defensive flank, until such time as the Thirteenth Corps was ready to pass through in a north-easterly direction.

"Exploitation" Divisions:
On the right, the 5th Australian Division, with the 8th and 15th Brigades in the first line and the 14th Brigade following in support.

On the left, the Third Australian Division, with the 10th and 11th Brigades in the first line and the 9th Brigade following in support.

The total frontage was equally divided between the two pairs of divisions, being about 3,500 yards to each. The battle was to be divided into two phases, the first to be executed by the Americans, under a timed barrage, the second, under open warfare conditions, by the Australians. It was intended that the Americans should penetrate to the "green line", an average distance of 3,500 yards, which took in the villages of Bellicourt, Nauroy, Bony and Gouy.

The Australians were to exploit eastward, but were limited to a further advance of 4,000 yards, overrunning Joncourt, Estrées and Beaurevoir. Should they reach that objective on the first day, they would have passed the last-known wired line, and the country beyond would be suitable for cavalry. Accordingly, I allotted to the 5th Cavalry Brigade, which had been placed under my orders, the role of passing through the Australian divisions, and carrying the exploitation still further east, in the direction of Montbrehain and Brancourt.

As it turned out, the whole of the objectives named were in our possession only on the forenoon of October 5th, instead of, as planned, by September 30th. The actual battle developed on totally different lines from those which I had planned, for reasons which I shall relate in due course. Little object would therefore be served in an explanation of the considerable mass of detailed arrangements which the original plan involved; these would also, by reason of their technical character, be more suitable for a text-book on tactics.

Suffice it to say that elaborate arrangements were made—and also partly utilised—for the rapid construction of four main roads from west to east, through the full width of the Hindenburg system. This work was to follow on the heels of the advance. The roles assigned to the tanks, the barrage artillery, the mobile artillery, the heavy artillery and the armoured cars were similar in character, although differing in detail from those carried out by them on August 8th.

On no previous occasion had the labour of preparation and the stress upon all commanders and staffs been so heavy, but all responded nobly. There were none who did not count the hours till zero hour, which was fixed for 5.50 a.m. on September 29th.

In appraising the long sustained fighting on the front of the Fourth Army which began on that day, and lasted a full week, regard must be had to contemporary events. The American First Army attack on St. Mihiel on September 11th had wrought fresh dislocation to the enemy's resources, and had created another sore spot on his long front. On September 26th the Americans and French again successfully attacked between Verdun and Rheims. On September 27th, the First and Third British Armies opened a great attack on a front of thirteen miles before Cambrai and the magnificent Canadian Corps captured Bourlon Wood and advanced to within a mile of Cambrai city. On September 28th, the Second British Army and the Belgians attacked between Ypres and the sea. All British Armies, except the Fifth, had, therefore, by that time developed active battle fronts. On September 29th the first French Army would co-operate with us, and on that day the battle front was to cover a total length of twenty-five miles.

The simultaneous engagement of so large a portion of the enemy's line in Belgium and France during the preceding three days had piled difficulty upon difficulty for him, and it was therefore not unreasonable to entertain two expectations—firstly, that our task would be rendered easier by the wide dispersion of the enemy's defensive energies, and, secondly, that he could hardly hope to survive a definite breach in his great defensive line at so critical a place as the Bellicourt tunnel. If that went, he would be secure nowhere, and his next possibility of making a stand would be on the line of the Meuse, even if not the line of the Rhine.

The day broke with a familiar mist, and the attack was launched punctually at the appointed time. Quite early in the day news came in that the Ninth Corps on my right hand had achieved an astonishing success, that Bellenglise had been captured, and that the deep canal had been successfully crossed in several places. It was the 46th Imperial Division to which this great success was chiefly due, a success achieved by most careful preparation and gallant execution. Lifebelts, rafts, boats, mats, portable bridges, and every device which ingenuity could suggest had been prepared beforehand for the actual crossing of the water in the canal. There can be no doubt that this success, conceived at first as a demonstration to distract attention from the Australian Corps front, materially assisted me in the situation in which I was placed later on the same day.

The first reports from my own front were in every way satisfactory, and it looked as if everything were going strictly to schedule. That morning the stream of messages pouring into my headquarters office, from special observers, from the air, from the line divisions, from the artillery, and from my liaison officers with neighbouring corps, exceeded in volume and import anything I had met with in my previous war experience. I have the typewritten precis of the "inwards" signal traffic before me as I write. Those received and laid before me on that day cover thirty closely typewritten foolscap pages.

The burden of the earlier messages all pointed to the same conclusion: "30th Division crossed the canal on time"; "1,000 prisoners, all going well"; "Bony captured"; "Tanks fighting round Bellicourt at 9 a.m."; "Bellicourt taken."

Those, omitting formal parts, were the burden of all the telegrams up to 10 a.m. They continued in such a favourable strain during the whole of the time that the two American divisions had command of the battle front.

The time for their arrival at the first objective—*i.e.*, the "green" line—had been computed to be at 9 a.m. The Australian divisions were to cross the green line at 11 a.m., and at the same hour to take over the command on the front of the battle. Two telegrams then came in which caused me serious anxiety. It may be of interest to set them out in detail:

Received at 11. 10 a.m. from 30th American Division:

Fighting in Bellicourt, owing to Germans having come down along the canal from the north. Fifth Australian Division hung up.

Received at 11. 12 a.m. from Third Australian Division:

We are dug in on west side of tunnel. Americans are held up in front of us.

These were only the first symptoms of a miscarriage of the plans. Evidences rapidly multiplied that all was not going well. But, concurrently, there came a stream of messages from the air that our troops and some of our tanks were east of both Bellicourt and Le Catelet.

The situation was therefore confused and uncertain, and it had to be diagnosed without delay. I hastened forward with all possible speed to get into personal touch with the situation and the divisional commanders. I soon formed the conclusion that probably both American divisions had successfully followed our barrage, and that numbers of their troops had really reached the green line, but that, once again, the "mopping up" procedure had been neglected. The enemy had reappeared in strength from underground *behind* the Americans, and was holding up the advance of the two Australian divisions to the second phase of the operation.

Subsequent developments and further inquiries entirely bore out these conclusions. On the front of the 27th American Division there had been difficulty from the start. A number of tanks allotted to that division had been put out of action, some by direct hits from artillery, others by land mines. It was currently believed that these were not enemy mines, but some which had been laid months before by our own Fifth Army as a measure of protection against the possible use of tanks by the enemy.

This had given the 27th Division a bad start. Only two out of its six assaulting Battalions had managed to catch up with and follow the barrage. The remainder could not get forward as far even as the artillery start line. Those Americans who did follow the barrage apparently forgot all about "mopping up". They reached Le Catelet and Gouy and entered those villages, only to find themselves surrounded on all sides by the enemy. A German officer prisoner informed us next day that 1,200 of these Americans had been taken prisoner.

The 30th American Division did not fare so badly. They got a good start with the barrage, but the broken condition of the ground, the intricate trench system and the confusion of wire and dug-outs brought about a loss of cohesion and of control. By the time Bellicourt was reached, the attacking troops had fallen some distance behind the barrage, and most of the weight had gone out of the attack.

Meanwhile, in this part of the field also, the enemy had reappeared from underground, and was still in strength on the west side of Bellicourt, now in the hands of the Americans, when the advanced guard of the Fifth Australian Division came upon them.

It was an unexpected situation for the Fifth Division. But without a moment's hesitation the leading troops took its measure. They deployed from the artillery formation in which they had been previously advancing into lines of skirmishers.

★★★★★★

"Artillery Formation" is an advance in numerous small infantry columns irregularly spaced both in frontage and depth. "Line of Skirmishers" is an advance in successive lines of men, the intervals between the men being from two to five paces, and between the lines from 50 to 100 paces.

★★★★★★

After hard fighting in the face of most vigorous resistance, they cleared away all opposition which lay between them and Bellicourt, and, sweeping forward through that village, carefully "mopping up" as they went, carried with them considerable numbers of the Americans whom they found there.

While this was happening, the Third Australian Division, deprived of the assistance either of artillery or of tanks, and in broad daylight, found themselves confronted with the difficult problem of carrying out the whole of the task which had been set for the 27th Division, because the reappearance of the enemy upon the ground successfully passed over by some of the Americans earlier in the day nullified all the value of that success.

It was about 2 p.m. before I had succeeded in gathering sufficient reliable information about the situation to enable me to arrive at a decision how to deal with it. By that hour the Fifth Division had advanced through Nauroy, and had passed across the Le Catelet line in that vicinity. The Third Division had managed to get obliquely astride of the line of the tunnel, its right being well across the main Hindenburg wire, while its left was still in the vicinity of the American start line of that morning. They had, however, succeeded in finally capturing Quennemont Farm. The whole of their advance into such a position had been hotly contested.

My troops were therefore, to all intents and purposes, astride of the Hindenburg main line, one division wholly on the east and the other division mainly on the west of it. The southern end of the tunnel was in my possession, the northern end was not.

My decision was forthwith to abandon the original plan which had taken so many days and so much labour to prepare, to take immediate measures for securing our gains for the day, and to organise a continuation of the battle next day on totally different lines. These were to conquer the remainder of the main Hindenburg trench system, in which the ruin of the village of Bony was the key position, by attacking it from the south towards the north, instead of from the west towards the east.

The first step in this plan was to ensure effective tactical contact between the right flank of the Third Division and the left flank of the Fifth Division. I framed an order that both divisions should take immediate steps to such an end. Telephone communication with both Gellibrand and Hobbs being momentarily interrupted, I was about to forward written orders by dispatch rider to each of them to the effect mentioned.

Before the messenger had time to leave, however, messages came in from both divisional commanders, each reporting that he had just secured tactical touch with the other in exactly the way which I wanted. I consider this a remarkable example of unity of thought. Each, without being able to consult the other or myself, had taken the very course which each correctly anticipated that I should decide to have taken. The German general staff used to boast in their writings that no other army approached theirs in this capacity for initiative by subordinates on lines in thorough unison with each other and with the policies of the higher command.

That the situation on my front, now held exclusively by Australians, would have been secure that night against a determined counter-attack I did not doubt, even though the fourteen Australian battalions now holding a line of some 9,000 yards would scarcely average 400 rifles apiece. However, nothing more than small local counter-attacks was attempted, and the hold which I had gained upon the main defences was not slackened. I feel sure, nevertheless, that the success of the Ninth Corps on my right in swarming across the canal from Bellenglise to Bellicourt had much to do with my immunity from interference; the enemy probably found himself with quite enough to do there in trying to re-establish his line further in rear, and this forbade him to materialise sufficient troops for any general counter-attack.

While I have felt obliged to state the facts in regard to the partial failure of the two American divisions to carry out their part of my battle plan, I desire, nevertheless, to do full justice to these troops. I have no hesitation in saying that they fought most bravely, and advanced to the assault most fearlessly; that the leaders, from the divisional generals downwards, did the utmost within their powers to ensure success. Nor must the very bad conditions under which the 27th Division had to start be forgotten. Our American Allies are, all things considered, entitled to high credit for a fine effort.

But it is, nevertheless, true that in this battle they demonstrated their inexperience in war, and their ignorance of some of the elementary methods of fighting employed on the French front. For these shortcomings they paid a heavy price. Their sacrifices, nevertheless, contributed quite definitely to the partial success of the day's operations, and although the comprehensive plan, which was to have carried my front beyond Beaurevoir on the very first day, had to be abandoned, the day's fighting ended with the two Australian divisions in quite a satisfactory position for a continuance of the operations on the next day.

To this there was, however, one important qualification. Air observers continued to report the presence of American troops between the Hindenburg Line and Le Catelet, and also in the latter village. Late that night an Australian artillery liaison officer managed to make his way back into our lines with the story that he had actually advanced with a battalion of Americans into Le Catelet, and that they were still there, although practically surrounded.

The 27th Division made many attempts to get into communication with them, but without avail. Beyond the report previously alluded to that they had subsequently been made prisoner, I have no information of their ultimate fate; but when patrols of the Third Division entered the village forty-eight hours later, there was no longer any sign of them. A number of small parties of Americans were, however, encountered and relieved as the further advance of the Third

Division progressed during the next two days.

The situation was profoundly embarrassing. With the mass of artillery at my disposal, it would have been a simple matter to cover the further advance of the Third Division so amply as to make it easy to master the northern half of the tunnel defences, especially if attacked end on. But so long as American troops or wounded were presumed to be lying out in front, I dared not use artillery at all, except on a very restricted scale. I felt justified, however, in bombarding isolated localities which patrols had definitely ascertained to be still in enemy hands; but nothing in the shape of adequate artillery support to the infantry could be attempted.

During the night of September 29th orders were issued to the Second American Corps to withdraw all advanced troops that could be reached, and to concentrate their regiments for rest and reorganisation, so as to be ready as soon as possible for re-employment. Very considerable numbers of American soldiers had become mixed up with the Australian battalions, and, in their eagerness, had gone forward with them, regardless of the particular roles or objectives which had been originally assigned to them. It was found to be a matter of some difficulty to induce these men to withdraw from the fighting and to rejoin their own units, so keen were they to continue their advance.

I also ordered the Second Australian Division to be brought up by bus from the Péronne area, and to take up a position of readiness just west of the Hindenburg Line. I foresaw that with the nature of the fighting before the Third and Fifth Divisions, it would not be very long before they would have to be relieved, and there was still the Beaurevoir Line of trenches to be overcome before the Hindenburg system could be claimed as taken in its entirety. This move was duly carried out, and the Second Division became available by the evening of October 1st in close support of the battle front.

The orders to the two line divisions for September 30th were to attack generally in a north-easterly direction. The immediate objectives of the Third Division were Bony village, the "Knob" and the northern entrance to the tunnel. The flanks of the two divisions were to meet on the Railway Spur, and the right of the Fifth Division was to swing forward in the direction of Joncourt, in sympathy with any advance made by the Ninth Corps to the south of them.

There was, as explained, no possibility of attempting anything like a methodical advance covered by a co-ordinated artillery barrage. Progress would depend upon the tenacity and skilful leading of the front-line troops, and reliance must be had more upon the bayonet and the bomb than upon external aids. It was, in a peculiar degree, a private soldier's battle.

The night of September 29th brought steady rain, and everybody was drenched to the skin. September 30th was a day of intense effort, slow and methodical hand-to-hand fighting, in a perfect tangle of trenches, with every yard of the advance vigorously contested; but by nightfall the line of the Third Division had advanced fully 1,000 yards. Its left had pivoted on the "Knoll", to the west of the Hindenburg Line. Gillemont Farm was by then securely in their hands; they had reached the southern outskirts of Bony village. Their right was well across the line of the canal, and joined the left flank of the Fifth Division on the Railway Spur. The Fifth Division had cleared the Le Catelet trench line of the enemy, and its right was by now well to the east of Nauroy.

Another day's fighting was still before both divisions, but the effect of the successful efforts of September 30th was speedily felt on October 1st. Overnight the enemy must have made up his mind that it was hopeless to try to retain any further hold upon the tunnel line, and his further resistance melted rapidly away. On October 1st events moved quickly; by 10 a.m. the Fifth Division reported the capture of Joncourt. By midday the whole of the village of Bony was in our hands, and at the same hour the air observers reported our patrols rapidly approaching the "Knob" and Le Catelet village.

By nightfall of October 1st the whole operation had been successfully completed. The northern entrance to the tunnel, the "Knob" and the whole of the Railway Spur were in our hands; our line ran just west of Le Catelet and east of Estrées and Joncourt; all isolated parties of Americans and all American wounded had been gathered in, and the whole situation had been satisfactorily cleared up from an artillery point of view.

Later the same night our patrols entered Le Catelet, which lay in a hollow below us, and found the village deserted except for a number of enemy wounded. The enemy, during that day, relinquished his last hold upon the famous tunnel defences, and withdrew precipitately eastwards to the Beaurevoir hill and northwards towards Aubencheul. Our total captures during the three days' operations amounted to 3,057 prisoners and 35 guns.

It had been a stiff fight, and the endurance of the infantry had been highly tested. The skill displayed by the Third Division in the course of the close trench fighting of September 30th was particularly noteworthy. The stress upon Major-General Gellibrand and his staff and infantry brigadiers had been severe. The several brigades and battalions had unavoidably become seriously mixed up. Control became very difficult, but was never completely lost.

This was illustrated by the following incident of the day's fighting. I had ascertained that the whole of the infantry of the division had been committed, and there were no reserves in the hands of the divisional commander. One battalion of the 9th Brigade was fighting under the orders of the 11th Brigade, another under that of the 10th Brigade. I took exception to this, and directed that a divisional reserve should be immediately reconstituted. In spite of the difficulties of communication, Gellibrand contrived to carry this intricate order into effect during the very climax of the fight.

Gellibrand was a man of interesting personality, more a philosopher and student than a man of action. His great personal bravery and his high sense of duty compensated in a great measure for some tendency to uncertainty in executive action. He had been a professional soldier, but before the war had retired into civil life. When the call came, he received a junior staff appointment with the First Division, but his outstanding merits soon gained him promotion. As a brigadier, he had, during 1916 and 1917, successfully led several of the Australian brigades. His command of the Third Division during the last five months of active fighting was characterized by complete success in battle. His temperament and methods sometimes involved him in embarrassments on the administrative side of his work; but he succeeded in retaining to the last the whole-hearted confidence of his troops.

I feel certain from my close observation of the course of events on September 30th and October 1st, that much of the success of the battle was due to Gellibrand's personal tenacity, and the assiduous manner in which he kept himself in personal touch from hour to hour with the forward situation and progress of his troops.

Immediately upon the conclusion of the fighting I issued the following message:

> Please convey to all commanders, staffs and troops of the Third and Fifth Australian Divisions my sincere appreciation of and thanks for their fine work of the past three days. Confronted at the outset of the operations with a critical situation of great difficulty, and hampered by inability to make full use of our ar-

tillery resources, these divisions succeeded in completely overwhelming a stubborn defence in the most strongly fortified sector of the Western Front. This was due to the determination and resource of the leaders and the grit, endurance and fighting spirit of the troops. Nothing more praiseworthy has been done by Australian troops in this war.

The operations entrusted to the corps had, by the night of October 1st, been substantially completed. Although the Beaurevoir defence line still lay to the east of us, the main canal defences, as far as the Le Catelet line, had been pierced, and a way had been opened for the Thirteenth Corps to pass across the line of the tunnel to be launched upon its task of turning the enemy out of the northern continuation of the Hindenburg Line by envelopment from the south.

It was impossible to call upon the Third and Fifth Divisions for any further effort. Their work had been most exhausting. Furthermore, the steady drain upon their resources, after sixty days of almost continuous battle activity, had so reduced their fighting strength, that a very drastic re-organisation had become necessary. This could only be effected by a complete withdrawal from the fighting zone.

Accordingly, arrangements were put in hand for the immediate relief of these two divisions. The Fifth Australian was relieved by the Second Australian Division, and the Third Australian Division by a division of the Thirteenth Corps. Both the relieved divisions, in the course of the next few days, followed the First and Fourth Australian Divisions into the grateful rest area which had been provided to the west and south-west of Amiens, and before they were again called upon for further front-line service hostilities had ended.

CHAPTER 16
Montbrehain and After

The successive withdrawals of the First, Fourth, Third and Fifth Australian Divisions from the battle zone during the period from September 22nd to October 2nd had been arranged with the Fourth Army commander about the middle of September. The corps had been continuously employed on front-line duty since April, and had already accomplished a considerable advance, for every inch of which it had been obliged to fight.

This consideration alone had earned for the corps a period of rest. But other important questions arose which affected the situation.

I have mentioned that early in 1918 all brigades of the Imperial Service had, owing to failing man-power, been reduced from four to three battalions each. In this reduction the Australian brigades participated only to a small extent during the fighting period. Every one of the Australian battalions had created great traditions; regimental *esprit* and pride of unit were very strong. The private soldier valued his battalion colour patch almost more than any other decoration.

My predecessor in the corps command had, during May, 1918, directed the disbandment of one battalion each of the 9th, 12th and 13th Brigades. This was due to the wastage resulting from the heavy fighting by these brigades on the Villers-Bretonneux front. The residues of the disbanded battalions were used as drafts to replenish the remaining three battalions of each brigade. It was doubtless a measure directed by necessity, as the flow of reinforcements was steadily diminishing.

Much lamentation was, however, caused among the officers and men who thus lost their battalion identity, both among those remaining in the field and those convalescing from wounds and sickness, who were thereby deprived of the hope of rejoining their former units. Through all these events I became fully alive to the difficulties which would present themselves when the evil day should arrive on which the fate of still other battalions would have to be decided. It was a day whose advent I was anxious to stave off until the last possible moment.

Throughout the summer and autumn, it became incumbent upon me to keep a close watch upon the fighting strengths of all the 57 Australian infantry battalions in the field. I had to consider the numbers actually present with the unit, the numbers likely to join from time to time from convalescent camps and hospitals, and the flow of new recruits from the Australian depots in England. Almost daily forecasts had to be made as to the probable strengths available on a given date in all the battalions likely to be employed in a given operation.

The full official strength of a battalion of infantry was 1,000 at the outbreak of the war, but a reduction to 900 had been authorised in July, 1918. No battalion in the army was ever for long able to maintain itself at a strength of 900. Indeed, experience went to show that so long as the strength did not fall below 600, a unit could quite well carry out, in battle, a normal battalion task, provided that frequent periods of short rest could be assured.

Towards the middle of September, 1918, the successful course of the fighting, and the moderate rate of net wastage—by which I mean the excess of battle losses over replenishments from the rear—had

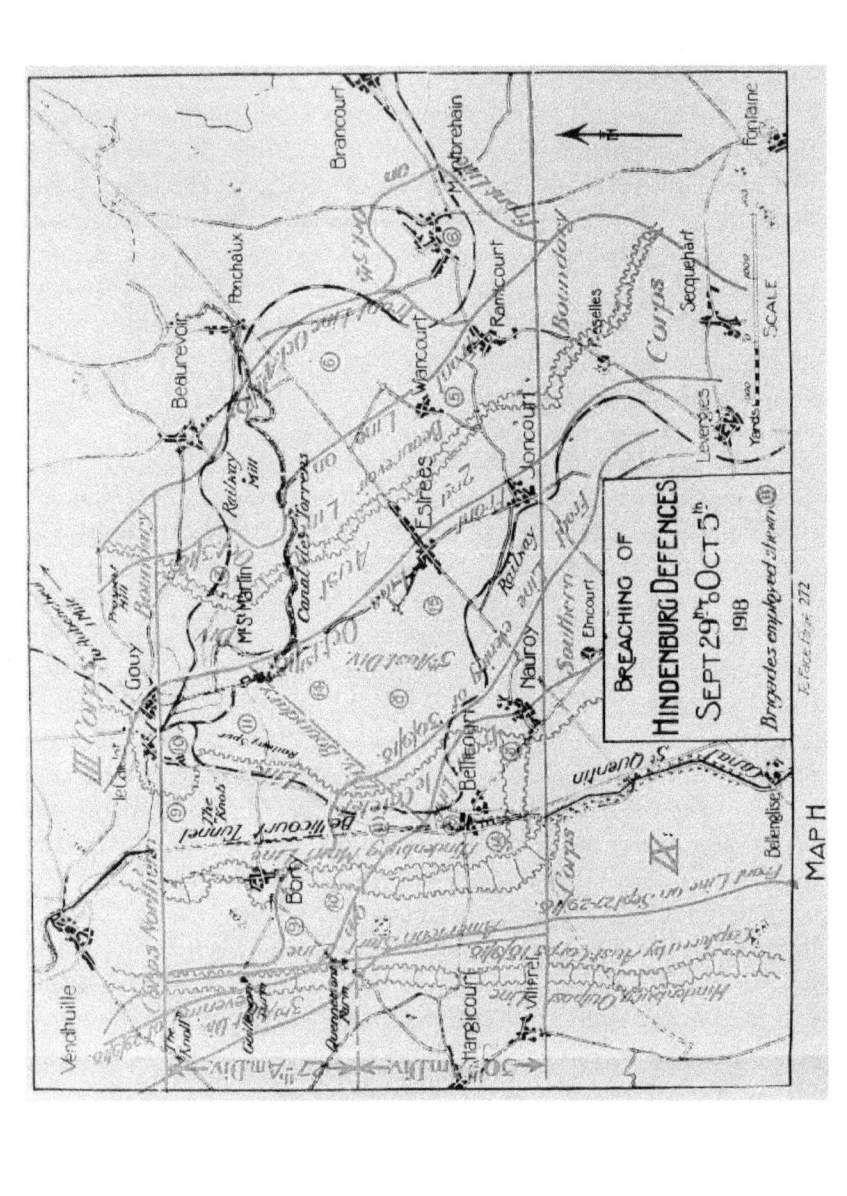

convinced me that there was every reason to hope that the strengths of the 57 battalions could be maintained at a useful standard until the end of the campaigning season of that year. If the war were to go on into 1919, and provided that the Australian Corps could be kept out of the line over the three winter months, thereby avoiding the daily wastage of trench duty, I felt able to guarantee that by the spring of 1919 the whole of these battalions would again have become replenished to a sufficient extent for a spring campaign.

It may have been an optimistic view; it may have savoured of a desire to postpone the evil day. But I felt assured that the disbandment of a number of additional battalions would seriously impair the fighting spirit of the whole Australian Corps. I was prepared to take the chance of being able to carry on until the end of 1918 with the whole 57 battalions retained intact. But I was not permitted to do so. At various times during the period June to August, 1918, an unimaginative department at G H.Q. kept harassing me with inquiries as to when it was proposed to conform to the new Imperial organisation in which all brigades were to be reduced to three battalions each. These inquiries were at first ignored, but early in September the adjutant-general became insistent for a reply.

I set out the whole position as I saw it, and strongly urged a postponement of the question until the corps should have completed the vitally important series of fighting operations on which it was then engaged. Looking back upon the course of events of that time, it is hardly credible now that, having regard to the reasons given, these representations should have been ignored. I procrastinated. Suddenly I received instructions from the War Office that some 6,000 men of the corps, who had served continuously since 1914, were to be given six months' furlough to Australia, and that they were to be held in readiness to entrain *en route* for Australia at forty-eight hours' notice.

These orders were received only two days before the Battle of Hargicourt. The First and Fourth Divisions, destined to fight in that battle, were those most affected by such a withdrawal of men, because these divisions contained the battalions and batteries which had been longest in the field. I could not, obviously, take up any attitude which would postpone the well-earned furlough of these veterans; nor had I the smallest inclination to do so. My case against the main proposal for an immediate extinction of additional battalions, was, however, weakened thereby.

The responsible authorities overruled my objections, and on Sep-

German Prisoners—captured at the battle of Chuignes, August 23rd, 1918.

Captured German Guns.—Park of Ordnance captured by the Australians during August, 1918.

tember 19th I received peremptory instructions to disband eight additional battalions forthwith. With many misgivings, I had no option but to comply. I called my divisional commanders together, and with them decided which battalions should suffer extinction.

It was a difficult choice, and created a situation of great difficulty. The whole of the personnel affected raised a very subordinate but none the less determined protest. One battalion after another very respectfully but very firmly took the stand that they did not wish to disband, and would prefer not to fight as dismembered and scattered portions of other battalions.

This attitude, perhaps, bordered upon insubordination, but it was conceived for a very worthy purpose. It was a pathetic effort, and elicited much sympathy from the senior commanders and myself.

On the eve of the great operations for the overthrow of the Hindenburg Line I found myself, therefore, in a sea of troubles, and threatened with the possibility of internal disaffection. To outsiders who could have no understanding of the situation this might imperil the fair fame and prestige of the Australian Army Corps.

Up to this stage the Fourth Army commander had been in no way concerned in the matter. The pressure upon me had come from the War Office and the adjutant-general's department. Lord Rawlinson's interests, however, now became vitally involved. I submitted the whole position to him. I pointed out how inopportune the time was for risking trouble of this nature. The order for disbandment, having been given, must of course stand, and obedience must be insisted upon; but a postponement of further action for fourteen days was desirable, if the opportunity of a decisive blow against the enemy was not to be imperilled by an impairment of the fighting spirit and goodwill of the Australian Corps.

Rawlinson accepted my views in their entirety, and used his authority and influence with the commander-in-chief. A postponement of action was authorised, and all the battalions which had been threatened with extinction, with one exception, were permitted to remain intact during the remainder of the fighting period. The exception was made in the case of the 59th and 60th Battalions (of the 15th Brigade), whose men most loyally made no demur at the immediate amalgamation of the two battalions for the purposes of the forthcoming operations.

By the end of September, therefore, three separate factors were operating to make a short withdrawal of the corps from the battle zone desirable.

These were, the long unbroken period of line service, the orders for the reorganisation of the brigades on a three-battalion basis, and the granting of Australian furlough to the veterans.

These were the reasons which brought about the decision that the whole of the Australian Corps should be sent for a period of rest in a coastal area as soon as the battle operations on which it had embarked had been brought to a successful conclusion.

Those operations were, on October 1st, almost completed. Only the Beaurevoir Line still remained to be mastered, and the Second Australian Division, which had been resting since its successes at Mont St. Quentin, was available to undertake that task. For the next three days the Australian Corps became, therefore, reduced to only one division (the Second Australian) in the line, with the 27th and 30th American Divisions in support.

The Second Division occupied the night of October 1st and the greater part of October 2nd in the process of taking over line duty from the Fifth Division, and in preparing for an attack timed for the next morning upon the Beaurevoir defences. I handed over the northern part of what had been the Australian Corps front, on the day previous, to the 50th Division (of the Thirteenth Corps), which had by now effected the passage of the tunnel line, and had deployed upon my left, facing north and north-east.

After these adjustments were made, the corps front, on the night of October 2nd, extended from Mont St. Martin through the eastern outskirts of Estrées and Joncourt, where I joined with the 32nd Division (now belonging to the Ninth Corps). It was a frontage of nearly 6,000 yards, an extraordinary length for the battle front of a single division. Our line lay parallel to and about 1,000 yards to the west of the Beaurevoir Line, and the attack for next day was designed to be delivered in a north-easterly direction. If the Beaurevoir Line itself were captured, the attack was to be pushed on beyond, in the endeavour to sweep the enemy off the prominent hill on which was situated the village of Beaurevoir. Concurrently the Thirteenth Corps would attack Prospect Hill, lying to the north-east of Gouy village.

The Beaurevoir Line was a fully-developed defensive system, with front, support and communication trenches, thoroughly traversed, well wired in, and still in good condition. In 1917 it would have been considered impossible to capture such a line of defence by such a force on such a frontage.

The Second Division deployed two of its brigades, the 5th on the right and the 7th on the left, with the 6th Brigade in reserve. The 5th Tank Brigade, now greatly reduced in numbers, and some Whippet Tanks co-operated in the attack. The assault was launched at 6.5 a.m. under a field artillery barrage. Considerable opposition was met with. The trenches were found strongly held, particularly with machine-guns, and the uncut wire seriously impeded the infantry.

The frontal attack of the 5th Brigade, nevertheless, achieved almost immediate success, although in some parts of the line there were centres of resistance which had to be enveloped before they yielded. The performance of the tanks on this day was disappointing. Most of the heavier tanks were disabled by artillery fire, while the Whippets found the Beaurevoir trench lines too wide to straddle. Nevertheless, the spirited action of the artillery made up for the loss of the assistance of the tanks, and by 11 a.m. the whole of the Beaurevoir Line in front of the 5th Brigade had been captured.

Further to the north, the 7th Brigade found the trenches almost end on to the direction of their advance, and the battle here speedily took on the form of pure trench fighting with bomb and bayonet, a type of fighting in which the Australian excels. Steady progress northwards was made.

The whole of the Beaurevoir Line over the full extent of the corps front was taken before midday, and although already very tired, the assaulting brigades pushed on beyond, to the ascent of the Beaurevoir Spur. On a knoll at its south-western extremity stood the stone base of the now wrecked Beaurevoir Mill, a prominent landmark visible for miles.

The spur and the vicinity of the mill were found to be strongly held, probably by fugitives driven out that morning from the Beaurevoir trenches. The weight of our attack spent itself on the slopes of the spur. The 6th Brigade was therefore launched at Beaurevoir Mill and village. Although some portion of our attack passed the mill and reached the village, our available infantry strength was not sufficient to mop it up satisfactorily, and the brigadier decided to establish for the night a secure line about 1,000 yards south-west of the village. The total captures by the Second Division on this day exceeded a thousand prisoners and many machine-guns—an astonishing performance for three weak brigades, fighting under open and exposed conditions.

The attack on Beaurevoir Hill had been undertaken chiefly to keep the enemy engaged and on the move, while an additional division of the Thirteenth Corps could be brought across the line of the tunnel and deployed into the battle line. The direction of the attack had been to the north-east. It now became necessary to readjust the general easterly line of advance by redistributing the army front between the three corps now in line. The greater part of October 4th was occupied in carrying out these arrangements, and the Second Division availed itself of the period to improve its line and the positions of parts of it by local attacks and the capture of tactical points along its front. On this day the division gathered in a further 800 prisoners and five guns.

By nightfall on October 4th the corps front, now reduced to 4,000 yards, ran generally north and south, well east of Wiancourt and just east of Ramicourt. The task of the Second Division and of the Australian Corps was completed, and in pursuance of arrangements previously made, the initial steps were taken on that day to hand over the Australian Corps front to the 27th and 30th American Divisions, which had, in the days intervening since September 29th, been reorganised and rested. They were to be given a place in the front battle line under the direct orders of their own Corps Headquarters (General Read).

To cover the interval of time necessary to enable the first of the American divisions (30th) to move up into line, General Rawlinson desired me to retain control of the battle front for one day longer, and avail myself of the time to make an endeavour to advance our line still further to the east.

I selected as a suitable objective the village of Montbrehain, which stood on a plateau that dominated any further advance.

The Second Division was instructed to carry out this attack early on October 5th, and I allotted to them one company of tanks, which was all that could be materialised in fighting trim at such short notice.

Rosenthal launched his attack at five minutes past six in the morning of October 5th. It was the 6th Brigade which led it. The village was full of machine-guns, but the gallant brigade dashed in with the bayonet, and methodically worked its way through the village to its eastern outskirts. A counter-attack developed about noon, and for a time about 400 yards of ground had to be yielded, but our foremost line was speedily restored with the assistance of a battalion of the 5th Brigade.

By nightfall our line ran completely around the eastern outskirts of the village of Montbrehain, the whole of which was in our possession. We took from it over 600 prisoners belonging to nine different German regiments.

What was even more interesting was that we came for the first time in the war upon French civilians, who had been under the domination of the enemy since the autumn of 1914. These unfortunate folk were found hidden away in cellars and underground shelters, and their joy at their deliverance from foreign bondage was pathetic. It was evident that the enemy had not had time to carry out the evacuation of the civilians, as had been his practice throughout the whole area over which the Australian Corps had hitherto advanced.

By the night of October 5th, the corps had, by the victory of Montbrehain, advanced its line to a point six miles to the east of the Bellicourt Tunnel, and had thereby confirmed the irretrievable collapse of the whole of the Hindenburg defences.

This achievement is, above everything else, an illustration, which should become classic, of the maxim that in war the *morale* is to the material as three to one. The enemy had all the advantages of position, of carefully prepared field works, of highly-organised defences, of detailed acquaintance with our lines of approach from the west, and of all the other tactical benefits of the defence.

Yet we had the advantage of moral factors. For the past nine weeks the enemy had suffered defeat after defeat. He had at one time been surprised and overwhelmed. He had at another time been driven from strong positions under conditions when surprise played no part. He had been defeated in gunnery, in the air, and in close infantry fighting. The *morale* of his troops had steadily declined. They no longer hoped for victory, but anticipated defeat. They knew that they were a beaten army.

The victory won in the series of battles from September 29th to October 5th was a victory of morale, the resolute determination of our troops to overcome all obstacles prevailing against the failing spirits of the defenders. It was a signal illustration that no defences, however powerful, can resist an energetically pressed assault, unless the defenders meet the attack with equal resolution. Verdun and the cliffs of Gallipoli are examples of resolute defence. Port Arthur and the Hindenburg Line are equally striking instances of the collapse of formidable field works through failure of the morale of the defenders.

Montbrehain was the last Australian battle in the Great War, and the fighting career of the Australian Army Corps had, as events turned out, come to an end. On that same day my Second Division was relieved by the 30th American Division, and I handed over command of the battle front to General Read. I had borne continuous responsibility, as a corps commander, for a section of the battle front in France varying from four to eleven miles for 128 consecutive days without a break.

On that same day, too, Prince Max of Baden accepted the programme of the President of the United States of America, and requested him to take in hand the restoration of peace. On behalf of the German Government he also asked for an immediate armistice on land, water and in the air.

The long-drawn-out negotiations which followed need only a brief reference. It was first necessary for the *Entente* Powers to agree upon a common line of action; then followed negotiations between the plenipotentiaries of the belligerents, and hostilities did not actually cease until after the conditions of the armistice had been signed in the early morning of November 11th.

During this period of five weeks, however, fighting went on. It was of an altogether different character from that in which the Australian Corps had been engaged. The enemy had no line of defence left in France. He was compelled to a retreat which became general along his whole front, and gathered momentum day by day. He gave up Lens, Armentières and the Aubers Ridge without a struggle, thus enabling the Second and Fifth Armies to advance to the occupation of Lille and the adjacent industrial centres.

A great army recoiling rapidly upon itself is beset with even greater difficulties than an army sweeping rapidly forward. If its retreat is not to be converted into a rout, time must be allowed for the methodical withdrawal, in proper sequence, of the whole complex organisation in rear of the battle front. Headquarters and hospitals, workshops and aerodromes, depots and supplies must be dismantled, packed and re-established further in rear; guns, transport and reserve troops must be withdrawn stage by stage, and, last of all, the fighting line must fall back in sympathy with the rate of withdrawal of all in rear.

Every hour's delay is an hour gained. Roads become congested, bridges overtaxed, cohesion and discipline are imperilled. An enforced withdrawal on so large a scale is one of the most difficult operations of war. The enemy's tactics during this period were, therefore, purely those of delay, achieved by the methodical destruction of bridges, tearing up of railways, and the blowing of great craters at every important road intersection. These methods impeded the advance of our armies quite as much as his rear-guards, who invariably yielded to the smallest demonstration of force.

Battles on the grand scale were now a thing of the past, and from the completion of the capture of the Hindenburg defences up to the signing of the Armistice there was no event in France of outstanding military importance.

The pursuit of the enemy towards the eastern frontiers of France and Belgium was, however, exhausting to the British and American troops on the front which the Australian Corps had vacated. It was only a question of time for the corps to be again called upon, this time to take its share of pursuit. The armistice negotiations were dragging out, and it was uncertain that they would be satisfactorily concluded. The Australian Corps had had a month for a pleasant rest along the banks of the Somme, between Amiens and Abbeville. It had had time to carry out the extensive reorganisations required by the War Office. On November 5th orders came for the corps once again to move up to the front.

The First and Fourth Divisions led the return to the battle zone. The remaining three divisions were to follow. My Corps Headquarters, on November 10th, commenced its move to Le Cateau, to occupy the very *château* which had been inhabited by General von der Marwitz, the commander of the Second German Army, against whom the Australian Corps had for so long been operating. I was actually on the way there on November 11th when the order arrived for the cessation of hostilities.

The Australian Army Corps was therefore not again employed, either in the final stages of pursuing the enemy out of France, or as part of the Army of Occupation on German territory.

The Prime Minister of Australia forwarded to me, the day after my arrival at Le Cateau, the following message:

> The Government and the people of Australia extend their heartiest congratulations on the triumphant conclusion of your great efforts. I am specially requested to convey to you their heartfelt thanks and deep admiration for your brilliant and great leadership, and for the way in which you and the brave men associated with you have borne the sufferings and trials of the past four years, and in common with the troops of all the Allied Nations brought the civilised peoples of the world through adversity to victorious peace. On behalf of the Government and the people of the Commonwealth, I assure you, and every Australian soldier in the field, that the Commonwealth is full of pride and admiration of their endurance and sacrifice. The Australian soldiers are entitled to, and shall receive, not only the thanks of a grateful people, but that treatment which their great

services deserve.

W.M. Hughes.

Not long after the conclusion of hostilities I was called upon by my government to undertake the organisation and direction of a special department to carry out the repatriation of the whole of the Australian Imperial Force, in Europe, Egypt, Salonika and Mesopotamia. This compelled me to sever, with much regret, my close and intimate association with the personnel of the army corps.

Before proceeding to England to establish the new department, I issued the following farewell order:

> Upon relinquishing the command of the Australian Army Corps, in order to take up the important and difficult work of the repatriation and demobilisation of the Australian Imperial Force, which has been entrusted to me by the Commonwealth Government, I desire to offer to all ranks of the corps a heartfelt expression of my gratitude to all for the splendid and loyal support which they have rendered to me during the past six months.
>
> It has been the period during which the corps has attained its highest development, as a fighting organism, of cohesion and efficiency. This has been brought about alike by the valour of the troops of all arms and services, and by the splendid devotion of commanders, staffs, and regimental officers, and has resulted in the series of brilliant victories which have contributed in so high a measure to the overthrow and utter collapse of our principal enemy.
>
> For the remainder of the period during which the corps will continue to act as a military body, held in readiness for any emergency that may arise during the peace negotiations, I am confident that every man will strive to do all in his power to uphold the great renown which the corps has so worthily won. But, having completed our task in the main object which brought us from our distant homeland, and having thereby safeguarded the future of our nation by the conquest of our most formidable enemy, we are now faced with another and an equally important task, namely, to prepare ourselves to resume our duties of citizenship and to assist individually and collectively in the reconstruction of the Australian Nation. Our numbers and our prestige place this opportunity in our hands,

and impose upon us this great responsibility.

I feel sure that every man in the corps will in this also worthily respond to the call of duty, and will co-operate loyally and self-sacrificingly in the realisation of all plans and projects which will be developed to so worthy an end.

CHAPTER 17

Results

The time has arrived when it is proper to take stock of gains and losses, and to endeavour to appraise, at its true value, the work done by the Australian Army Corps during its long-sustained effort of the last six months of its fighting career.

It has become customary to regard the actual captures of prisoners and guns as a true index of the degree of success which has attended any series of battle operations. Every soldier knows, however, that such a standard of judgment, applied alone, would render but scant justice. The actual captures in any engagement depend more upon the state of morale of the enemy and the temperament of the attacking troops than upon the military quality of the battle effort considered as a whole. While large captures necessarily imply great victories, it does not by any means follow that small captures imply the reverse.

Nevertheless, judged by such a purely arbitrary standard, the performances of the Australian Army Corps during the period under review are worthy of being set out in particular detail.

From March 27th, when Australian troops were for the first time interposed to arrest the German advance, until October 5th, when they were finally withdrawn from the line, the total captures made by them were:

Prisoners   29,144
Guns   338

No accurate record was ever kept of the capture of machine-guns, trench mortars, searchlights, vehicles and travelling kitchens or pharmacies, nor of the quantity of artillery ammunition, which alone must have amounted to millions of rounds.

During the advance, from August 8th to October 5th, the Australian Corps recaptured and released no less than 116 towns and villages. Every one of these was defended more or less stoutly. This count of them does not include a very large number of minor hamlets, which were unnamed on the maps, nor farms, brick-fields, factories, sugar refineries, and similar isolated groups of buildings, every one of which had been fortified and converted by the enemy into a stronghold of resistance.

Although the amount of territory reoccupied, taken by itself, is ordinarily no criterion of value, the whole circumstances of the relentless advance of the Australian Corps make it a convenient standard of comparison. The total area of all the ground fought over, from the occupation of which the enemy was ejected, amounted in the period under consideration to 394 square miles.

A much more definite and crucial basis for evaluating the military successes of the corps is the number of enemy divisions actually engaged and defeated in the course of the operations. Very accurate records of these have been kept, and every one of them was identified by a substantial contribution to the list of prisoners taken. An analysis of this investigation produced the following results:

The total number of separate enemy divisions engaged was thirty-nine. Of these, twenty were engaged once only, twelve were engaged twice, six three times, and one four times. Each time "engaged" represents a separate and distinct period of line duty for the enemy division referred to.

Up to the time of the armistice we had definitely ascertained that at least six of these thirty-nine enemy divisions had been entirely disbanded as the result of the battering which they had received. Their numberings have already been given. It is more than probable that several other divisions shared the same fate, by reason of the number of prisoners actually taken, and the other casualties known to have been inflicted. Up to the time when the signing of the armistice precluded further inquiries, absolutely conclusive evidence of their disappearance had not been obtained.

In such an analysis it is possible to go even further, and to compare the tangible results achieved with the relative strength of the forces engaged. The Australian Army Corps of five divisions represented 9½ *per cent.* of the whole of the remaining 53 divisions of the British Army engaged on the Western Front. Its captures in prisoners, by the same comparison, and within the period reviewed—*i.e.*, March 27th to October 5th—was 23 *per cent.*, in guns 23½ *per cent.*, and in territory reoccupied was 21½ *per cent.* of the whole of the rest of the British Army. The ratio, therefore, of the results to the strengths, as between the five Australian divisions and the whole of the rest of the British Army, was as follows:

Prisoners	2.42	times
Territory	2.24	"
Guns	2.47	"

It is not, however, by the mere numerical results disclosed by such a comparison that the work of the Australian Army Corps should be judged. If a broad survey be made of the whole of the 1918 campaign, I think that the decisive part which the corps took in it will emerge even more convincingly.

Such a survey will show that the whole sequence of events may be divided into five very definite and clearly-marked stages. The first was the arrest and bringing to naught of the great German spring offensive; the second was the conversion of the enemy's offensive strategy into a distinct and unqualified defensive. Next followed the great, initial and irredeemable defeat of August 8th, which, according to the enemy's own admissions, was the beginning of the end. Then came the denial to the enemy of the respite which he sought on the line of the Somme, which might well have helped him to recover himself for another year of war; and, finally, there was the overthrow of his great defensive system, on which he relied as a last bulwark to safeguard his hold upon French soil, a hold which would have enabled him to bargain for terms.

It must never be forgotten that whatever claims may be made to the contrary, Germany's surrender was precipitated by reason of her military defeat in the field. Her submarine campaign, disappointing to her expectations as it had been, was still a potent weapon. Her fleet was yet intact. Our blockade was grievous, but she did in fact survive it, even though it continued in force for a full eight months after her surrender. The defection of Bulgaria and the collapse of Turkey might conceivably be a source of increased military strength, even if one of greater political weakness. Had she been able to hold us at bay in France and Belgium for but another month or six weeks, she could have been assured of a respite of three months of winter in which to organise a levy *en masse*. Who can say that the stress of another winter and the prospect of another year of war might not have destroyed the Entente combination against her?

On these grounds I believe that the real and immediate reason for the precipitate surrender of Germany on October 5th, 1918, was the defeat of her Army in the field. It followed so closely upon the breaching of the Hindenburg defences on September 29th to October 4th, that it cannot be dissociated from that event as a final determining cause. Whether this view be correct or not, I think that the claim may fairly be made for the Australian Army Corps, that in each of the stages of the operations which led to this military overthrow, the corps played an important, and in some of them a predominating, part. No better testimony for such a conclusion can be adduced than the admissions of Ludendorff himself.

Narrowing our survey of the closing events of the campaign to a consideration of the fighting activities of the Australian Corps, I would like to emphasize the remarkable character of that effort. Deprived of the advantage of a regular inflow of trained recruits, and relying practically entirely for any replenishments upon the return of its own sick and wounded, the corps was able to maintain an uninterrupted fighting activity over a period of six months. For the last sixty days of this period the corps maintained an unchecked advance of thirty-seven miles against the powerful and determined opposition of a still formidable enemy, who employed all the mechanical and scientific resources at his disposal.

Such a result alone, considered in the abstract and quite apart from any comparison with the performances of other forces, is a testimony, on the one hand, to the pre-eminent fighting qualities of the Australian soldier considered individually, and, on the other hand, to the collective capacity and efficiency of the military effort made by the corps. I doubt whether there is any parallel for such a performance in the whole range of military history.

As regards the troops themselves, the outstanding feature of the campaign was their steadily rising morale. Always high, it was, in spite of fatigue and stress, never higher than in the closing days. A stage had been reached when they regarded their adversary no longer with cautious respect but with undisguised contempt.

On the part of the troops it was a remarkable feat of physical and mental endurance to face again and yet again the stress of battle. To the infantry a certain measure of periodical rest was accorded, but the artillery and technical services had scarcely any respite at all. Almost every day of the whole period they worked and fought, night and day, under the fire of the enemy's batteries, and under his drenching, suffocating gas attacks, for our battery positions were the favourite targets for his gas bombardments.

On the part of the staffs it was a period of ceaseless toil, both mental and physical. The perfection of the staff work, its precision,

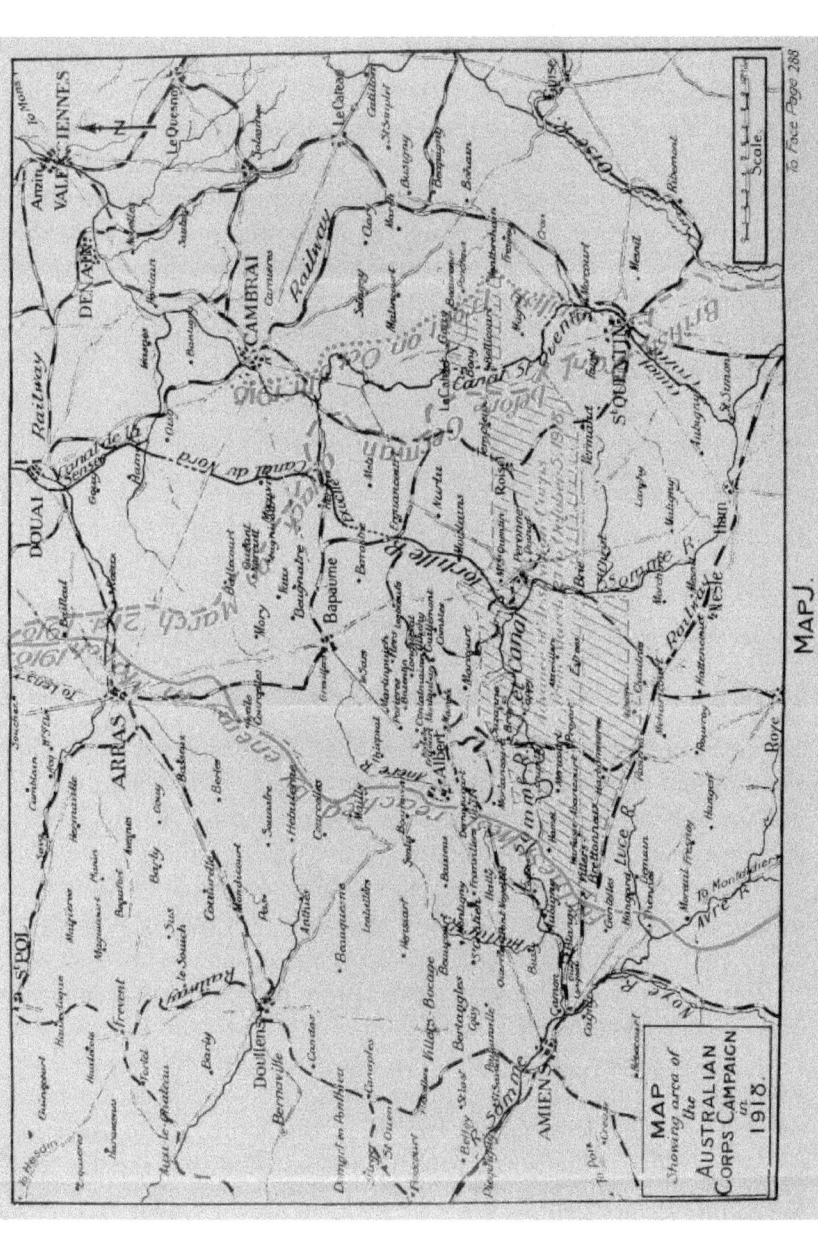

MAP J.

its completeness, its rapidity, its whole-souled devotion to the service of the troops, were the necessary conditions for the victories which were won.

Another outstanding feature was the uniformity of standard achieved by all the five divisions, as well as the wonderful comradeship which they displayed towards each other. Omitting altogether the performances of any one of them in the previous years of the war, it is noteworthy that all so fully seized the opportunities that presented themselves, that each could boast of outstanding achievements during this period—the First Division for its capture of Lihons and the Battles of Chuignes and Hargicourt, the Second Division for Mont St. Quentin and Montbrehain, the Third for Bray, Bouchavesnes and Bony, the Fourth for Hamel and Hargicourt, and the Fifth for Péronne and Bellicourt.

I must also pass in brief review the losses which the corps suffered during its advance. From August 8th to October 5th the total battle casualties were as follows:

Killed	3,566
Died of wounds	1,432
Wounded	16,166
Missing	79
Total	21,243

Averaging these losses over all five divisions for the whole period, they amount to a wastage from all causes of seventy men per division per day, which must be regarded as extraordinarily moderate, having regard to the strenuous nature of the fighting, the great results achieved, and the much higher rate of losses incurred by Australian troops during the previous years of the war. Even during periods of sedentary trench warfare, the losses averaged forty per division per day.

The total losses of the army corps during this period were, indeed, only a small fraction of Australia's contribution to the casualty roll for the whole period of the war. It was the least costly period, for Australia, of all the fighting that her soldiers underwent. Had it been otherwise, the effort could not have been maintained for so long, nor could the spirit of the troops have been sustained. It was the low cost of victory after victory which spurred them on to still greater efforts.

Of the causes which contributed to so gratifying a result, much credit must be given to the great development in 1918 of mechanical aids, in the form of tanks, and to a considerable augmentation of aeroplanes, artillery and Lewis guns. Of all these the corps proved eager to avail itself to the full. But the main cause is, after all, the recognition of a principle of text-book simplicity, which is that a vigorous offensive is in the long run cheaper than a timorous defensive. No war can be decided by defensive tactics. The fundamental doctrine of the German conception of war was the pursuit of the unrelenting offensive; it was only when the *Entente* Armies, on their part, were able and willing themselves to put such a doctrine into practice that our formidable enemies were overcome.

It may be that hereafter I may be charged with responsibility for so relentlessly and for so long committing the troops of the corps to a sustained aggressive policy. Such criticisms have already been whispered in some quarters. But I am sure that they will not be shared by any of the men whom it was my privilege to command. They knew that an offensive policy was the cheapest policy, and the proof that they accepted it as the right one was their ever-rising morale as the campaign developed.

"Feed your troops on victory", is a maxim which does not appear in any text-book, but it is nevertheless true. The aim and end of all the efforts and of all the heavy sacrifices of the Australian nation was victory in the field. Nothing that could be done could lead more swiftly and more directly to its fulfilment than an energetic offensive policy. The troops themselves recognised this. They learned to believe, because of success heaped upon success, that they were invincible. They were right, and I believe that I was right in shaping a course which would give them the opportunity of proving it.

There are some aspects of the Australian campaign to which, before closing this memoir, I should like to make brief reference. Success depended first and foremost upon the military proficiency of the Australian private soldier and his glorious spirit of heroism. I do not propose to attempt here an exhaustive analysis of the causes which led to the making of him. The democratic institutions under which he was reared, the advanced system of education by which he was trained—teaching him to think for himself and to apply what he had been taught to practical ends—the instinct of sport and adventure which is his national heritage, his pride in his young country, and the opportunity which came to him of creating a great national tradition, were all factors which made him what he was.

Physically the Australian Army was composed of the flower of the youth of the continent. A volunteer army—the only purely volunteer army that fought in the Great War—it was composed of men carefully selected according to a high physical standard, from which, happily, no departure was made, even although recruiting began to fall off in the last year of the war, and there were some who had proposed a more lenient recruiting examination. The cost to Australia of delivering each fighting man, fully trained, to the battle front was too great to permit of any doubt whether the physical quality of the raw material would survive the wear and tear of war.

Mentally, the Australian soldier was well endowed. In him there was a curious blend of a capacity for independent judgment with a readiness to submit to self-effacement in a common cause. He had a personal dignity all his own. He had the political sense highly developed, and was always a keen critic of the way in which his battalion or battery was "run", and of the policies which guided his destinies from day to day.

His intellectual gifts and his "handiness" made him an apt pupil. It was always a delight to see the avidity with which he mastered the technique of the weapons which were placed in his hands. Machine-guns, Lewis guns, Mills' bombs, Stokes' mortars, rifle grenades, flares, fuses, detonators, Very lights, signal rockets, German machine-guns, German stick bombs, never for long remained a mystery to him.

At all schools and classes, he proved a diligent scholar, and astonished his instructors by the speed with which he absorbed and bettered his instruction. Conservatism in military methods was no part of his creed. He was always mentally alert to adopt new ideas and often to invent them.

His adaptability spared him much hardship. He knew how to make himself comfortable. To light a fire and cook his food was a natural instinct. A sheet of corrugated iron, a batten or two, and a few strands of wire were enough to enable him to fabricate a home in which he could live at ease.

Psychologically, he was easy to lead but difficult to drive. His imagination was readily fired. War was to him a game, and he played for his side with enthusiasm. His bravery was founded upon his sense of duty to his unit, comradeship to his fellows, emulation to uphold his traditions, and a combative spirit to avenge his hardships and sufferings upon the enemy.

Taking him all in all, the Australian soldier was, when once understood, not difficult to handle. But he required a sympathetic handling, which appealed to his intelligence and satisfied his instinct for a "square deal".

Very much and very stupid comment has been made upon the discipline of the Australian soldier. That was because the very conception and purpose of discipline have been misunderstood. It is, after all, only a means to an end, and that end is the power to secure co-ordinated action among a large number of individuals for the achievement of a definite purpose. It does not mean lip service, nor obsequious homage to superiors, nor servile observance of forms and customs, nor a suppression of individuality.

Such may have been the outward manifestations of discipline in times gone by. If they achieved the end in view, it must have been because the individual soldier had acquired in those days no capacity to act intelligently and because he could be considered only in the mass. But modern war makes high demands upon the intelligence of the private soldier and upon his individual initiative. Any method of training which tends to suppress that individuality will tend to reduce his efficiency and value. The proverbial "iron discipline" of the Prussian military ideal ultimately broke down completely under the test of a great war.

In the Australian Forces no strong insistence was ever made upon the mere outward forms of discipline. The soldier was taught that personal cleanliness was necessary to ensure his health and well-being, that a soldierly bearing meant a moral and physical uplift which would help him to rise superior to his squalid environment, that punctuality meant economy of effort, that unquestioning obedience was the only road to successful collective action. He acquired these military qualities because his intelligence taught him that the reasons given him were true ones.

In short, the Australian Army is a proof that individualism is the best and not the worst foundation upon which to build up collective discipline. The Australian is accustomed to team-work. He learns it in the sporting field, in his industrial organisations, and in his political activities. The team-work which he developed in the war was of the highest order of efficiency. Each man understood his part and understood also that the part which others had to play depended upon the proper performance of his own.

The gunner knew that the success of the infantry depended upon his own punctilious performance of his task, its accuracy, its punctuality, its conscientious thoroughness. The runner knew what depended upon the rapid delivery at the right destination of the message which he carried. The mule driver knew that the load of ammunition entrusted to him must be delivered, at any sacrifice, to its destined battery; the infantryman knew that he must be at his tape line at the appointed moment, and that he must not overrun his allotted objective.

The truest test of battle discipline was the confidence which every leader in the field always felt that he could rely upon every man to perform the duty which had been prescribed for him, as long as breath lasted, and that he would perform it faithfully even when there was no possibility of any supervision.

Thus, the sense of duty was always very high, and so also was the instinct of comradeship. A soldier, a platoon, a whole battalion would sooner sacrifice themselves than "let down" a comrade or another unit. There was no finer example of individual self-sacrifice, for the benefit of comrades, than the stretcher-bearer service, which suffered exceedingly in its noble work of succouring the wounded, and exposed itself unflinchingly to every danger.

The relations between the officers and men of the Australian Army were also of a nature which is deserving of notice. From almost the earliest days of the war violence was done to a deep rooted tradition of the British Army, which discouraged any promotion from the ranks, and stringently forbade, in cases where it was given, promotion in the same unit. It was rare to recognise the distinguished service of a ranker; it was impossible for him to secure a commission in his own regiment.

The Australian Imperial Force changed all that. Those privates, corporals and sergeants who displayed, under battle conditions, a notable capacity for leadership were earmarked for preferment. If their standard of education was good, they received commissions as soon as there were vacancies to fill; if not, they were sent to Oxford or Cambridge to be given an opportunity of improving both their general and their special military knowledge.

As a general rule, they came back as commissioned officers to the very unit in which they had enlisted or served. They afforded to all its men a tangible and visible proof of the recognition of merit and capacity, and their example was always a powerful stimulus to all their former comrades.

There was thus no officer caste, no social distinction in the whole force. In not a few instances, men of humble origin and belonging to the artisan class rose, during the war, from privates to the command of battalions. The efficiency of the force suffered in no way in

The Toll of Battle—an Australian gun-team destroyed by an enemy shell, September 1st, 1918.

Inter-Divisional Relief—The 30th American and the 3rd Australian Divisions passing each other in the "Roo de Kanga," Péronne, during the "relief" after the capture of the Hindenburg Line, October 4th, 1918.

consequence. On the contrary, the whole Australian Army became automatically graded into leaders and followers according to the individual merits of every man, and there grew a wonderful understanding between them.

The duties and responsibilities of the officers were always put upon a high plane. They had, during all military service with troops, to dress like the men, to live among them in the trenches, to share their hardships and privations, and to be responsible for their welfare. No officer dared to look after his own comfort until every man or horse or mule had been fed and quartered, as well as the circumstances of the moment permitted. The battle prowess of the Australian regimental officer and the magnificent example he set have become household words.

Then there must be a word of recognition of the work of the devoted and able staffs. It was upon them, after all, that the principal burden of the campaign rested. Upon them, their skill and industry, depended the adequacy of all supplies and their proper distribution, the precision of all arrangements for battle, the accuracy of all maps, orders and instructions, the clearness of messages and reports, the completeness of the information on which the commander must base his decisions, and the correct calculations of time and space for the movement of troops, guns and transport. Their watchword was "efficiency".

"The staff officer is the servant of the troops." This was the ritual pronounced at the initiation of every staff officer. It was a doctrine which contributed powerfully to the success of the staff work as a whole. It meant that the staff officer's duties extended far beyond the mere transmission of orders. It became his business to see that they were understood, and rightly acted upon, and to assist in removing every kind of difficulty in their due execution. The importance of accurate and reliable staff work can be understood when it is realised that no mistake can happen without ultimately imposing an added stress upon the most subordinate and most helpless of all the components of an army—the private soldier. An error in a clock time, the miscarriage of a message, the neglect to issue an instruction, a misreading of an order, an omission from a list of names, a mistake in a computation, an incomplete inventory, are bound in the long run to involve an added burden somewhere upon some private soldier.

The staff of the Australian Army Corps, its divisions and brigades, consisted during the last six months almost entirely of Australians, many of them belonging to the permanent military forces of the

Commonwealth, but more still men who, before the war, followed civilian occupations. Among both categories the quality of the staff work steadily grew in efficiency, speed and accuracy, and during the last period of active fighting it reached a very high standard indeed.

Had it been otherwise, I could not have carried out either the rapid preparations for several of the greater battles, or the frequent and complex interchanges of divisions which alone rendered it possible for me to keep up a continuous pressure on the enemy, or the readjustments throughout the whole of the very large area always under my jurisdiction which became necessary as the advance proceeded.

No reference to the staff work of the Australian Corps during the period of my command would be complete without a tribute to the work and personality of Brigadier-General T.A. Blamey, my chief of staff. He possessed a mind cultured far above the average, widely informed, alert and prehensile. He had an infinite capacity for taking pains. A Staff College graduate, but not on that account a pedant, he was thoroughly versed in the technique of staff work, and in the minutiae of all procedure.

He served me with an exemplary loyalty, for which I owe him a debt of gratitude which cannot be repaid. Our temperaments adapted themselves to each other in a manner which was ideal. He had an extraordinary faculty of self-effacement, posing always and conscientiously as the instrument to give effect to my policies and decisions. Really helpful whenever his advice was invited, he never obtruded his own opinions, although I knew that he did not always agree with me.

Someday the orders which he drafted for the long series of history-making military operations upon which we collaborated will become a model for staff colleges and schools for military instruction. They were accurate, lucid in language, perfect in detail, and always an exact interpretation of my intention. It was seldom that I thought that my orders or instructions could have been better expressed, and no commander could have been more exacting than I was in the matter of the use of clear language to express thought.

Blamey was a man of inexhaustible industry, and accepted every task with placid readiness. Nothing was ever too much trouble. He worked late and early, and set a high standard for the remainder of the large corps staff of which he was the head. The personal support which he accorded to me was of a nature of which I could always feel the real substance. I was able to lean on him in times of trouble, stress and difficulty, to a degree which was an inexpressible comfort to me.

To the commanders of the five divisions I have already made detailed allusion. They were all renowned leaders. To all the brigadiers of infantry and artillery and to the heads of the Administrative Services who laboured under them, the limitations of space forbid my making any individual reference. But they were all of them men to whose splendid services Australia owes a deep debt of gratitude. In their hands the honour of Australia's fighting men and the prestige of her arms were in safe keeping.

None but men of character and self-devotion could have carried the burden which they had to bear during the last six months of the war. In spite of stress and difficulty, unremitting toil and wasted effort, weary days and sleepless nights, fresh task piling upon the task but just begun, labouring even harder during periods of so-called rest than when their troops were actually in the line, this gallant band of leaders remained steadfast of purpose, never faltered, never lost their faith in final victory, never failed to impress their optimism and their unflinching fighting spirit upon the men whom they commanded.

It may be appropriate to end this memoir on a personal note. I have permitted myself a tone of eulogy for the triumphant achievements of the Australian Army Corps in 1918, which I have endeavoured faithfully to portray. Let it not be assumed on that account that the humble part which it fell to my lot to perform afforded me any satisfaction or prompted any enthusiasm for war. Quite the contrary.

From the far-off days of 1914, when the call first came, until the last shot was fired, every day was filled with loathing, horror, and distress. I deplored all the time the loss of precious life and the waste of human effort. Nothing could have been more repugnant to me than the realisation of the dreadful inefficiency and the misspent energy of war. Yet it had to be, and the thought always uppermost was the earnest prayer that Australia might for ever be spared such a horror on her own soil.

There is, in my belief, only one way to realise such a prayer. The nation that wishes to defend its land and its honour must spare no effort, refuse no sacrifice to make itself so formidable that no enemy will dare to assail it. A League of Nations may be an instrument for the preservation of peace, but an efficient army is a far more potent one.

The essential components of such an army are a qualified staff, an adequate equipment and a trained soldiery. I state them in what I believe to be their order of importance, and my belief is based upon the lessons which this war has taught me. In that way alone can Australia secure the sanctity of her territory and the preservation of her independent liberties.

Such a creed is not militarism, but is of the very essence of national self-preservation. For long years before the war it was the creed of a small handful of men in Australia, who braved the indifference and even the ridicule of public opinion in order to try to qualify themselves for the test when it should come. Four dreadful years of war have served to convince me of the truth of that creed, and to confirm me in the belief that the men of the coming generation, if they love their country, must take up the burden which these men have had to bear.

Appendix A

Grouping into Australian divisions of artillery and infantry brigades, during the period May to October, 1918, and the general officers commanding them:

FIRST DIVISION (Glasgow):
- *Artillery*, 1st and 2nd Brigades (Anderson).
- *Infantry*, 1st Brigade (Mackay).
- 2nd ,, (Heane).
- 3rd ,, (Bennett).

SECOND DIVISION (Rosenthal):
- *Artillery*, 4th and 5th Brigades (Phillips).
- *Infantry*, 5th Brigade (Martin).
- 6th ,, (Robertson).
- 7th ,, (Wisdom).

THIRD DIVISION (Gellibrand):
- *Artillery*, 7th and 8th Brigades (Grimwade).
- *Infantry*, 9th Brigade (Goddard).
- 10th ,, (McNicoll).
- 11th ,, (Cannan).

FOURTH DIVISION (Maclagan):
- *Artillery*, 10th and 11th Brigades (Burgess).
- *Infantry*, 4th Brigade (Brand).
- 12th ,, (Leane).
- 13th ,, (Herring).

FIFTH DIVISION (Hobbs):
- *Artillery*, 13th and 14th Brigades (Bessel-Browne).
- *Infantry*, 8th Brigade (Tivey).
- 14th ,, (Stewart).
- 15th ,, (Elliott).

The 3rd, 6th and 12th Artillery Brigades were corps troops not forming part of any division. The 9th Artillery Brigade was disbanded at the end of 1916.

Appendix B

In order to illustrate the nature of the individual fighting carried out by the Australian Corps, during the period covered by this book, the following very small selection has been made from the official records of deeds of gallantry by individual soldiers. In every one of these twenty-nine cases, the Victoria Cross has been awarded by His Majesty the King:

No. 4061, Sergeant Stanley Robert MacDougall,
47th Battalion, A.I.F.

At Dernancourt, on morning of 28th March, 1918, the enemy attacked our line, and his first wave succeeded in gaining an entry. Sergt. MacDougall, who was at a post in a flank company, realised the situation, and at once charged the enemy's second wave single-handed with rifle and bayonet, killing 7 and capturing the machine-gun which they had. This he turned on to them, firing from the hip, causing many casualties, and routing that wave.

He then turned his attention to those who had entered, until his ammunition had run out, all the time firing at close quarters, when he seized a bayonet and charged again, killing three men and a German officer, who was just about to kill one of our officers. He then used a Lewis Gun on the enemy, killing many and enabling us to capture 33 prisoners. His prompt action saved the line and enabled us to stop the enemy advance.

Lieutenant Percy Valentine Storkey,
19th Battalion, A.I.F.

Lieut. Storkey was in charge of a platoon which took part in the attack at Bois de Hangard on morning of 7th April, 1918. On emerging from the wood, the enemy trench line was encountered, and Lieut. Storkey found himself with 6 men. While continuing his move forward, a large enemy party—about 80 to 100 strong—armed with several machine-guns, was noticed to be holding up the advance of the troops on the right. Lieut. Storkey immediately decided to attack this party from the flank and rear, and while moving forward to the attack, was joined by Lieut. Lipscomb and four men. Under the leadership of Lieut. Storkey, this small party of 2 officers and 10 other ranks charged the enemy position with fixed bayonets, driving the enemy out, killing and wounding about 30 and capturing the remainder, *viz.*: 3 officers and 50 men, also one machine-gun.

Lieutenant Clifford William King Sadlier,
51st Battalion, A.I.F.

For conspicuous gallantry on the night of 24-25th April, 1918, during a counter-attack by his battalion on strong enemy positions south of Villers-Bretonneux, east of Amiens. Lieut. Sadlier's platoon, which was on the left of the battalion, had to advance through a wood, where they encountered a strong enemy machine-gun post, which caused casualties and prevented the platoon from advancing. Although himself wounded, this officer at once collected his bombing section, and led them against the machine-guns, succeeding in killing the crews and capturing two of the guns. By this time Lieut. Sadlier's party were all casualties, and he alone attacked a third enemy machine-gun with his revolver, killing the crew of four and taking the gun. In doing so, he was again wounded, and unable to go on.

No. 1914, Sergeant William Ruthven,
22nd Battalion, A.I.F.

For most conspicuous bravery and daring in action during the attack at Ville-sur-Ancre, near Albert, on 19th May, 1918. During the advance Sergeant Ruthven's company suffered numerous casualties, and his company commander was severely wounded. He then assumed command of his portion of the assault, took charge of the Company Headquarters, and rallied the sections in his vicinity. As the leading wave approached its objective, it was subjected to heavy fire from an enemy machine-gun at 30 to 40 yards' range, directly in front. This N.C.O., without hesitation, at once sprang out, threw a bomb which landed beside the post, and immediately rushed the position, bayoneting one of the crew and capturing the gun. He then encountered some of the enemy coming out of a shelter. He wounded two, captured six others in the same position, and handed them over to an escort from the leading wave, which had now reached the objective.

Sergeant Ruthven then reorganised our men in his vicinity, and established a post in the second objective. Enemy movement was then seen in a sunken road about 150 yards distant. Without hesitation, and armed only with a revolver, he went over the open alone and rushed the position, shooting two Germans who refused to come out of their dug-out. He then single-handed mopped up this post, and captured the whole of the garrison, amounting in all to 32, and kept them until assistance arrived to escort them back to our lines. During the remainder of the day this gallant N.C.O. set a splendid example of leadership, moving up and down his position under fire, supervising consolidation and encouraging his men.

No. 1327, Corporal Phillip Davey, M.M.,
10th Battalion, A.I.F.

In a daylight operation against the enemy position near Merris on June 28th, 1918, Corporal Davey's platoon advanced 200 yards and captured part, of enemy line. While the platoon was consolidating, the enemy pushed a machine-gun forward under cover of a hedge, and opened fire from close range, inflicting heavy casualties and hampering work. Alone Corporal Davey moved forward in the face of a fierce point-blank fire, and attacked the gun with hand grenades, putting half the crew out of action. Having used all available grenades, he returned to the original jumping-off trench, secured a further supply and again attacked the gun, the crew of which had in the meantime been reinforced. He killed the crew, 8 in all, and captured the gun. This gallant N.C.O. then mounted the gun in the new post and used it in repelling a determined counter-attack, during which he was severely wounded in both legs, back and stomach.

No. 3399, Private (Lance-Corporal) Thomas Leslie Axford, M.M.,
16th Battalion, A.I.F.

For conspicuous gallantry and initiative during the operations against Vaire and Hamel Woods, east of Corbie, on the morning of the 4th July, 1918. When the barrage lifted and the infantry advance commenced, the platoon of which he is a member was able to reach the first enemy defences through gaps which had been cut in the wires. The adjoining platoon got delayed in uncut barbed wire. This delay enabled the enemy machine-guns to get into action, and enabled them to inflict a number of casualties among the men struggling through the wires, including the company commander, who was killed. L.-Corporal Axford, with great initiative and magnificent courage, at once dashed to the flank, threw his bombs amongst the machine-gun crews; followed up his bombs by jumping into the trench, and charging with his bayonet.

Unaided he killed ten of the enemy and took 6 prisoners; he threw the machine-guns over the parapet, and called out to the delayed platoon to come on. He then rejoined his own platoon, and fought with it during the remainder of the operations. Prior to the incidents above-mentioned, he had assisted in the laying out of the tapes for the jumping-off position, which was within 100 yards of the enemy.

When the tapes were laid, he remained out as a special patrol to ensure that the enemy did not discover any unusual movement on our side.

No. 1936, Private Henry Dalziel,
15th Battalion, A.I.F.

For his magnificent bravery and devotion to duty during operations near Hamel Wood, east of Corbie, on 4th July, 1918. He was No. 2 of a Lewis Gun Section, and at the commencement of our advance his company met with determined resistance from Pear Trench strong point, which was strongly garrisoned and manned by numerous machine-guns. This strong point, undamaged by our artillery fire, was protected by strong wire entanglements. A heavy concentration of machine-gun fire caused heavy casualties and held up our advance. His Lewis Gun came into action and silenced enemy guns in one direction, when another enemy gun opened up from another direction.

Private Dalziel dashed at it, and with his revolver killed or captured the entire crew and gun, and allowed our advance to continue. He was severely wounded in the hand, but carried on and took part in the capture of the final objective. He twice went over open ground under heavy enemy artillery and machine-gun fire to where our aeroplanes had dropped some boxes of ammunition, and carried back a box on each occasion to his gun, and though suffering from considerable loss of blood, he filled magazines and served his gun until severely wounded through the head.

No. 1689A, Corporal Walter Ernest Brown, D.C.M.,
20th Battalion, A.I.F.

For gallant service on the morning of 6th July, 1918, north-east of Villers-Bretonneux, east of Amiens. This N.C.O. was one of an advanced party from his battalion making arrangements with the Battalion then in the line for relief by his own battalion. As such he was under no obligation to participate in any offensive operations before his battalion took over the line. During the night of 5th-6th July the company to which he was attached carried out a minor operation resulting in the capture of a small system of enemy trench. Early on the morning of 6th July an enemy strong post, about 70 yards distant, caused the occupants of the newly-captured trench great inconvenience by persistent sniping. It was decided to rush this post.

Hearing of this, Corporal Brown, on his own initiative, crept out along the shallow trench towards the enemy post, and then made a dash across No Man's Land towards this post. An enemy machine-gun opened fire from another trench, and he had to take cover by lying down. He later made another dash forward, and succeeded in reaching his objective. With a Mills grenade in his hand, he stood at the door of a dug-out and called on the occupants to surrender. One of the enemy rushed out, a scuffle ensued, and Corporal Brown knocked him down with his fist. Loud cries of '*Kamerad*' were then heard, and from the dug-out an officer and eleven other ranks appeared. Driving them before him, Corporal Brown brought back the complete party as prisoners to our line.

Lieutenant Albert Chalmers Borella, M.M.,
26th Battalion, A.I.F.

For exceptional gallantry in the attack near Villers-Bretonneux, on the 17th-18th July, 1918. Whilst leading his platoon with the first wave, Lieut. Borella noticed an enemy machine-gun firing through our barrage—he ran out ahead of his men into the barrage, shot two German machine-gunners with his revolver, and captured the gun. He then led his party, now reduced to ten men and two Lewis Guns, further on, against Jaffa Trench, which was very strongly held, but using his revolver, and later a rifle, with great effect, Lieut. Borella shot down the enemy right and left, and set such a splendid example, that the garrison were quickly shot and captured. Two large dug-outs were bombed here and thirty prisoners taken.

After reorganisation the enemy counter-attacked twice in strong force, on the second occasion outnumbering Lieut. Borella's platoon by ten to one; but he showed such coolness and determination, that the men put up an heroic resistance, and twice repulsed the enemy with very heavy loss. It is estimated that from 100 to 150 Germans were killed in this vicinity. When Lieut. Borella refused his left flank about 40 yards during the first counter-attack he sent his men back one at a time, and was himself the last to leave, under heavy fire.

Lieutenant Alfred Edward Gaby,
28th Battalion, A.I.F.

During the attack east of Villers-Bretonneux, near Amiens, on the morning of 8th August, 1918, this officer led his company with great dash, being well in front. On reaching the wire in front of the enemy-trench, strong opposition was encountered. The enemy were holding a strong point in force about 40 yards beyond the wire, and commanded the gap with four machine-guns and rifles. The advance was at once checked. Lieut. Gaby found another gap in the wire, and entirely by himself approached the strong point, while machine-guns and rifles were still being fired from it. Running along the parapet, still alone, and at point-blank range, he emptied his revolver into the garrison, drove the crews from their guns, and compelled the surrender of 50 of the enemy, with four machine-guns.

He then quickly reorganised his men and led them on to his final objective, which he captured and consolidated. On the morning of the 11th August, 1918, during an attack east of Framerville, Lieut. Gaby again led his company with great dash on to the objective. The enemy brought heavy rifle and machine-gun fire to bear upon the line, but in the face of this heavy fire Lieut. Gaby walked along his line of posts, encouraging his men to quickly consolidate the line. While engaged on this duty he was killed by an enemy sniper.

No. 2742 Private Robert Matthew Beatham,
8th Battalion, A.I.F.

For conspicuous gallantry and devotion to duty during the attack north of Rosières on 9th August, 1918. Private Beatham showed such heroism and courage, that he inspired all officers and men in his vicinity in a wonderful manner, When the advance was held up by heavy machine-gun fire, Private Beatham dashed forward and, assisted by one man, bombed and fought the crews of four enemy machine-guns, killing ten of them and capturing ten others. The bravery of the action greatly facilitated the advance of the whole battalion and prevented casualties. In fighting the crew of the first gun he was shot through the right leg, but continued in the advance. When the final objective was reached and fierce fighting was taking place, he again dashed forward and bombed the machine-gun that was holding our men off, getting riddled with bullets and killed in doing so.

No. 506, Sergeant Percy Clyde Statton, M.M.,
40th Battalion, A.I.F.

For most conspicuous gallantry and initiative in action near Proyart on 12th August, 1918. The platoon commanded by Sergeant Statton reached its objective, but the remainder of the battalion was held up by heavy machine-gun fire. He skilfully engaged two machine-gun posts with Lewis Gun fire, enabling the remainder of his battalion to advance. The advance of the battalion on his left had been brought to a standstill by the heavy enemy machine-gun fire, and the first of our assaulting detachments to reach the machine-gun posts were put out of action in taking the first gun.

Armed only with a revolver, in broad daylight, Sergeant Statton at once rushed four enemy machine-gun posts in succession, disposing of two of them, killing five of the enemy. The remaining two posts retired and were wiped out by Lewis Gun fire. This N.C.O.'s act had a very inspiring effect on the troops who had been held up, and they cheered him as he returned. By his daring exploit he enabled the attacking troops to gain their objective. Later in the evening, under heavy machine-gun fire, he went out again and brought in two badly-wounded men.

Lieutenant Lawrence Dominic McCarthy,
16th Battalion, A.I.F.

This officer is especially brought to notice for his wonderful gallantry, initiative and leadership on the morning of the 23rd August, 1918, when an attack was being made near Madame Wood, west of Vernandivukkers. The objectives of this battalion were attained without serious opposition. The battalion on the left flank were less fortunate. Here several well-posted machine-gun posts were holding up the attack, and heavy fire was being brought to bear on our left flank. When Lieut. McCarthy realised the situation, he at once engaged the nearest machine-gun post; but still the attacking troops failed to get forward. This officer then determined to attack the nearest post. Leaving his men to continue the fire fight, he, with two others, dashed across the open and dropped into a disused trench which had been blocked.

One of his two men was killed whilst doing this. He was now right under the block over which the enemy machine-gun was firing. The presence of head cover prevented the use of bombs. He therefore tunnelled a hole through the bottom of the block, through which he inserted his head and one arm. He at once shot dead the two men firing the gun.

He then crawled through the hole he had made, and by himself charged down the trench. He threw his limited number of Mills bombs among the German garrison and inflicted more casualties. He then came in contact with two German officers, who fired on him with their revolvers. One of these he shot dead with his revolver, the other he seriously wounded. He then charged down the trench, using his revolver and throwing enemy stick bombs, and capturing three more enemy machine-guns. At this stage, some 700 yards from his starting point, he was joined by the N.C.O., whom he had outdistanced when he crawled through the hole in the trench block mentioned above.

Together they continued to bomb up the trench, until touch was established with the Lancashire Fusiliers, and in the meanwhile yet another machine-gun had been captured. A total of 5 machine-guns and 50 prisoners (37 unwounded and 13 wounded) was captured, while Lieut. McCarthy during his most amazing and daring feat had, single-handed, killed 20 of the enemy. Having cleared up a dangerous situation, he proceeded to establish a garrison in the line. Whilst doing this he saw a number of the enemy getting away from neighbouring trenches. He at once seized a Lewis Gun and inflicted further casualties on the enemy.

Lieutenant William Donovan Joynt,
8th Battalion, A.I.F.

For conspicuous gallantry and devotion to duty during the attack on Herleville Wood, near Chuignes, on 23rd August, 1918. Early in the advance Lieut. Joynt's company commander was killed; he immediately took charge of the company and led them with courage and skill. A great deal of the success of the operation in this portion of the sector was directly due to his magnificent work. When the advance was commenced the battalion was moving into support to another battalion.

On approaching Herleville Wood, the troops of the leading battalion lost all their officers and became disorganised. Under very heavy fire, and having no leaders, they appeared certain to be annihilated. Lieut. Joynt grasped the situation, and rushed forward in the teeth of very heavy machine-gun and artillery fire over the open. He got the remaining men under control, and worked them into a piece of dead ground, until he could reform them. He manoeuvred his own men forward, and linked them up with the men of the other battalion.

He then made a personal reconnaissance, and found that the fire from the wood was holding the whole advance up, the troops on his flanks suffering very heavy casualties. Dashing out in front of his men, he called them on, and by sheer force of example inspired them into a magnificent frontal bayonet attack on the wood. The audacity of the move over the open staggered the enemy, and Lieut. Joynt succeeded in penetrating the wood and working through it. By his leadership and courage, a very critical situation was saved, and on this officer rests to the greatest extent the success of the brigade's attack.

When the battalion on our left was held up on Plateau Wood, and was suffering severe casualties, Lieut. Joynt, with a small party of volunteers, worked right forward against heavy opposition, and by means of hand-to-hand fighting forced his way round the rear of the wood, penetrating it from that side, and demoralising the enemy to such an extent that a very stubborn and victorious defensive was changed into an abject surrender. He was always in the hardest pressed parts of the line, and seemed to bear a charmed life. He was constantly ready to run any personal risk and to assist flank units. He continually showed magnificent leadership, and his example to his men had a wonderful effect on them, causing them to follow him cheerfully in his most daring exploits. He continued to do magnificent work until he was badly wounded by shell fire in the legs.

No. 23, Private (Lance-Corporal) Bernard Sydney Gordon,
41st Battalion, A.I.F.

During the operations of the 26-27th August, 1918, east of Bray, this N.C.O. showed most conspicuous gallantry and devotion to duty in the face of the enemy. He led his section through heavy enemy shelling to its objective, which he consolidated. Then single-handed he attacked an enemy machine-gun which was enfilading the company on his right, killed the man on the gun, and captured the post, which contained one officer (a captain) and 10 men. After handing these over at Company Headquarters, he returned alone to the old system of trenches, in which were many machine-guns; entered a trench and proceeded to mop it up, returning with 15 prisoners in one squad and 14 in another, together with two machine-guns.

Again, he returned to the system, this time with a trench mortar gun and crew, and proceeded to mop up a further portion of the trench, bringing in 22 prisoners, including one officer and 3 machine-guns. This last capture enabled the British troops on our left to advance, which they had not been able to do owing to machine-gun fire from these posts. His total captures were thus 2 officers and 61 other ranks, together with 6 machine-guns, and with the exception of the trench mortar assistance, it was absolutely an individual effort and done entirely on his own initiative.

No. 726, Private George Cartwright,
33rd Battalion, A.I.F.

For most conspicuous valour and devotion to duty. On the morning of the 31st August, 1918, during the attack on Road Wood, south-west of Bouchavesnes, near Péronne, Private Cartwright displayed exceptional gallantry and supreme disregard for personal danger in the face of a most withering machine-gun fire. Two companies were held up by a machine-gun firing from the south-western edge of the wood. Without hesitation, this man stood up, and walking towards the gun, fired his rifle from his shoulder. He shot the No. 1 Gunner; another German manned the gun, and he killed him; a third attempted to fire the gun and him he also killed.

Private Cartwright then threw a bomb at the post, and on its exploding, he rushed forward, captured the gun and nine Germans. Our line then immediately rushed forward, loudly cheering him. This magnificent deed had a most inspiring effect on the whole line; all strove to emulate his gallantry. Throughout the operation Private Cartwright displayed wonderful dash, grim determination and courage of the highest order.

> Lieutenant Edgar Thomas Towner, M.C.,
> 2nd Australian Machine-gun Battalion.

On 1st September, 1918, in the attack on Mont St. Quentin, near Péronne, this officer was in charge of 4 Vickers guns operating on a front of 1,500 yards. During the early stages of the advance an enemy machine-gun was causing casualties to our advancing infantry. Locating the gun, Lieut. Towner dashed ahead alone, and succeeded in killing the crew with his revolver, capturing the gun, and then, by turning it against the enemy, inflicted heavy casualties on them. Advancing then past a copse from which the enemy were firing, he brought his guns into action, placing his fire behind the enemy and cutting them off.

On their attempting to retire before the advancing infantry, and finding they were prevented by this machine-gun fire, the party of 25 Germans surrendered. He then reconnoitred alone over open ground exposed to heavy machine-gun and snipers' fire, and by the energy, foresight and the promptitude with which he brought fire to bear on further enemy groups, enabled the infantry to reach a sunken road.

On moving his guns up to the sunken road, he found himself short of ammunition, so went back across the open under heavy fire and obtained a German gun, and brought it and boxes of ammunition into the sunken road. Here he mounted and fired the gun in full view of the enemy, causing the enemy to retire further, and enabling infantry on the flank, who were previously held up, to advance. Enemy machine-gunners having direct observation, flicked the earth round and under this gun, and played a tattoo along the top of the bank. Though one bullet went into his helmet and inflicted a gaping scalp wound, he continued firing. Subsequently he refused to go out to have his wound attended to, as the situation was critical and his place was with his men. Later in the day the infantry were obliged to retire slightly, and one gun was left behind.

Lieut. Towner, seeing this, dashed back over the open, carried the gun back in spite of terrific fire, and brought it into action again. He continued to engage the enemy wherever they appeared, and put an enemy machine-gun out of action. During the following night he insisted on doing his tour of duty along with the other officers, and his coolness and cheerfulness set an example which had a great effect on the men. To steady and calm the men of a small detached outpost, he crawled out among the enemy posts to investigate. He remained out about an hour, though enemy machine-guns fired continuously on the sector, and the Germans were moving about him. He moved one gun up in support of the infantry post, and patrolled the communication saps which ran off this post into the German line during the remainder of the night. Next morning, after his guns assisted in dispersing a large party of the enemy, he was led away utterly exhausted, 30 hours after being wounded."

No. 2358, Sergeant Albert David Lowerson,
21st Battalion, A.I.F.

At Mont St. Quentin, north of Péronne, on the 1st September, 1918, this N.C.O. displayed courage and tactical skill of the very highest order during the attack on this village. Very strong opposition was met with early in the attack, and every foot of ground was stubbornly contested by the enemy located in very strong positions. This N.C.O.'s example during the fighting was of the greatest value. He moved about, regardless of the heavy enemy machine-gun fire, directing his men, encouraging them to still greater effort, and finally led them on to the objective. On reaching the objective, he saw that the left attacking party had not met with success, and that the attack was held up by an enemy strong post, heavily manned with 12 machine-guns. Under the heaviest sniping and machine-gun fire Sergeant Lowerson rallied seven men around him into a storming party, and deployed them to attack the post from both flanks, one party of three being killed immediately.

He himself then rushed the strong point, and, with effective bombing, inflicted heavy casualties on the enemy, and captured the post containing 12 machine-guns and 30 prisoners. Though severely wounded in the right thigh, he refused to leave the front line until the prisoners had been dispatched to the rear, and the organisation and consolidation of the post by our men had been completed. When he saw that the position was thoroughly secure, he returned to the rear, but refused to leave the battalion until forced to evacuate two days later by the seriousness of his wound. This act was the culminating point of a series of most gallant performances by this N.C.O. during the fighting extending over a week.

No. 1584A, Private William Matthew Currey,
53rd Battalion, A.I.F.

During the attack on Péronne, on the morning of 1st September, 1918, Private Currey displayed most conspicuous gallantry and daring. During the early stage of the advance the battalion was suffering heavy casualties from a 77 mm. field gun, that was firing over sights at very close range. Private Currey, without hesitation, rushed forward, and despite a withering machine-gun fire that was directed on him from either flank, succeeded in capturing the gun single-handed after killing the entire crew. Later, when continuing the advance, an enemy strong point, containing 30 men and two machine-guns, was noticed, which was holding up the advance of the left flank.

Private Currey crept around the flank, and engaged the post with a Lewis Gun, causing many casualties. Finally, he rushed the post single-handed, killing four, wounding two, and taking one prisoner, the survivors running away. It was entirely owing to his gallant conduct that the situation was relieved, and the advance enabled to continue.

After the final stage of the attack, it was imperative that one of the companies that had become isolated should be withdrawn. This man at once volunteered to carry the message, although the ground to be crossed was very heavily shelled and continuously swept by machine-gun fire. He crossed the shell and bullet-swept area three times in the effort to locate the company, and on one occasion his box respirator was shot through by machine-gun bullets, and he was gassed. Nevertheless, he remained on duty, and after finding the isolated company, delivered the message, and returned with very valuable information from the company commander. Owing to the gas poisoning from which he was suffering Currey had shortly afterwards to be evacuated.

No. 6939, Private Robert Mactier,
23rd Battalion, A.I.F.

On the morning of 1st September, 1918, during the operation entailing capture of Mont St. Quentin, this man stands out for the greatest bravery and devotion to duty. Fifteen minutes before zero two bombing patrols were sent to clear up several enemy strong points close to our line, but they met with very stubborn resistance and no success, and the battalion was unable to move on to its Jumping Off Trench. Mactier, single-handed and in daylight, then jumped out of the trench from the leading company, rushed past the block, closed with and killed the machine-gun garrison of 8 men with his revolver and bombs, and threw the enemy machine-gun over the parapet.

He rushed forward another 20 yards and jumped into another strong point held by a garrison of 6 men, who immediately surrendered. Continuing to the next block through the trench, an enemy gun, which had been enfilading our flank advancing troops, was swung on to him; but he jumped out of the trench into the open, and disposed of this third post and gun crew by bombing them from the rear. Before he could get into this trench, he was killed by enemy machine-gun at close range. In the three posts which Mactier rushed, 15 of the enemy were found killed and 30 taken prisoners.

No. 1876, Corporal Alexander Henry Buckley,
54th Battalion, A.I.F.

For most conspicuous gallantry and devotion to duty at Péronne during the operations on 1st-2nd September, 1918. After passing the first objective, his half company and part of the company on the flank were held up by an enemy machine-gun nest. With one man he rushed the post, shooting 4 of the occupants and taking 22 prisoners. Later on, reaching a moat, another machine-gun nest commanded the only available footbridge. Whilst this was being engaged from a flank, this N.C.O. endeavoured to cross the bridge and rush the post, but was killed in the attempt.

Throughout the advance he had displayed great initiative, resource and courage, being a great inspiration to his men. In order to avert casualties amongst his comrades and to permit of their advance, he voluntarily essayed a task which practically meant certain death. He set a fine example of self-sacrificing devotion to duty and bravery.

No. 2631, Corporal Arthur Charles Hall,
54th Battalion, A.I.F.

For most conspicuous gallantry, brilliant leadership and devotion to duty during the operations at Péronne on 1st and 2nd September, 1918. A machine-gun post in the enemy front line was holding up the advance; alone, this N.C.O. rushed the position, shot 4 of the occupants as he advanced, and captured 9 others and 2 machine-guns.

Then, crossing the objective with a small party, he reconnoitred the approaches to the town, covering the infiltration of the remainder of the company. During the mopping up he continuously—in advance of the main party—located enemy posts of resistance, and then personally led parties to the assault. In this way he captured many small parties of prisoners and machine-guns.

On the morning of 2nd September, during a heavy barrage on the newly consolidated position, a man of his platoon was severely wounded. Seeing that only immediate medical attention could save him, Corporal Hall volunteered and carried the man out of the barrage, handed him to a stretcher-bearer, and immediately returned to his post. This company was heavily engaged throughout the day, only one officer remaining unwounded.

No. 1153, Private (Lance-Corporal) Laurence Carthage Weathers, 43rd Battalion, A.I.F.

On the 2nd September, 1918, during operations north of Péronne, Lance-Corporal Weathers was one of an advanced bombing party operating well forward of our attacking troops. Just before the attack reached its final objective it was held up by the enemy, who occupied a trench in great numbers. After an hour's continuous fighting Lance-Corporal Weathers went forward alone in face of heavy enemy fire and located a large body of them.

He immediately attacked the enemy with bombs and killed the senior officer; then made his way back to our lines and, securing a further supply of bombs and taking three men with him, he went forward and again attacked under very heavy fire. On reaching the enemy position, he jumped up on the parapet of the trench and threw bombs among the Bosche. He then signalled for his comrades to come up, and the remainder of the enemy, seeing this, surrendered. When counted, the number of prisoners totalled 100 and 3 machine-guns.

No. 3244, Private James Park Woods, 48th Battalion, A.I.F.

For conspicuous gallantry and devotion to duty during the operations near Le Verguier, north-west of St. Quentin, on the 18th September, 1918. Woods formed one of a party of three to patrol the right flank. He encountered a very formidable enemy strong point, consisting of about 25 men with four heavy and two light machine-guns. This strong point commanded the greater portion of our position, and it was of the utmost importance to us, insomuch as it gave us a commanding view of the whole canal system. The strong point was situated at the junction of four enemy fire trenches, apparently sited with a view to protecting the approaches to the village of Bellenglise. Private Woods, appreciating the great importance of this position, and realising the necessity for its immediate capture, fearlessly attacked with his rifle and bayonet, capturing one of the enemy and wounding the second with his bayonet, forcing the remainder to retire.

After the capture of the strong point, it was found that one of the party was wounded. Private Woods, although himself slightly gassed, stubbornly defended the post. The enemy ascertaining that only two men opposed them, immediately attempted to recapture the strong point. The counter-attack by the enemy was carried out with at least 30 men attacking up the three trenches and across the open ground. This meant that Private Woods was attacked from both flanks and the front. He fearlessly jumped on the parapet, and opened fire on the attacking enemy, inflicting several casualties.

During this operation he was exposed to very heavy machine-gun, rifle fire and bombing, but with dogged determination he kept up his fire, thus holding up the enemy until help arrived, enabling the enemy counter-attack to be repulsed with heavy losses. The capture of this strong post was the means of securing our flank, which had previously been in the air, and also enabled us to get in touch with the troops on our flank.

No. 6594, Sergeant Gerald Sexton,
13th Battalion, A.I.F.

In the attack near Le Verguier, north-west of St. Quentin, on the 18th September, 1918, Sergeant Sexton displayed the most conspicuous bravery and performed deeds which, apart from their gallant nature, were in a great measure responsible for the battalion's success. On the southern edge of the village of Le Verguier the enemy fought hard, and serious opposition had to be crushed. During the whole period of the advance, Sergeant Sexton was to the fore dealing with enemy machine-guns by firing from the hip as he advanced, rushing enemy posts, and performing feats of bravery and endurance, which are better appreciated when one realises that all the time he fired his Lewis Gun from the hip without faltering or for a moment taking cover.

Immediately the attack commenced, Sergeant Sexton's Lewis Gun Section was confronted by an enemy machine-gun. He called out to his section to follow, rushed the machine-gun and killed the crew. He then called out to the rest of the company to follow, but they had not gone far when they encountered some bombers and riflemen about 70 yards in front of the company. Sexton rushed the trench, firing his gun from the hip, and killed or took prisoner all the members of the post. Continuing, he entered a copse, and killed or took prisoner another party of the enemy. The advance continued over the ridge at Le Verguier to where Sexton was met by Lieut. Price, who pointed out a party of the enemy manning a bank, and a field gun in action which was causing casualties and holding up a company.

There was also a trench mortar in action. Sergeant Sexton did not wait, but firing a few short bursts as he advanced, and calling out to his section to follow, rushed down the bank and killed the gunners on the field gun. Dashing out on to a flat under fire from two hostile machine-guns directed on him, he killed 12 more of the enemy. Paying no heed to the machine-gun fire, he returned to the bank, and after firing down some dug-outs, induced about 30 of the enemy to surrender. Owing to his action the company on the left of the battalion was able to continue the advance where they had been definitely held up, and were suffering from the effects of the field gun. When the advance was continued from the first to the second objective, the company was again held up by two machine-guns on the right and one on the left. In conjunction with a platoon, Sexton engaged the machine-gun on the left, firing all the while from the upright position, a fearless figure which, according to eye-witnesses, inspired everyone.

To have taken cover would have been more prudent, but Sexton realised that prompt action was essential, and did not wait to assume the prone position. Silencing this gun, he turned his attention to the two machine-guns on the right and silenced them. He then moved forward into a trench, killing quite a number of the enemy and, advancing along a sap, took a few prisoners. Further on he was responsible for a few more small posts, and, on the final objective, being given a responsible post on the left of his company, he engaged a machine-gun which was firing across the company front, and thus enabled his company to dig in. This completed, he went forward down a sunken road and captured several more prisoners.

Major Blair Anderson Wark, D.S.O.,
32nd Battalion, A.I.F.

During the period 29th September-1st October, 1918, in the operations against the Hindenburg Line at Bellicourt, and the advance through Nauroy, Etricourt, Magny La Fosse and Joncourt, Major Wark, in command of the 32nd Battalion, displayed most conspicuous gallantry and set a fine example of personal bravery, energy, coolness, and control under extremely difficult conditions. On 29th September, under heavy artillery and machine-gun fire at very close range from all sides and in a dense fog, Major Wark, finding that the situation was critical, moved quickly forward alone and obtained sufficient information regarding the situation in front to be able to lead his command forward. At this time American troops were at a standstill and disorganised, and Major Wark quickly organised more than 200 of them, and attached them to his leading companies and pressed forward.

By his prompt action in the early stages of the battle he narrowly averted what would have resulted in great confusion on the part of the attack-troops. Still moving fearlessly at the head of his leading companies, and at most times far out in advance, attended only by a runner, he cheered his men on, and they swept through the Hindenburg defences towards Nauroy. Pushing quickly through Nauroy, and mopping up the southern portion of the village, the process yielding 50 prisoners, the battalion swung towards Etricourt. Still leading his assaulting companies, he observed a battery of 77 mm. guns firing point-blank into his rear companies and causing heavy casualties. Calling on a few of his men to him he rushed the battery, capturing the 4 guns and 10 of the crew; the remainder of the crew fled or were killed.

Moving rapidly forward with only two N.C.O.'s, he surprised and captured 50 Germans near Magny la Fosse. Quickly seizing this opportunity, he pushed one Company forward through the village and made good the position. Having captured his objectives for the day, and personally reconnoitring to see that his flanks were safe, he found his command in a very difficult and dangerous position, his left flank being exposed to the extent of 3,000 yards on account of the 31st Battalion not being able to advance. He, after a strenuous day's fighting, set about the selection and reorganisation of a new position, and effected a junction with British troops on the right and 31st Battalion on the left, and made his line secure. At 6 a.m. on 30th September, he again led his command forward to allow of the troops on the right being able to advance. The men were tired and had suffered heavily, but he personally led them, and his presence amongst them inspired them to further efforts.

On October 1st, 1918, his battalion was ordered to advance at very short notice. He gave his orders for the attack, and personally led his troops forward. A nest of machine-guns was encountered, causing casualties to his men. Without hesitation and regardless of personal risk, he dashed forward practically into the muzzles of the guns and under an exceptionally heavy fire and silenced them, killing or capturing the entire crews. Joncourt and Mill Ridge were then quickly captured and his line consolidated. His men were practically exhausted after the three days' heavy fighting, but he moved amongst them from post to post, across country swept by heavy and continuous shell and machine-gun fire at point-blank range, urged them on and the line was made secure.

Throughout he displayed the greatest courage and devotion to duty, coupled with great tact and skill, and his work, together with the reports based on his own personal observations, which he forwarded, were invaluable to the brigade. It is beyond doubt that the success achieved by the brigade during the heavy fighting on 29th and 30th September and 1st October was due to this officer's gallantry, determination, skill and great courage.

No. 1717, Private John Ryan,
55th Battalion, A.I.F.

For conspicuous gallantry and devotion to duty, and for saving a very dangerous situation under particularly gallant circumstances during an attack against the Hindenburg defences on 30th September, 1918. In the initial assault on the enemy's positions this soldier went forward with great dash and determination, and was one of the first men of his company to reach the trench which was their objective. Seeing him rush in with his bayonet with such exceptional skill and daring, his comrades were inspired and followed his example. Although the enemy shell and machine-gun fire was extremely heavy, the enemy trench garrison was soon overcome. In the assault the attacking troops were weakened by casualties, and, as they were too few to cover the whole front of attack, a considerable gap was left between Private Ryan's battalion's left and the unit on the flank.

The enemy counter-attacked soon after the objective was reached, and a few succeeded in infiltrating through the gap, and taking up a position of cover in rear of our men, where they commenced bombing operations. The section of trench occupied by Private Ryan and his comrades was now under fire from front and rear, and for a time it seemed that the enemy was certain to force his way through. The situation was critical and necessitated prompt action by someone in authority. Private Ryan found that there were no officers or N.C.O.'s near; they had become casualties in the assault. Appreciating the situation at once, he organised the few men nearest him, and led them out to attack the enemy with bomb and bayonet. Some of his party fell victims to the enemy's bombs, and he finally dashed into the enemy position of cover with only 3 men.

The enemy were three times their number, but by skilful bayonet work they succeeded in killing the first three Germans on the enemy's flank. Moving along the embankment. Private Ryan alone rushed the remainder of the enemy with bombs. It was while thus engaged he fell wounded, but his dashing bombing assault drove the enemy clear of our positions. Those who were not killed or wounded by his bombs fell victims to our Lewis Gunners as they retired across No Man's Land. A particularly dangerous situation had been saved by this gallant soldier, whose display of determined bravery and initiative was witnessed by the men of the two attacking battalions, who, inspired and urged by it, fought skilfully and bravely for two days.

Lieutenant Joseph Maxwell, M.C., D.C.M.,
18th Battalion, A.I.F.

On 3rd October, 1918, he took part as a platoon commander in an attack on the Beaurevoir-Fonsomme Line near Estrées, north of St. Quentin. His company commander was severely wounded soon after the jump off, and Lieut. Maxwell at once took charge of the company. When the enemy wire was reached, they were met by a hail of machine-gun fire, and suffered considerable casualties, including all other officers of the company. The wire at this point was six belts thick, each belt being 20 to 25 feet wide. Lieut. Maxwell pushed forward single-handed through the wire, and attacked the most dangerous machine-gun. He personally killed three of the crew, and the remaining four men in the post surrendered to him with a machine-gun. His company followed him through the wire and captured the trenches forming their objective.

Later, it was noticed that the company on his left was held up in the wire by a very strong force on the left flank of the battalion. He at once organised a party and moved to the left to endeavour to attack the enemy from the rear. Heavy machine-gun fire met them. Lieut. Maxwell again dashed forward single-handed at the foremost machine-gun, and with his revolver shot five of its crew, so silencing the gun. Owing to the work of this party, the left company was then able to work a small force through the wire, and eventually to occupy the objective and mop up the trenches. In the fighting prior to the mopping up, an English-speaking prisoner, who was captured, stated that the remainder of the enemy were willing to surrender.

Lieut. Maxwell and two men, with this prisoner, walked to a post containing more than twenty Germans. The latter at once seized and disarmed our men. Lieut. Maxwell waited his chance, and then with an automatic pistol which he had concealed in his box respirator, shot two of the enemy and with the two men escaped. They were pursued by rifle fire, and one was wounded. However, Lieut. Maxwell organised a small party at once, attacked and captured the post.

Second Lieutenant George Morby Ingram, M.M., 24th Battalion, A.I.F.

During the attack on Montbrehain, east of Péronne, on 5th October, 1918, this officer was in charge of a platoon. About 100 yards from the Jumping Off Trench severe enemy machine-gun fire was encountered from a strong post which had escaped our artillery fire, and the advance was thus held up. Lieut. Ingram dashed out, and, under cover of the fire of a Lewis Gun, rushed the post at the head of his men. This post contained 9 machine-guns and 42 Germans, who fought until our men were within 3 yards of them. They were killed to a man—Lieut. Ingram accounting for no less than 18 of them. A number of enemy posts were then observed to be firing on our men from about 150 yards further forward, and the company moved forward to attack them, but severe casualties were sustained.

The company commander had been badly wounded, and the company sergeant-major and several others, who attempted to lead the advance, were killed. Our barrage had passed on, and no tanks were near. Lieut. Ingram quickly seized the situation, rallied his men in the face of murderous fire, and, with magnificent courage and resolution, led them forward. He himself rushed the first post, shot 6 of the enemy, and captured a machine-gun, thus overcoming a very serious resistance. By this time the company had been reduced from 90 to about 30 other ranks; but this officer, seeing enemy fire coming from a quarry, to his left front, again led his men forward and rushed the quarry. He jumped into the quarry amongst enemy wire, and his men followed and proceeded to mop up a large number of the enemy who were in bivouacs there.

He then observed an enemy machine-gun firing from the ventila-

Australian Artillery—moving up to the front, through the Hindenburg wire, October 2nd, 1918.

Advance during Battle—Third Division Infantry and Tanks advancing to the capture of Bony, October 1st, 1918.

tor of a cellar, through a gap in the wall of a house about 20 yards away. Without hesitation and entirely alone he scrambled up the edge of the quarry, ran round the rear of the house, and entering from the far side, shot the enemy gunner through the ventilator of the cellar. He fired several more shots into the cellar, then, seeing some enemy jumping out of the window of the house, he burst open a door, rushed to the head of the stairs leading into the cellar, and forced 62 of the enemy to surrender.

He now found he was out of touch with the company on his left flank, so went out alone and made a personal reconnaissance under heavy fire, and succeeded in gaining touch with the left company, which had lost all its officers. Having returned to his company, he personally placed a post on his left flank to ensure its safety, and then reconnoitred and established two posts on his right flank. All this was done in the face of continuous machine-gun and shell fire.

Appendix C

Corps Orders for the Battle of August 8th, 1918

The following were the complete orders issued by the Australian Army Corps for the battle of August 8th, 1918. They form only a small part of the whole of the orders which were required for the operation. There were, in addition, detailed orders by the Corps Artillery Headquarters, the heavy artillery, the chief engineer, and each of the five divisions and fifteen brigades, and also by the Administrative Services of the corps.

On the question of the form of the orders, the most expedient course was found to be the one here adopted—namely, that of issuing a numbered series of battle instructions, each dealing comprehensively with a separate subject matter:

Battle Instructions No. 1

1. The Australian Corps will attack the enemy from the Villers-Bretonneux-Chaulnes Railway exclusive to the River Somme, inclusive, at a date and hour to be notified.

The Canadian Corps will co-operate on the right, south of the railway (inclusive), and the Third Corps on the left, north of the Somme.

2. *General Method of Attack.*—The Australian Corps will attack on a two-division front. The attack will be carried out in three phases. Divisional boundaries and objectives are shown on the attached map.

(*i*) *First Phase.*—The 2nd and 3rd Australian Divisions will form up on a taped line prior to zero, and will attack with tanks under a creeping artillery barrage. Their objective is shown by a Green line on the attached map. On arrival at their objective they will consolidate.

(*ii*) *Second Phase.*—The 5th and 4th Australian Divisions, organised in brigade groups, will advance in open warfare formations, from the first objective passing through 2nd and 3rd Australian Divisions respectively. Their objective is shown in Red on the map.

(*iii*) *Third Phase.*—The 5th and 4th Australian Divisions will exploit their success and seize the old British line of Defences marked Blue on the map, and establish themselves defensively on this line.

(*iv*) The 1st Australian Division will be in Corps Reserve.

(*v*) A detailed programme of the action will be issued.

3. *Assembly.*—In order to free as many troops from line duty as possible, 2nd and 3rd Australian Divisions will arrange to hold the front with one infantry brigade on each divisional sector. This will be completed before daybreak on 5th August.

To prevent any troops arriving at their objectives in an exhausted condition through a long march, troops detailed to the farthest objectives must be quartered nearest the starting line prior to Zero.

The brigades of 2nd and 3rd Australian Divisions not holding the line will be quartered in rear of all brigades of 5th and 4th Australian Divisions respectively prior to Zero night. This will be completed before daybreak on 5th August.

The allotment of areas for quartering during this stage will be made by mutual arrangement between divisional commanders concerned. The allotment of routes and times of movement in accordance with the corps programme will be arranged similarly.

On Zero night the brigades of 2nd and 3rd Australian Divisions not in the line will make their approach march to their tape lines through the area occupied by 5th and 4th Australian Divisions respectively.

4. *Artillery.*

(*i*) The artillery available consists of:
        18 Field Artillery Brigades.
        12 Heavy Artillery Brigades.

(*ii*) G.O.C., R.A., Aust. Corps, will command all artillery of the corps during the first phase of the operation.

(*iii*) For the second phase G.O.C., R.A., Aust. Corps, will allot:

(*a*) Three field artillery brigades to 5th and 4th Aust. Divisions for distribution to infantry brigade groups. These will include the 5th and 4th Aust. Divisional Artillery respectively.

(*b*) Three brigades of field artillery and one battery of 60-pdr. Heavy artillery allotted to each of the 5th and 4th Aust. Divisions for employment as may be ordered by the divisional commanders.

(*c*) The remainder of the field artillery and the heavy artillery to Corps Reserve.

(*iv*) Heavy Artillery will be pushed forward by G.O.C., R.A., to protect the troops in the second objective.

5. *Tanks.*—Instructions for the distribution and employment of tanks will be issued later.

6. *Engineers.*—Engineers and pioneers will be distributed for work as follows from midnight on 6th-7th instant:

(*i*) Corps Pool under Chief Engineer—
    1 Field Coy. from 4th Aust. Div.
    1 Field Coy. from 5th Aust. Div.
    2 Field Coys. from 2nd Aust. Div.
    2 Field Coys. from 3rd Aust. Div.
    3 Army Troops Coys. Engineers
    5th Aust. Pioneer Bn.
    3rd Aust. Pioneer Bn

(*ii*) With divisions:

2nd Aust. Pioneer Bn. will serve 2nd and 3rd Aust. Divisions. 2 Coys. to each.

4th Aust. Pioneer Bn. will serve 4th and 5th Aust. Divisions. 2 Coys. to each.

Divisional commanders will control:

2nd Aust. Division—1 Field Coy. and 2nd Aust. Pioneer Bn. (less 2 Coys.)

3rd Aust. Division—1 Field Coy. and 2 Coys. 2nd Aust. Pioneer Bn.

4th Aust. Division—2 Field Coys. and 4th Aust. Pioneer Bn. (less 2 Coys.).

5th Aust. Division—2 Field Coys. and 2 Coys. 4th Aust. Bn. (less 2 Coys.).

Tunnellers will be detailed to each division for dug-out exploration.

Chief Engineer, Aust. Corps, will arrange for the distribution in accordance with this.

Chief Engineer will issue instructions for the withdrawal and storing of demolition charges of bridges for which the Corps is responsible, and for the return of engineer personnel employed on this work to their units.

7. Deputy Director of Medical Services will arrange for the distribution of medical units.

BATTLE INSTRUCTIONS No. 2

Secrecy

(*a*) It is of first importance that secrecy should be observed and the operation carried out as a surprise.

Commanders will take all possible steps to prevent the scope or date of the operation becoming known except to those taking part. Any officer, N.C.O., or man discussing the operation in public, or communicating details regarding it to any person, either soldier or civilian, not immediately concerned, will be severely dealt with.

(*b*) All movement of troops and transport will take place by night, whether in the forward or back areas of the Australian Corps, on and after 1st August, except where absolutely necessary to move by day.

(*c*) O.C., No. 3 Squadron, A.F.C., will arrange for aeroplanes to fly over the Australian Corps Army area during days when flying is possible, and to report to Corps H.Q. any abnormal movement of troops or transport within our lines.

(*d*) Work on back lines will be continued as at present, so that there may be no apparent change in our attitude.

(*e*) Commanders will ensure that the numbers of officers reconnoitring the enemy's positions is limited to those for whom such reconnaissance is essential.

Nothing attracts attention to an offensive more than a large number of officers with maps looking over the parapet and visiting Observation Posts.

Commanding officers of units holding the front line should report at once to higher authority any disregard of these orders.

BATTLE INSTRUCTIONS No. 3

Communications and Headquarters

1. Communications will be carefully organised to ensure the maintenance of communication throughout the advance and after its conclusion.

2. (*i*) Headquarters of Divisions will be established as follows:

2nd Australian Division—Glisy
5th Australian Division—Blangy-Tronville Château
Advanced Headquarters in dug-outs at Railway cutting
3rd Australian Division—Bussy
4th Australian Division—Corbie

(*ii*) Headquarters of brigades and battalions will be selected in advance, as far as this can be done, and all concerned will be notified of their proposed locations.

3. Report Centres in advance of the heads of buried cables will be selected in each Divisional Sector and details prepared for the organisation of communications back to cable head.

4. The following mounted troops are detailed to divisions:
To 2nd Australian Division—1 Troop 13th L.H.
3rd Australian Division—1 Troop 13th L.H.
4th Australian Division—2 Troops 13th L.H.
5th Australian Division—2 Troops 13th L.H.

Divisions will inform O.C., 13th Light Horse, as to the time and place at which the Light Horse will report.

The Cyclist Section now with divisions will remain.

5. The employment of wireless will be exploited to the full.

6. Popham panels will be employed for communication between infantry and aeroplanes.

Battle Instructions No. 4

Artillery

(a) Ammunition will be dumped at or near gun positions as follows:

18-pdr	600 rounds
4.5" Howitzer	500 rounds
60-pdr	400 rounds
6" guns	400 rounds
6" Howitzers	400 rounds
8" Howitzers	400 rounds
9.2" Howitzers	400 rounds
12" Howitzers	400 rounds

Arrangements should be made to commence dumping this ammunition as soon as feasible. Echelons will be kept full.

(b) Boundaries between Corps as regards bombardment and counter-battery work coincide with the boundaries between Corps shown on map issued with Australian Corps "Battle Instructions No. 1", dated 1st August, 1918.

BATTLE INSTRUCTIONS NO. 5

Tanks

1. Tanks are available as follows:

5th Tank Brigade.
Mark V. Tanks—2nd Battalion— Lieut.-Col. E. D Bryce, D.S.O
Mark V. Tanks—8th Battalion— Lieut.-Col. The Hon. J.D.Y. Bingham, D.S.O.
13th Battalion— Lieut.-Col. P. Lyon
Mark V. (Star) Tanks—15th Battalion— Lieut.-Colonel Ramsey-Fairfax
No. 1 G.C. Coy. (24 Carrying Tanks)— Major W. Partington, M.C.

2. *Mark V. Tanks* are allotted as follows:

13th Battalion (Lieut.-Col. Lyon), less one company, to 3rd Australian Division.

2nd Battalion (Lieut.-Col. Bryce), plus one company 13th Battalion attached, to be employed with the two right Divisions—two companies to be allotted to each division.

8th Battalion (Lieut.-Col. The Hon. J.D.Y. Bingham) to 4th Australian Division.

One company of the 8th Battalion will be employed in support. It will be specially charged with the function of maintaining the attack at the junction of divisions throughout the advance as far as the second objective.

Command will be effected through battalion commanders in each case except that Lieut.-Col. Bryce will be responsible for command of all Mark V. Tanks allotted to both 2nd and 5th Australian Divisions.

3. After the capture of the first objective, tanks detailed to 2nd and 3rd Australian Divisions will rally and will be employed to support the advance of the 5th and 4th Australian Divisions respectively.

4. After the capture of the second objective, tanks will rally. One company will remain in close support in each divisional sector; the remainder will be withdrawn to positions to be arranged between divisional and tank commanders.

5. Mark V. (Star) Tanks are allotted as follows:
>1½ companies (18 tanks) to the 5th Australian Division.
1½ companies (18 tanks) to the 4th Australian Division.
These tanks are allotted for the capture of the blue line.

6. *Carrying Tanks* are allotted as follows:
>2nd and 3rd Australian Divisions—3 tanks each.
4th and 5th Australian Divisions—9 tanks each.

7. Orders for forming up and movement to the Start Line will be issued by G.O.C., 5th Tank Brigade.

Battalion commanders detailed to divisions will be responsible for all liaison duty in connection with the tanks.

8. For tactical purposes tanks will be placed under the command of infantry commanders to whose commands they are allotted.

BATTLE INSTRUCTIONS NO. 5A

Assembly of Tanks

1. *Preliminary Movement.*

Tanks will be assembled in concealed positions in the forward area under the orders of the 5th Tank Brigade prior to night Y/Z.

2. *Advance to Start Line.*

On night Y/Z the tanks allotted to troops attacking the first objective will commence to move forward at 9.30 p.m. to the Tank Start Line. They will move with full engines to a line not nearer to the Tank Start Line than 3,000 yards. From there they will continue the movement forward to the Tank Start Line, moving at a slow rate and as quietly as possible. The Tank Start Line will be approximately 1,000 yards in rear of the infantry taped line.

Tanks will leave the Tank Start Line at such times as will allow them to catch up to the infantry as the barrage lifts at zero plus three minutes.

3. *Concealment of Engine Noise.*

To conceal the noise of the engines during the advance of the tanks, the 5th Brigade R.A.F. will arrange to have planes flying continuously over the Corps area from 9.30 p.m. until midnight on Y/Z night, and from zero minus one hour onward to zero.

4. *Tanks allotted to Second Objective.*

The tanks allotted to the second objective will form up independently under the orders of the 5th Tank Brigade in consultation with

G.O.'s C., 4th and 5th Australian Divisions. These tanks will be formed up when the aeroplanes are in the air during the hours laid down in para. 3.

5. *Liaison Company.*

The company of the 8th Tank Battalion detailed to act in support, and to ensure liaison in the battle line at the junction of divisions, will detail a half-company to each wave of tanks, *vide* paras. 2 and 4 above.

Divisions will detail special liaison parties of infantry to work in co-operation with this company.

6. *Re-assembly.*

As soon as the blue line has been reached, G.O.C. 5th Australian Division will arrange to release the 2nd Tank Battalion, less the attached company. This battalion will then be withdrawn. The remainder of the tanks, less one company allotted to remain in support of each of the 4th and 5th Australian Divisions, will be withdrawn when ordered by Divisional Commanders, *vide* Battle Instructions No. 5, para. 4.

7. *Smoke Grenades.*

Divisions will ensure that a proportion of smoke rifle grenades accompanies each infantry detachment detailed to the blue line and which accompanies each of the Mark V. (Star) Tanks.

BATTLE INSTRUCTIONS NO. 6

Artillery

1. *Preparation.*

Active counter-battery work and harassing fire will be maintained.

Such registration as is necessary will be carried out under cover of this fire. A detailed programme for this will be arranged in each divisional sector.

The necessity for concealing the increase in the number of guns on the front must be borne in mind, and on no account should a large number of guns be employed at any one time. Counter preparation and S.O.S. plans during the period of preparation for the attack will be drawn up accordingly.

Normal fire should, so far as possible, be carried out from positions other than those in which batteries will be emplaced during the battle.

2. *Heavy Artillery.*

(*a*) In view of the nature of the enemy's defences, the fire of the majority of the heavy howitzers, employed for purposes other than counter-battery work, will be used during the barrage to engage special strong points or localities.

(b) Throughout the advance beyond the green line enemy centres of resistance will be kept under fire until such time as the progress of the infantry renders this inadvisable. A map will be issued to show the times at which heavy artillery fire will cease on zones and special localities.

(c) At least two-thirds of the available heavy artillery will be employed for counter-battery purposes.

Heavy concentrations of fire will be directed on the different groups of enemy artillery.

3. G.O.C., R.A., will prepare plans for dealing with a heavy development of hostile fire on zero night. He will also prepare a plan to deal with any attempt at a deliberate gas bombardment of the Villers-Bretonneux area on zero night.

BATTLE INSTRUCTIONS NO. 7

Programme of Action

1. *Capture of First Objective.*

(a) Forming-up troops detailed to the capture of the first objective will be deployed on the Forming-up Line one hour before zero hour.

(b) *Artillery Programme.*

(i) The field artillery 18-pdr. barrage will open at zero 200 yards in advance of the forming-up line.

At zero plus three minutes the barrage will commence to advance; lifts will be 100 yards at 2-minute intervals. There will be two lifts at this rate.

The rate will then decrease to lifts of 100 yards every 3 minutes. There will be eight lifts at this rate.

From the eleventh lift inclusive until the green line is reached lifts will be of 100 yards each at 4-minute intervals.

(ii) The 4.5" Howitzer barrage will move 200 yards in advance of the 18-pdr. barrage.

(iii) A protective barrage will be maintained in front of the green line until zero plus four hours. During this period approximately fifty *per cent.* (50%) of the guns remaining in the barrage will be employed in a protective line barrage; the remainder will be employed to search and sweep deeply into the enemy's position. At zero plus four hours all barrage fire will cease.

Barrage Maps will be issued later.

2. *Capture of Second and Third Objectives.*

(*a*) *Assembly.*—5th and 4th Australian Divisions will select and mark positions for the assembly of their troops.

These areas will be selected in liaison with tank commanders and with the 2nd and 3rd Australian Divisions respectively, to prevent movement to them clashing with the approach march of these divisions and that of the tanks. This requires careful co-ordination between each pair of divisions and tank commanders.

(*b*) *Command.*—At zero plus four hours, responsibility for the battle front will pass to G.O.C., 5th Australian Division, in the right sector, and to G.O.C., 4th Australian Division, in the left sector.

(*c*) *The Advance.*—5th and 4th Australian Divisions will time their advance so that the leading troops cross the first objective (green line) at zero plus four hours.

(*d*) From zero plus four hours the advance will be continued under the conditions of open warfare.

BATTLE INSTRUCTIONS NO. 8

Roads

1. A map is forwarded herewith showing the organisation of the road system in the captured territory.

2. The Chief Engineer will issue the necessary instructions for the preparation of these roads for traffic.

3. All light traffic which is capable of moving across country will do so and will avoid main roads.

4. Mule tracks will be a divisional responsibility.

5. Artillery advancing with the 5th and 4th Australian Divisions will carry forward a proportion of bridges. Arrangements should be made as soon as possible for the development of tracks, making use of the routes taken by the artillery over these bridges.

6. The Amiens-Longueau-Villers-Bretonneux main road, as far east as the cross roads in N.26.c., will be reserved for the exclusive use of the Cavalry Corps from 9.30 p.m. on Y/Z night until 8 a.m. on Z day. After 8 a.m. on Z day it will be available for the Australian and Cavalry Corps. Assistant Provost Marshal, Australian Corps, will arrange for the control of the traffic on this road throughout.

Chief Engineer, Australian Corps, will prepare short avoiding roads at the cross roads at N.26.c. to cross the north-east or south-west corner to avoid congestion at this spot.

BATTLE INSTRUCTIONS NO. 9
Light Signals, Message Rockets, Smoke

1. *Light Signals.*

(a) *Australian Corps.*

The following Light Signals will be employed in the Australian Corps:

S.O.S. Signal, No. 32 grenade—showing green over green over green. Allotment 500 per Division.

Success Signal, No. 32 grenade—showing white over white over white. Allotment 600 per Division.

A small reserve of each of these grenades is held at Corps Headquarters.

No other Light Signals will be laid down by corps. There is no objection to the use within divisions of a Very Light for the local indication of targets between infantry and tanks.

(b) *Other Formations.*

Light Signals of other formations are as follows:

Formation.	Signal.	Meaning.
(i) Cavalry Corps.	White star turning to red on a parachute fired from 1¼" Very pistol.	"Advanced troops of Cavalry are here."
(ii) Third Corps.	No. 32 grenade, green over green over green.	"S.O.S."
	No. 32 grenade, white over white over white.	"Success signal, *i.e.*, we have reached objective."
	One white Very light.	"Barrage is about to lift."
(iii) Canadian Corps	No. 32 grenade, red over red over red.	"S.O.S." will also mean (a) "We are held up and cannot advance without help." (b) "Enemy is counter-attacking."
	No.32 grenade, green over green over green.	"(a) Lift your fire. We are going to advance. (b) Stop firing."
	Three white Very lights in quick succession.	"We have reached this point."

Remark.—In the case of (*a*) a smoke rocket (No. 27 grenade) will also be fired in the direction of the obstruction to indicate its position.

(*c*) Special care must be taken by the artillery on the right flank of the corps that all officers and N.C.O.'s are acquainted with these signals, so that no mistake may arise as regards the difference in the S.O.S. Signals of the Australian and Canadian Corps.

2. *Message-carrying Rockets.*
Allotment of Message-carrying Rockets is 80 per division.

3. *Smoke.*
(*a*) Artillery smoke will be as follows:
(*i*) 3 rounds per gun will be fired during the first three minutes of the artillery barrage.

(*ii*) 3 rounds per gun will be fired in quick succession on the arrival of the field artillery barrage at the artillery halt line covering the first objective.

(*iii*) In the event of wet weather a small proportion of smoke will be used in the barrage to replace the smoke and dust caused by the burst of the shells in dry weather. This will not be sufficient to confuse the effect with that of the smoke shells prescribed in paragraph 3 (a) (*i*) and (*ii*).

(*b*) *Screening beyond the First Objective.*

15th Wing, Royal Air Force, will arrange to screen the advance of the tanks and infantry from special localities in advance of their first objective by dropping phosphorus bombs.

Divisions and G.O.C., 5th Tank Brigade, will inform Australian Corps Headquarters as early as possible of the localities which they desire screened.

A map will be issued showing times at which it is anticipated that the infantry will make good certain zones. Phosphorus bombs will not be dropped within these zones at any time after it is anticipated that the infantry will have occupied them.

BATTLE INSTRUCTIONS NO. 10

Intelligence and Disposal of Prisoners of War

1. *Battalion Intelligence Police.*

One German speaker and two searchers will be allotted to each battalion for use as follows:

(a) *German Speaker.*

(*i*) To secure immediate identifications quickly, so that identifications will reach Corps Headquarters as speedily as possible of enemy units on the battle front.

(*ii*) To secure immediate information required by the battalion commander as regards enemy dispositions, assembly positions, orders for counterattack, etc.

(*iii*) To be in charge of the two searchers and separate important documents, orders, maps, etc., translate and convey information of moment to the immediate commander.

(*b*) *Two Searchers.*

The two searchers under the German speaker systematically search the battlefield, enemy positions, suspected headquarters, dead, etc., for papers, documents, maps, etc., have them packed in sandbags, and sent through the usual channels to the Corps Cage as quickly as possible.

This personnel should carry torches and, besides rifles or revolvers, bombs are recommended as being useful for dealing with any of the enemy who may be found in dug-outs.

2. *Divisional Intelligence Officers.*

Divisional Intelligence Officers will go forward to an Advanced Divisional Collecting Cage, with a view to obtaining, as soon as possible, information of immediate tactical importance.

The cage will be connected by telephone to Divisional H.Q., and important information obtained should be transmitted as quickly as possible to Divisional and Brigade H.Q.

The main points on which immediate information is required from prisoners are:

The Order of Battle, Units seen, Distribution of the Enemy's Forces, Method of holding the Line, Assembly Positions, Counter-attack Orders and Intentions.

This information will be wired to their respective Divisional Headquarters and repeated to Corps Headquarters and Corps Cage by Divisional Intelligence Officers.

Divisional Intelligence Officers will not detain prisoners longer than is necessary to obtain this tactical information of immediate importance.

In case a large number of prisoners are captured, they will detain only one or two from each regiment, and will not delay the passage of the remainder to the Corps Cage.

Any further information required from prisoners by Divisions or lower formations can always be obtained by telephone from the Corps Cage.

3. *Searching of Prisoners,*
(a) *Officers and N.C.O.'s.*

Officers and N.C.O.'s will be searched as soon as possible after capture by a responsible officer or N.C.O., and all documents taken from them sent back with them (in sacks, labelled by regiments, if a number are captured) to the Divisional Intelligence Officer, at such place as this officer has prearranged.

It is left to the discretion of Divisional Intelligence Officers as to what documents, maps, etc., taken from prisoners they hold back for the information of Brigade and Divisional Commanders. When this is done, Corps "I" will be informed by wire, priority if necessary, of the nature of the documents, etc., held back, and of any points of immediate tactical importance they may contain.

As soon as possible after information has been extracted from them, the documents will be forwarded on to the Corps Cage. Arrangements can be made by Corps, if notified that documents are ready to be sent on, to fetch them by motorcyclist or cycle.

(b) *Other Ranks.*

Prisoners other than officers and N.C.O.'s will be searched on their arrival at the Corps Cage. Their papers, etc., will be taken from them and put into sacks labelled according to regiments.

(c) All ranks should understand that a prisoner's pay-book, identity disc, and personal belongings should not be taken from him. Escorts and guards will be warned to take special precautions to prevent prisoners from destroying papers.

4. *Separation of Officers, N.C.O.'s and Men.*

Care will be taken that officers, N.C.O.'s and privates are all separated from one another at once, and are not allowed to communicate with one another.

Prisoners who have been interrogated should not be allowed to mix with those who have not yet been interrogated.

5. *Notification of Locality of Capture.*

It is essential that, when prisoners are sent back, information be sent with them which will show where they were captured. Information as to the battalion which made the capture is a useful indication.

6. *Authorised Persons only to converse with Prisoners.*

It is most important that no officer or N.C.O., except those duly authorised, be allowed to interrogate or converse with prisoners.

7. *Prisoners of War Cage.*

The Advanced Corps Cage will be situated at Vecquemont, N.11.b.8.7. and the Rear Corps Cage at N.2.c.3.7.

Intelligence Officers and personnel will be stationed here, and will carry out a more detailed interrogation and sort out captured documents.

The Advanced Corps Cage will be connected by telephone to Corps H.Q.

8. *Prisoners.*

The following procedure will be adopted for the disposal of prisoners:

After capture they will be escorted to the Advanced Divisional Collecting Cage, for examination by the Divisional Intelligence Officer, who, after he has finished with them, will send them back to the Advanced Corps Cage.

The sending back of prisoners should be carried out as quickly as possible, and several escorts should be arranged for them to be passed back without any unusual delay. Instructions should be issued to ensure that too many men are not employed on escort duty.

In the forward area directing notices should be placed to show the route to be taken to the Advanced Divisional Collecting Cage.

Traffic control personnel should be conversant with the method of disposing of prisoners.

9. *Identifications.*

The importance of passing on all identifications as speedily as possible to Corps "I" cannot be too strongly impressed on all concerned. It is essential that special efforts be made to wire at once, as soon as identifications are made and the locality in which obtained.

10. *Maps and Photographs.*

The following maps are being issued:

(*i*) A large issue of 1/20,000 No. 62. D. South-East regular series for distribution to all officers.

(*ii*) 1/20,000 Map Message Form, for distribution down to N.C.O.'s.

(*iii*) A small issue of 1/10,000 Maps of forward area only.

(*iv*) 1/20,000 Barrage Map, for distribution down to Company Commanders.

(*v*) 1/40,000 Organisation Map, together with notes on the enemy.

The following special photographs are being issued:

(*a*) A Mosaic of each divisional front, squared and contoured and freely annotated, for distribution down to N.C.O.'s.

(*b*) Oblique Photographs of each divisional front, for distribution to all officers.

BATTLE INSTRUCTIONS No. 11
Co-Operation of Infantry and Aircraft

1. *Contact Aeroplanes.*

(i) *Indication of position by flares.*

(*a*) Red ground flares will be used to indicate the infantry positions to contact aeroplanes. They will be lit by infantry in the most advanced line only.

(*b*) A contact aeroplane will fly along the line of the first objective at zero plus 2 hours 30 minutes. Flares will be called for by the aeroplane sounding a succession of "A's" on the Klaxon horn and by firing a white Very Light. If the aeroplane fails to mark the line accurately, it will repeat its call ten minutes later.

Should the infantry not have reached the line of the objective at the time laid down above, the contact aeroplane will return at half-hour intervals until flares are shown.

(*c*) A contact aeroplane will fly along the line of the second objective at zero plus 6 hours 30 minutes. It will call for flares, and the same procedure will be followed on this objective as on the first objective until the flares are seen.

(*d*) A contact aeroplane will fly over third objective at zero plus 7 hours, when the procedure laid down for the first objective will be observed until the flares are shown.

(*e*) Divisions will organise message-dropping stations in the vicinity of their Headquarters.

(ii) *Other means of identifying the position of the Infantry.*

(*a*) *Rifles.*—Three or four rifles laid parallel across the top of the trench.

(*b*) *Metal Discs.*—Metal discs will be used as reflectors by flashing in the sun. This method has been successful even on days which have not been particularly bright.

The disc is most easily carried sewn to the Small Box Respirator, and can be used in this way without inconvenience.

2. *Counter-attack Planes.*

(*a*) From zero hour counter-attack planes will be constantly in the air, with the object of observing hostile concentrations or abnormal movement.

(b) In the event of an enemy concentration indicating a counter-attack, the counter-attack aeroplane will signal this information to the artillery by wireless. In the case of a counter-attack actually developing a white parachute flare will be fired by the aeroplane in the direction of the troops moving for the impending counter-attack, for the information of the infantry.

3. *Ammunition-carrying Aeroplanes.*

(a) Aeroplanes will be detailed to transport ammunition from zero plus 2 hours 30 minutes.

(b) Vickers guns will display a white "V" at the point where ammunition is to be dropped. The arms of the "V" to be 6 feet in length and 1 foot in width. The apex of the "V" to point towards the enemy.

(c) Ammunition aeroplanes will have the under-side of the lower planes painted black for a distance of 2½ feet from the tips.

BATTLE INSTRUCTIONS NO. 12

Consolidation

1. *Divisions allotted to First Objective.*

(a) *Consolidation.*—As soon as the first objective has been captured troops will dig in.

(b) *Troops holding present front line.*—The brigades of 2nd and 3rd Australian Divisions holding the line on the night prior to zero will remain in their battle positions until all troops detailed to the attack have passed through. They will then be organised and prepared to move to meet any emergency.

2nd Australian Division will be prepared to detach its brigade to act in support of 5th Australian Division, and 3rd Australian Division to detach its brigade in support of 4th Australian Division.

(c) *Reorganisation of Troops on First Objective.*—As soon as the whole of the troops detailed to the capture of second (red line) and third (blue line) objectives have passed through the line of the first objective, 2nd and 3rd Australian Divisions will organise the defence of their sectors on the first objective in depth in each brigade sub-sector. Units will be reorganised, and those not detailed to the defence of the line will be withdrawn into support and held in readiness for eventualities.

At least one battalion in each brigade sub-sector should be withdrawn in this way.

2. *Second Objective.*

Consolidation.—As soon as the second objective (the red line) has been captured, the position will be thoroughly consolidated. Arrangements will be made to ensure a supply of engineering material for this.

3. *Main Line of Resistance.*

(*a*) When the third objective (the blue line) is attained, it will be organised and consolidated as the main line of resistance.

(*b*) If the enemy is able to develop an immediate counter-attack, or if he has a definite plan, and the troops available in close reserve for the defence of the blue line, it may not be possible to reach the third objective.

In this case the second objective (red line) will become the main line of resistance, and will be consolidated and organised in depth accordingly.

(*c*) Definite plans will be prepared to deal with either case. The Corps must be prepared, as early as possible, to fight a stiff defensive battle on the main line of resistance.

BATTLE INSTRUCTIONS NO. 13

1. The 5th Australian Division will move into its assembly area by Brigade Groups as follows:

"A" Brigade Group on the night 4th–5th August from Montières to Camon and Rivery area. Quarters have been arranged for one brigade, less one battalion. Shelters will be drawn from Area Commandant, Camon, for this battalion.

"B" Brigade Group from Allonville area to forward area.

"C" Brigade Group from Vaux area to Allonville area.

2. For the purposes of staging, Poulainville will be included as one of the battalion areas of the Allonville Brigade area.

The camp in Bois De Mai has been allotted for the use of the 5th Division nucleus.

It is left to the discretion of the G.O.C., 5th Australian Division, as to whether the battalion at Poulainville moves on the night of 4th August.

3. On the night 5th–6th August the 5th Australian Division will continue its move into its allotted assembly grounds in the forward area.

4. Rear parties are to be left in charge of all camps until handed over to the Area commandant.

Battle Instructions No. 14
Armoured Car Battalion

1. The 17th Armoured Car Battalion has been placed at the disposal of the Australian Corps, and will join the 5th Tank Brigade shortly.

2. This battalion is organised in two companies of eight (8) armoured cars each. Each armoured car carries one forward and one rear Hotchkiss gun.

3. One and a half (1½) companies are allotted to the 5th Australian Division, and half (½) a company will remain in Corps Reserve.

The half company detailed to remain in Corps Reserve will select a position of assembly in Square 0.26, and will occupy this position by 9.30 p.m. on Y/Z night. During the action its orders will be transmitted through the 5th Australian Divisional Signal Service. The Commander will arrange with the 5th Australian Division accordingly.

4. As soon as the battalion commander or his representative reports to the 5th Tank Brigade, he will be instructed to report to the general staff, Australian Corps, and then to Headquarters, 5th Australian Division.

Battle Instructions No. 14A
Armoured Car Battalion

1. The 17th Armoured Car Battalion is being given definite roles in accordance with paragraph 3 of Battle Instructions No. 14. The roles assigned to this battalion may carry the cars forward for a considerable distance into enemy territory, and may necessitate their returning through other Divisional Sectors than that of the 5th Australian Division.

2. British Armoured Cars can be recognised by the red and white band markings which are similar to those of the British tanks.

3. All troops will be warned of the possibility of our armoured cars coming into our own sector, and of the way in which they are marked.

Battle Instructions No. 15
Zero Hour—Synchronization of Watches

1. *Zero Hour.*

Zero hour will be notified in writing from Australian Corps Headquarters by noon on the day prior to zero.

2. *Synchronization of Watches.*

Watches will be synchronised by officers detailed by Australian Corps Headquarters, who will visit Headquarters in the following order, leaving Corps Headquarters shortly after noon and 6 p.m. on Y day:

(*a*) One officer to Headquarters Heavy Artillery, 3rd Australian Division and 4th Australian Division.

(*b*) One officer to 2nd Australian Division and 5th Australian Division.

BATTLE INSTRUCTIONS NO. 16

Aircraft

1. The Air Forces which will operate on the Australian Corps front during the battle will be as follows:

(*a*) Corps Squadron—3rd Australian Squadron.

(*b*) 5th Tank Brigade—8th Squadron.

(*c*) The 22nd Wing, consisting of eight Scout Squadrons, which will be exclusively employed in engaging ground targets by bombing and machine-gunning along the whole army front.

(*d*) One night-bombing squadron—101st Bombing Squadron.

(*e*) One Reconnaissance Squadron—48th Squadron.

Four additional day-bombing squadrons and three additional night-bombing squadrons are being obtained from other wings for co-operation with the above, making 19 squadrons in all.

2. *Low-flying Scouts.*

The low-flying scouts of the 22nd Wing are being detailed on an even distribution to the Corps front. They will operate in two phases, *viz.*:

(*a*) From zero to zero plus four hours eastward from the green line.

(*b*) From zero plus four hours onwards eastwards from the red line. In each phase favourable targets will be engaged in addition to the targets marked by the green and red lines.

3. *Markings on Planes.*

The following will be the special markings of machines allotted to special duties:

(*a*) Contact patrol machines—Rectangular panels 2' by 1' on both lower planes about three feet from the fuselage.

(*b*) Machines working with tanks—Black band on middle of right side of tail.

4. *Ammunition-carrying Squadron.*

Aeroplanes carrying small arms ammunition will drop it at points as laid down in Battle Instructions No. 11, para. 3 (*b*). The first ammunition-carrying planes will arrive over the battlefield at zero plus seven hours.

5. *Aeroplane Smoke Screens.*

In addition to carrying small arms ammunition, this squadron will be employed to drop phosphorus smoke bombs to obstruct the enemy's view.

The areas to be screened and the time at which the screening in each case shall cease in order not to interfere with the advance of the infantry will be shown on a map to be issued later.

BATTLE INSTRUCTIONS NO. 17

Artillery Arrangements for the Last Night Before Zero

1. *S.O.S.*

(*i*) Each line division will arrange for four field artillery brigades, or an equivalent number of guns, to fire on S.O.S. lines at any time up to zero minus fifteen minutes.

(*ii*) From zero minus fifteen minutes until zero hour S.O.S. arrangements will be inoperative.

2. *Heavy Artillery.*

In the event of the enemy opening a gas bombardment on the Villers-Bretonneux area, arrangements have been made for the co-operation of the Canadian Corps Heavy Artillery in an artillery counter-attack on enemy batteries. The Canadian Corps will deal with the enemy artillery about Wiencourt and Marcelcave. Fire will be opened, on application, direct between the two Corps Headquarters.

G.O.C., R.A., Australian Corps, will arrange details with G.O.C., R.A., Canadian Corps.

BATTLE INSTRUCTIONS NO. 18

These are not reproduced. They refer only to Wireless Code Calls prescribed for all units.

BATTLE INSTRUCTIONS NO. 19

Liaison Arrangements

1. Officers are detailed for liaison duties as follows:

(*a*) At Canadian Corps Headquarters—Capt. Shearman, D.S.O., M.C.

(*b*) At Third Corps Headquarters—Major R. Morrell, D.S.O.

(*c*) With 1st Australian Division—To be notified.

(*d*) With 2nd Australian Division—Major H. Page, M.C.

(*e*) With 3rd Australian Division—Lt.-Col. A.R. Woolcock, D.S.O.
(*f*) With 4th Australian Division—Major G.F. Dickinson, D.S.O.
(*g*) With 5th Australian Division—Lt.-Col. N. Marshall, D.S.O.

2. The main function of the liaison officer is to relieve the Staff of the fighting formation of the necessity of:
(*a*) Supplying information to Australian Corps Headquarters.

(*b*) Collecting information from Corps Headquarters for transmission to the formation for whom they are carrying out liaison duties. It is their function to save the staff as far as possible, and not to get in the way. At the same time, they are expected to keep Corps Headquarters and the formation to which they are attached fully informed of events.

3. Direct telephone lines exist between Australian Corps Headquarters and neighbouring corps.

For the battle there is a special general staff switchboard with direct lines to 2nd, 3rd, 4th and 5th Australian Divisions.

4. An information bureau will be established in a marquee to be erected on the lawn in front of the Headquarters offices. Major W.W. Berry will be in charge of this bureau. It will be provided with a telephone, writing material, maps, etc.

Liaison officers from other formation at Australian Corps Headquarters will be accommodated in this marquee.

During the battle officers whose business does not require them to visit the General Staff Office will make all inquiries at this office for information as to the progress of the operations.

BATTLE INSTRUCTIONS NO. 20

Cavalry

1. The First Cavalry Brigade, plus one company of Whippet Tanks attached, comes under the command of the Australian Corps Commander at 9 p.m. on Y/Z night.

2. Its function is to assist in carrying out the main cavalry role by seizing any opportunity which may occur to push through this corps front.

3. The First Cavalry Brigade will operate north of the Amiens-Chaulnes railway in conjunction with 5th Australian Division. It will move from its assembly position in Square n.32 under orders of G.O.C., 1st Cavalry Division, *via* the southern side of Bois de L'Abbé. It will cross to the north side of the railway east of Villers-Breton-

neux.

It will push forward patrols to keep in touch with 8th and 15th Australian Brigades.

After crossing the railway, the main body of 1st Cavalry Brigade will march roughly parallel to it, keeping close touch with the remainder of 1st Cavalry Division to the south.

4. If a break in enemy's resistance occurs, the remainder of the 1st Cavalry Division may be employed in support of 1st Cavalry Brigade.

5. Command of 1st Cavalry Brigade will pass from Australian Corps to the 1st Cavalry Division when the infantry reaches the red line unless the brigade is required in the area south of the Australian Corps to exploit success gained before that hour. This will be determined by G.O.C., 1st Cavalry Division, who will inform Australian Corps and 5th Australian Division, and issue orders direct to 1st Cavalry Brigade.

BATTLE INSTRUCTIONS NO. 21

Notification of Date and Time of Battle

1. Reference paragraph 1 of General Staff Memo. No. AC/42, dated 7th instant, Zero will be 4.20 a.m. 8th instant.

ALSO FROM LEONAUR
AVAILABLE IN SOFTCOVER OR HARDCOVER WITH DUST JACKET

THE FALL OF THE MOGHUL EMPIRE OF HINDUSTAN *by H. G. Keene*—By the beginning of the nineteenth century, as British and Indian armies under Lake and Wellesley dominated the scene, a little over half a century of conflict brought the Moghul Empire to its knees.

LADY SALE'S AFGHANISTAN *by Florentia Sale*—An Indomitable Victorian Lady's Account of the Retreat from Kabul During the First Afghan War.

THE CAMPAIGN OF MAGENTA AND SOLFERINO 1859 *by Harold Carmichael Wylly*—The Decisive Conflict for the Unification of Italy.

FRENCH'S CAVALRY CAMPAIGN *by J. G. Maydon*—A Special Correspondent's View of British Army Mounted Troops During the Boer War.

CAVALRY AT WATERLOO *by Sir Evelyn Wood*—British Mounted Troops During the Campaign of 1815.

THE SUBALTERN *by George Robert Gleig*—The Experiences of an Officer of the 85th Light Infantry During the Peninsular War.

NAPOLEON AT BAY, 1814 *by F. Loraine Petre*—The Campaigns to the Fall of the First Empire.

NAPOLEON AND THE CAMPAIGN OF 1806 *by Colonel Vachée*—The Napoleonic Method of Organisation and Command to the Battles of Jena & Auerstädt.

THE COMPLETE ADVENTURES IN THE CONNAUGHT RANGERS *by William Grattan*—The 88th Regiment during the Napoleonic Wars by a Serving Officer.

BUGLER AND OFFICER OF THE RIFLES *by William Green & Harry Smith*—With the 95th (Rifles) during the Peninsular & Waterloo Campaigns of the Napoleonic Wars.

NAPOLEONIC WAR STORIES *by Sir Arthur Quiller-Couch*—Tales of soldiers, spies, battles & sieges from the Peninsular & Waterloo campaingns.

CAPTAIN OF THE 95TH (RIFLES) *by Jonathan Leach*—An officer of Wellington's sharpshooters during the Peninsular, South of France and Waterloo campaigns of the Napoleonic wars.

RIFLEMAN COSTELLO *by Edward Costello*—The adventures of a soldier of the 95th (Rifles) in the Peninsular & Waterloo Campaigns of the Napoleonic wars.

AVAILABLE ONLINE AT **www.leonaur.com**
AND FROM ALL GOOD BOOK STORES

ALSO FROM LEONAUR
AVAILABLE IN SOFTCOVER OR HARDCOVER WITH DUST JACKET

OFFICERS & GENTLEMEN by *Peter Hawker & William Graham*—Two Accounts of British Officers During the Peninsula War: Officer of Light Dragoons by Peter Hawker & Campaign in Portugal and Spain by William Graham.

THE WALCHEREN EXPEDITION by *Anonymous*—The Experiences of a British Officer of the 81st Regt. During the Campaign in the Low Countries of 1809.

LADIES OF WATERLOO by *Charlotte A. Eaton, Magdalene de Lancey & Juana Smith*—The Experiences of Three Women During the Campaign of 1815: Waterloo Days by Charlotte A. Eaton, A Week at Waterloo by Magdalene de Lancey & Juana's Story by Juana Smith.

JOURNAL OF AN OFFICER IN THE KING'S GERMAN LEGION by *John Frederick Hering*—Recollections of Campaigning During the Napoleonic Wars.

JOURNAL OF AN ARMY SURGEON IN THE PENINSULAR WAR by *Charles Boutflower*—The Recollections of a British Army Medical Man on Campaign During the Napoleonic Wars.

ON CAMPAIGN WITH MOORE AND WELLINGTON by *Anthony Hamilton*—The Experiences of a Soldier of the 43rd Regiment During the Peninsular War.

THE ROAD TO AUSTERLITZ by *R. G. Burton*—Napoleon's Campaign of 1805.

SOLDIERS OF NAPOLEON by *A. J. Doisy De Villargennes & Arthur Chuquet*—The Experiences of the Men of the French First Empire: Under the Eagles by A. J. Doisy De Villargennes & Voices of 1812 by Arthur Chuquet.

INVASION OF FRANCE, 1814 by *F. W. O. Maycock*—The Final Battles of the Napoleonic First Empire.

LEIPZIG—A CONFLICT OF TITANS by *Frederic Shoberl*—A Personal Experience of the 'Battle of the Nations' During the Napoleonic Wars, October 14th-19th, 1813.

SLASHERS by *Charles Cadell*—The Campaigns of the 28th Regiment of Foot During the Napoleonic Wars by a Serving Officer.

BATTLE IMPERIAL by *Charles William Vane*—The Campaigns in Germany & France for the Defeat of Napoleon 1813-1814.

SWIFT & BOLD by *Gibbes Rigaud*—The 60th Rifles During the Peninsula War.

AVAILABLE ONLINE AT **www.leonaur.com**
AND FROM ALL GOOD BOOK STORES

ALSO FROM LEONAUR
AVAILABLE IN SOFTCOVER OR HARDCOVER WITH DUST JACKET

A DIARY FROM DIXIE *by Mary Boykin Chesnut*—A Lady's Account of the Confederacy During the American Civil War

FOLLOWING THE DRUM *by Teresa Griffin Vielé*—A U. S. Infantry Officer's Wife on the Texas frontier in the Early 1850's

FOLLOWING THE GUIDON *by Elizabeth B. Custer*—The Experiences of General Custer's Wife with the U. S. 7th Cavalry.

LADIES OF LUCKNOW *by G. Harris & Adelaide Case*—The Experiences of Two British Women During the Indian Mutiny 1857. A Lady's Diary of the Siege of Lucknow by G. Harris, Day by Day at Lucknow by Adelaide Case

MARIE-LOUISE AND THE INVASION OF 1814 *by Imbert de Saint-Amand*—The Empress and the Fall of the First Empire

SAPPER DOROTHY *by Dorothy Lawrence*—The only English Woman Soldier in the Royal Engineers 51st Division, 79th Tunnelling Co. during the First World War

ARMY LETTERS FROM AN OFFICER'S WIFE 1871-1888 *by Frances M. A. Roe*—Experiences On the Western Frontier With the United States Army

NAPOLEON'S LETTERS TO JOSEPHINE *by Henry Foljambe Hall*—Correspondence of War, Politics, Family and Love 1796-1814

MEMOIRS OF SARAH DUCHESS OF MARLBOROUGH, AND OF THE COURT OF QUEEN ANNE VOLUME 1 by A. T. Thomson

MEMOIRS OF SARAH DUCHESS OF MARLBOROUGH, AND OF THE COURT OF QUEEN ANNE VOLUME 2 by A. T. Thomson

MARY PORTER GAMEWELL AND THE SIEGE OF PEKING *by A. H. Tuttle*—An American Lady's Experiences of the Boxer Uprising, China 1900

VANISHING ARIZONA *by Martha Summerhayes*—A young wife of an officer of the U.S. 8th Infantry in Apacheria during the 1870's

THE RIFLEMAN'S WIFE *by Mrs. Fitz Maurice*—*The Experiences of an Officer's Wife and Chronicles of the Old 95th During the Napoleonic Wars*

THE OATMAN GIRLS *by Royal B. Stratton*—The Capture & Captivity of Two Young American Women in the 1850's by the Apache Indians

AVAILABLE ONLINE AT **www.leonaur.com**
AND FROM ALL GOOD BOOK STORES

www.ingramcontent.com/pod-product-compliance
Lightning Source LLC
Chambersburg PA
CBHW030358100426
42812CB00028B/2760/J